REDISCOVER THE HIDDEN NEW JERSEY

RIVERGATE REGIONALS Rivergate Regionals is a collection of books published by Rutgers University Press focusing on New Jersey and the surrounding area. Since its founding in 1936, Rutgers University Press has been devoted to serving the people of New Jersey and this collection solidifies that tradition. The books in the Rivergate Regionals Collection explore history, politics, nature and the environment, recreation, sports, health and medicine, and the arts. By incorporating the collection within the larger Rutgers University Press editorial program, the Rivergate Regionals Collection enhances our commitment to publishing the best books about our great state and the surrounding region.

REDISCOVER THE HIDDEN NEW JERSEY

Second Edition

Russell Roberts

RUTGERS UNIVERSITY PRESS

New Brunswick, New Jersey and London

Library of Congress Cataloging-in-Publication Data

Roberts, Russell, 1953– [Discover the hidden New Jersey]
    Rediscover the hidden New Jersey / Russell Roberts.—Second edition.
        pages cm.—(Rivergate regionals)
    Revised edition of: Discover the hidden New Jersey. New Brunswick, N.J. : Rutgers University
Press, 1995.
    Includes bibliographical references and index.
    ISBN 978-0-8135-6945-1 (pbk. : alk. paper)—ISBN 978-0-8135-6946-8 (e-book)
    1. New Jersey—History—Miscellanea. 2. New Jersey—History—Anecdotes. I. Title.
    F134.5.R6 2014
    974.9—dc23
    2014017565

A British Cataloging-in-Publication record for this book is available from the British Library.

Visit our website: http://rutgerspress.rutgers.edu

Manufactured in the United States of America

To Megan—because without her I am nothing

Contents

Preface to the Second Edition

As I thought about what to say for this updated edition, I thought about all the changes that have occurred since the first edition was published in 1995.

I thought about all the books I've written since then, and all the thousands of words that have poured out of my writing pen in the form of articles and many other types of writing. Maybe I never achieved my goal of being as well-known as Hemingway—I suspect he wasn't too worried anyway—but my work will survive in libraries and other places for some time. At least that's something we will have in common.

I also thought about all the changes that have occurred in writing during that time. When I was writing the first edition, the idea that so much of the information that I had to dredge up out of libraries, badly lit microfilm, and historical societies would be available with a few computer keystrokes on the Internet would have been ludicrous. Then again the idea of writing a book is in and of itself ludicrous—much of it is done alone, with no idea if all your hard work is ultimately going to result in something good or something cringe-worthy—that maybe I should have seen it coming.

Then I thought about the book itself. If you had told me twenty years ago that I'd someday be writing a preface for a second edition, I'd have smiled and figured you were delusional. Nobody sets out to write a good book, or a bad book; you just write it because you have to, because it's as important as breathing to you, and hope that people won't use it to line the bottom of their birdcages. I'm just glad that the first edition was so well received and hope that I didn't deprive too many birds.

I finally thought about myself. I'm no longer a young writer struggling to carve out a career. No longer intent on letting myself be defined by my work, I've realized with the passage of years that you can only be defined by the type of life you lead. By now the same thing has happened to me that has happened to everyone else—life—and I hope I've learned that the destination isn't as important as the journey.

I hope you'll enjoy the journey this second edition of the book provides.

REDISCOVER
THE
HIDDEN
NEW
JERSEY

New Jersey Firsts

George Washington may have been "first in war, first in peace, and first in the hearts of his countrymen," but New Jersey has been first in a lot of things as well.

The vast number of "firsts" that have occurred in the state, from technological breakthroughs and important scientific discoveries to more whimsical achievements such as the invention of the first drive-in movie theater, would fill a book by themselves. Those who put down New Jersey should remember that without this state, there would be no baseball, college football, movies, electric lights, boardwalks, public libraries, condensed soup, or a multitude of other things both important and enjoyable. All these got their start in New Jersey—the "first state" of innovation and ingenuity.

If you're driving along in Camden County and you blink, you might miss it—but then you'd be missing one of New Jersey's most significant firsts, as well as an important African American milestone.

At first blush, there's nothing overly special about the town of Lawnside. It seems like just another pleasant New Jersey community full of hardworking people. According to the 2010 United States Census, nearly three thousand folks (2,945) called Lawnside's 1.408 acres home.

However, a quick peak behind the curtain reveals that Lawnside's relatively small size does not reflect its enormity in United States history. In 1926, Lawnside became the first independent self-governing African American community north of the Mason-Dixon Line in America.

According to the authoritative *Encyclopedia of New Jersey,* people of African descent began settling in the area in the 1700s. As the concept and practice of abolitionism spread throughout the region, both free blacks and escaped slaves were attracted to the area.

Early in the nineteenth century an African American named Peter Mott came to what was then called Free Haven. Mott had been born sometime around 1810 across the river in Delaware. However, at this time Delaware was a slave state, which likely accounts for the antislavery Mott's relocation.

At Free Haven Mott found love, marrying Virginia-born Elizabeth Ann Thomas in 1833. Mott became a business success, but it was another type of endeavor for which we remember him today. His home became a "station" on the Underground Railroad. Mott and his wife were instrumental in helping African Americans fleeing the evils of slavery to escape further north in the U.S. and even into Canada. At great personal risk to himself, Mott would take them in his horse-drawn wagon to their next stop in towns like Haddonfield and Moorestown.

Mott died in 1881. By then, Free Haven was called Snow Hill as often as it was Free Haven. The name reportedly came from its slightly higher elevation and the white sand of its landscape, which gave it a "snow on the mountain top" appearance.

The Peter Mott house in Lawnside.

When the railroad came to town the station was renamed "Lawnton." From there it was an easy jump to "Lawnside," which was adopted in 1907. At that time the area was still part of Centre Township, but there was a growing movement to make Lawnside its own distinct community. The New Jersey legislature agreed, and on March 23, 1926, New Jersey Governor A. Harry Moore signed a bill dissolving Centre Township and incorporating the Borough of Lawnside. One month later, on April 20, a special election was held in Lawnside to elect governing officials. With that election, the community blazed its name into the history books as the first independent self-governing African American community in America north of the Mason-Dixon Line.

Today the Peter Mott House has been preserved thanks to some far-sighted people and serves as a museum and headquarters for the Lawnside Historical Society.

In June 1822, a man was fishing at Lake Hopatcong when he suddenly got one of those ideas that are typically shown in cartoons with a light bulb over the head. The man was George P. Macculloch, and his idea was to construct a canal that would use the lake's water to connect the Passaic and Delaware Rivers. Whether that is a fish story is open to debate, but the result of his brainstorm was another New Jersey first—the Morris Canal, which some historians feel was the first in the United States to use the inclined plane. That may or may not be true, but what's undeniable is that the Morris Canal was considered a technological marvel in its day.

When you think of canals, your mind goes to a waterway that connects two other bodies of water. Normally you think of something long and relatively straightforward, with locks used when necessary to compensate for differences in water levels.

Not so the Morris Canal. To call it "straightforward" is to call Michael Jordan "adequate" at basketball. The 107-mile-long Morris Canal was a mountain climber, the Sir Edmund Hillary of canals; from sea level at New York Harbor, the Morris Canal trekked upward 914 feet to near Lake Hopatcong, then traveled downward 760 feet to its lowest level at Phillipsburg (Warren County) on the Delaware River. For those of us bad in math, that's a total of 1,674 feet of elevation change—more elevation change than any other transportation canal in the world.

Before the Morris Canal was a water-soaked gleam in anyone's eyes, George Washington had called for a canal system as a way to bring the diverse new American nation together; however, it was the overwhelming success of the Erie Canal, completed in 1825, that put canal building on the new nation's front burner. Unfortunately, using just locks to deal with the elevation problems would not work for the Morris Canal because of the amount of water needed. Fortunately, in 1796 Robert Fulton (he of future steamboat fame) had published a paper entitled *Treatise on the Improvement of Canal Navigation*. In it Fulton devised a system of using inclined planes instead of locks to deal with elevation on canal routes. His inclined plane idea became the key to building the canal.

So, armed with a good idea, the technology to achieve it, and an urgent need to find a better way to transport goods (especially anthracite coal from Pennsylvania) to market than just with horse-drawn wagons, the Morris Canal was begun in 1825. Professor James Renwick took Fulton's inclined plane ideas and adapted them for use on the waterway. Remarkably, the state of New Jersey had no role in building the canal. This was accomplished by private investors, who sold 20,000 shares of stock at $100 per share to raise the funds. By 1831 the canal was completed from Newark to Phillipsburg; five years later it ran all the way to Jersey City.

The canal was a brilliant mixture of engineering. When faced with elevations of twenty feet or less, locks were used; more than that and the inclined plane was utilized. The final cost of the waterway when it was completed to Newark in 1831 was a little over two million dollars.

At its peak the canal transported a variety of materials besides coal, such as cider, vinegar, beer, whiskey, wood, sugar, lime, bricks, hay, hides, iron ore, lumber, and manure. It would be nice to say that the canal was a decadeslong hit and led to prosperity for all concerned, but its only profitable years were from 1860 to 1869, half of which were Civil War years, which caused unusually large amounts of cargo to be shipped throughout the United States. Beginning in the late 1840s, the railroad, which had been steadily emerging as a transportation source, began cutting into the canal's business. Eventually, the railroad took over most of the coal shipping, which severely hurt canal profits. That, combined with the fact that the center of the coal industry had moved west of the Appalachian Mountains, ended the canal's days. In 1922 the state of New Jersey took over most of the canal and soon afterward declared it obsolete. The canal was broken up and its real estate sold. Some pieces were saved for posterity, and they still exist today. Some of the sections have been incorporated into parks, nature trails, and the like—a reminder of the time when water, water may have been everywhere, but New Jersey was the one to figure out how to climb it.

Sometime around 1930, night after night, in the driveway of his home in Riverton, a New Jersey man sat in his car, intently watching a movie screen that he had nailed to a tree, on which was playing a film from a projector perched on top of the automobile. Sometimes, he would even turn on the lawn sprinkler while the movie was going on and sit there, in the car, watching the movie while the water poured down around him. Anyone who saw him might well have shaken his (or her) head, and that's perfectly understandable. What they could not possibly know was that what they were witnessing was not the actions of a raging eccentric, but rather the birth of an American icon: the drive-in movie theater.

The man sitting in his car and watching movies "in the rain" was Richard M. Hollingshead Jr. His father, Richard Hollingshead Sr., owned the Whiz Auto Products Company, which had correctly anticipated the switch from the horse to the horseless carriage by dumping their line of harness products for a full line of automobile soaps, polishes, and related products, thus becoming quite successful. Born on February 25, 1900, Hollingshead Junior joined his father's company after completing his education. It was a job for life, as are most jobs in a family business, but the young man was restless. He wanted to make his own mark in the world.

Hollingshead took his first steps on the path that would lead to the drive-in when he realized that cars and movies were two things that people refused to surrender, no matter how tight money became. He then analyzed the reasons why people didn't want to go to the movies: "The mother says she's not dressed; the husband doesn't want to put on his shoes; the question is what to do with the kids; then how to find a babysitter; parking the car is difficult or maybe they have to pay for parking; even the seats in the theater may not be comfortable to contemplate."

Having defined the problem, Hollingshead next sought the solution. In the driveway of his home, he set a 1928 Kodak projector on the hood of his car, nailed a makeshift movie screen onto a nearby tree, and placed a radio behind the screen to provide sound. Then the erstwhile inventor sat in his car and watched the film unwind. No matter what he did—including using the lawn sprinkler to simulate rain—he liked it. The car was convenient, roomy, and private; no more annoying loudmouths talking behind you, no more people crinkling candy wrappers during a crucial scene, and no more tight, uncomfortable theater seats.

Over the next few months, Hollingshead worked out the bugs in his idea. He figured out that by elevating each row of cars slightly, people in cars in the back would be able to see as well as those in the front. He found a company that would build a fifty-foot-wide projection screen. For adequate sound he contacted RCA Victor in Camden, which devised "controlled directional sound," basically a fancy name for three centrally located speakers (the infamous in-car speaker did not appear until the late 1940s) that would blast the sound all at once throughout the entire theater lot.

Having solved these problems, by spring 1933 Hollingshead was ready to unleash his invention on the world—or at least on New Jersey. A crew of workmen, many taken off the relief rolls, descended on a site on Crescent Boulevard in Pennsauken Township (most reports erroneously give the location of the first theater as the Admiral Wilson Boulevard in Camden) on May 16, 1933, to begin building the outdoor theater. Construction took a mere three weeks and cost an estimated $30,000. On June 6, the world's first "Automobile Movie Theater" opened for business.

"Sit In Your Car—See and Hear MOVIES" trumpeted the huge sign outside the theater. The cost was ninety-five cents per person, or one dollar for an entire carload. The first film was *Wife Beware*, starring Adolphe Menjou.

The grand opening was a glorious success. The lot was jammed, thanks in part to a clever marketing campaign by Hollingshead. Besides giving out passes to many Philadelphia and Camden media outlets, he also ran ads targeting particular groups that he thought the drive-in concept would appeal to. One of the ads, for example, showed a rather large woman trying to squeeze into a tiny indoor theater seat (much to the dismay of the surrounding patrons).

"The world's first Automobile Theatre opened on Crescent Boulevard last night with more than 600 motorists attending the initial performance," announced the next day's *Camden Courier* under a headline reading "600 Motorists See Open-Air Movies." The story went on to say that "beer and lunches" would be on sale the following week and that features with "all dull or uninteresting parts omitted" would be shown three times nightly.

Unfortunately, business died off quickly after that triumphant first night. Hollingshead ultimately sold the theater to a man who "moved" it to Union, New Jersey. In later years, Hollingshead contended that his biggest problem was getting movie distributors to give him first-run films (a problem that forever plagued drive-ins, which always seemed to be playing *Attack of the Killer Tomatoes* while the local indoor theater was showing the latest blockbuster).

In reality, several factors contributed to the demise of the first drive-in. The sound was poor, and often not synchronized with the film; many cars were situated at odd angles to the screen, which made viewing difficult; and, the price was high for what was, essentially, a novelty experience. Most importantly, with the windows rolled up, cars quickly became steam baths on New Jersey's humid, sticky summer nights; with the windows down, the state's other hot weather terror—the voracious Jersey mosquito—snacked on theater patrons with a vengeance. (Realizing that heat would be a problem, Hollingshead had planted more than two hundred trees around the theater.)

Nearly twenty years later, fueled by the mass migration to the suburbs, the lack of indoor theaters there, and cheap gas, the drive-in came into its own. During the 1950s, drive-ins almost single-handedly enabled films to stave off the onslaught of television. For Hollingshead, however, there were no laurels, even belated ones, from Hollywood. The inventor of the drive-in died on May 13, 1975, ignored by the industry to which he had contributed so much.

Today, New Jersey has just one drive-in left, which is similar to other states, that have just one or two. Some states have none (Alaska, Delaware, Hawaii, and Louisiana). So, hurry; time's running out for you to see such cinematic classics as *Mad Monkey Kung Fu* in the comfort of your own car. And that's sad (or is it?).

DID YOU KNOW?

One movie that invariably pops up on lists of favorite drive-in films is *The Blob*, the 1958 original with Steve McQueen, filmed right next door in Phoenixville, Pennsylvania—which just goes to show you that you can't keep a gelatinous green thing down.

Today, *E Pluribus Unum* (which means, roughly, "from many, one") is found on all United States coins. The first state to adopt that motto was New Jersey, back in 1786, when it placed the saying on so-called "horsehead" cents. Other states didn't follow suit until several years later.

Hot air ballooning has become an extremely popular pastime all over the world. It's especially widespread in France, where the large, colorful balloons are a common sight floating over the countryside. Indeed, it was a Frenchman who made the first airborne passenger flight in the Western Hemisphere—right here in New Jersey!

On January 9, 1793, a farmer working in his field in Deptford Township looked up to behold a wondrous sight. Floating down at him from out of the sky was a huge, round object with a wicker basket underneath. Even more amazing was that inside the wicker basket was what appeared to be a man, who was shouting something at him in a language the farmer had never heard before.

As the object settled down in his field, thoughts of witches, devils, and the like must have raced through the farmer's mind. Yet, pushing these fears aside, he ran toward the strange object to see for himself what had landed so unceremoniously in his field.

Seeing the farmer approaching, the man in the wicker basket climbed out and tried talking to him, but neither could understand a word the other said. Then the man showed the farmer a letter, which also had little effect, since the farmer couldn't read. Finally, the man reached into the wicker basket and pulled out the universal communicator: wine. Soon he and the farmer were toasting each other's friendship—which was fortunate, because other people were arriving who had also seen the strange object, and one of them had a gun.

Luckily, the man with the gun could read. He took the letter from the man and read it to the small group. The letter identified the balloonist as a Frenchman named Jean-Pierre Blanchard and guaranteed him safe passage wherever he landed. It was signed by President George Washington.

With the mention of Washington's name the mood in the field instantly changed from wariness to friendliness. Blanchard later recorded in his journal: "In the midst of profound silence was it [the letter] read with a loud and audible voice. How dear the name of Washington is to this people! With what eagerness they gave me all possible assistance, in consequence of his recommendation."

Blanchard had taken off from Philadelphia earlier that day, in the midst of bands playing, people waving handkerchiefs, and cannons booming. President George Washington had been on hand to wish the balloonist good luck and give him a letter of safe conduct.

At a few minutes past ten o'clock in the morning, Blanchard's balloon lifted off from the yard of the Walnut Street Prison. Taking a southeasterly course, the balloon floated over the Delaware River and the surrounding countryside until coming to rest in Deptford. The fifteen-mile trip would have taken several hours by horseback or carriage, but the French adventurer had made the journey in less than sixty minutes.

The small group brought the flying Frenchman and his balloon to a nearby farmhouse. There they wrote down what they had seen: "These may certify, that we the subscribers saw the bearer, Mr. Blanchard, settle in his balloon in Deptford Township, County of Gloucester, in the state of New Jersey, about fifteen miles from Philadelphia, about ten o'clock 56 minutes, A.M. Witness our hands the ninth day of January, Anno Domini, 1793." It was signed by Everard Bolton, Joseph Griffith, Joseph Cheesman, Samuel Taggart, Amos Castell, and Zara North.

Later, after he returned to Philadelphia, Blanchard went to Washington's home, where he presented the president with the unusual two-country flag (the French Tricolor was on one side, the Stars and Stripes on the other) that he had carried on his trip.

The young Frenchman had hoped that the fanfare of this trip would be the start of a successful career for him demonstrating his ballooning skills in the United States, where the sport was unknown. Unfortunately, his hopes were doomed to failure. Although Blanchard had sold tickets to spectators of his historic flight at the then-stratospheric price of five dollars apiece, he failed to make money on the venture and returned to Europe. There he continued to support himself through ballooning until he had a heart attack while on a flight over Paris in 1808. Although he managed to land safely, he died the following year.

This is a first that most drivers in New Jersey probably wish would have been a "last"—the invention of the first traffic circle.

Today, of course, traffic circles are distinguished mainly by the vast number of expletives muttered by approaching drivers. But in 1925, when they were first unveiled to the general public in Camden County, traffic circles were hailed as a wonderful innovation that would—get ready to laugh—help reduce bottlenecks and accidents.

The first traffic circle in the United States was Airport Circle in Camden County. It was named for Central Airport, which was then located on the north side of Route 130. When the circle was opened, much of Camden and Burlington Counties were farmland, and the roads were not heavily traveled. The circle, modeled after the roundabouts and rotaries of Great Britain, was considered a marvelous alternative to traffic signals as a way to manage traffic.

But ingenuity soon gave way to inanity. Just as the opening of Philadelphia International Airport in the early 1950s sounded the death knell for Central Airport, so did the post–War II building boom that swept through New Jersey mean the end of a traffic circle's effectiveness. By the 1960s, as farmland was replaced by homes, offices, and retail outlets, and the vehicles these spawned poured onto the highways, traffic circles had become the very thing they were supposed to guard against: traffic bottlenecks. All those cars piling willy-nilly into circles became reminiscent of mice racing around a maze with no exit and no hope.

In the 1980s, the New Jersey Department of Transportation began to phase out the once-revolutionary traffic circle. However, as of 2014, there were still approximately forty traffic circles in New Jersey ready, willing, and able to confuse and annoy drivers.

The next New Jersey first concerns a man with a broad face and a little round belly that shakes when he laughs like a bowl full of jelly. No, it's not your Uncle Fred after Thanksgiving dinner, but Santa Claus, who looks the way he does today thanks to the artistic talents of a Morristown resident named Thomas Nast.

Nast was born in Landau, Bavaria, in 1840. When he was six his parents emigrated to the United States, where they settled in New York. Young Thomas displayed his artistic ability at an early age; in 1855, at age fifteen, after just two years of formal schooling, he got an illustrator's job with *Leslie's Illustrated Newspaper*. His first published drawing showed a crowd boarding a ferry for Elysian Fields in Hoboken.

In 1862, Nast moved to the leading periodical of the day, *Harper's Weekly*. This was the second—and one of the bloodiest—year of the Civil War; thousands upon thousands of Americans lost their lives in places with names like Antietam, Gaines' Mill, and Shiloh. The war was never far from anyone's thoughts and was certainly the major story at *Harper's*. To Nast fell the job of illustrating the war for *Harper's* readers, through drawings of battles, the soldier's life in camp, and other scenes. He did his job well; his drawings kept northern sympathies for the war strong during those dark days when Confederate victories were causing the Union flame to flicker uncertainly. (Ulysses S. Grant later said that "[Nast] did as much as any man to preserve the Union and bring the war to an end.")

Drawing battles, death, and man's inhumanity to man was a wearying, depressing chore, so one supposes that Nast jumped at the chance to inject a little joy into his work. This opportunity came during late December 1862; Germans have always had a strong Christmas tradition, and so it was natural for Nast to draw, for the first time, the symbol of Christmas—Santa Claus—in a cartoon that appeared on the cover of the January 3, 1863, issue of *Harper's*. The drawing is entitled "Santa in Camp" and shows St. Nicholas dispensing gifts to Union soldiers. Inside this same issue, Nast drew a few Santa scenes to help counterbalance the generally depressing pictures throughout of lonely soldiers stuck in cold and snowy camps, aching for the warmth of home and hearth during the holiday season.

The Santa Claus that Nast drew (and soon began to refine, in other holiday issues of *Harper's*) was a far cry from what had been done before. Previously, the jolly old elf had been shown as a short, stumpy man with a thin, hawklike face and sharp features. (In fact, one drawing in 1837 verges on being outright scary, depicting Santa with coal-black eyes and a sinister smile, leering over his shoulder at the reader from the fireplace.) The beard, when one was present, was usually short and scruffy, and Santa's garb ran the gamut from an overcoat and pants to an Arabian prince type of suit, complete with puffy sleeves.

Nast gave Santa a complete makeover. He made Santa friendlier by rounding and softening his features and by putting the now-famous twinkle in his eye. He lengthened Santa's beard to modern-day levels and gave him the large, portly (or, as we would say in today's politically correct world, "weight-challenged") frame that is so familiar today. For his clothing, the artist dressed Santa in a furry suit with a large black belt around the middle.

Nast continued to draw Santa Claus for years to come, even after his political cartoons, which established such symbols as the Republican elephant and the Democratic donkey, made him famous. His Christmas sketches were a phenomenal success, not just because of Santa Claus but because the artist captured the joy and excitement of the holiday so perfectly.

As time went on, Nast gave Santa a few more contemporary characteristics, such as his toy-making workshop and a large book in which he recorded the names of good and bad children. The final touch came when, for a series of color paintings for a book about Santa, Nast depicted him in a red suit, which he trimmed in white fur to add a little contrast. (Before this, Nast had always drawn Santa in black and white and had assumed that his suit was fawn-colored.)

Nast was a firm believer in politics as an instrument of national self-improvement. His beautiful three-story Morristown home, known as Villa Fontana, played host to numerous important personages from both the United States and abroad. Although internationally famous, Nast did not hesitate to use his talent to aid his hometown. He drew huge cartoons showing scenes from the Revolutionary War and Washington's life for the Centennial Celebration at Washington's Headquarters in Morristown. Nast also provided scenery for local theater productions and contributed a self-portrait for the cover of a cookbook that was sold to benefit Morristown Memorial Hospital.

Sadly, Nast did not find the happiness in later life that he had given so many others through his art. Disgusted by the political corruption spawned in the wake of the Civil War, he left *Harper's* in 1886, although his influence had diminished considerably before that. During his final years a series of financial crises plagued him, and he was forced to give up his home. In 1902, down on his luck, he gratefully accepted the consular post in Guayaquil, Ecuador. But on December 7, 1902, after just six months in residence there, he died of yellow fever at the still-young age of sixty-two.

There's nothing unique anymore about being served food in your car, thanks to carhops and those ubiquitous and incomprehensible drive-through speakers found at virtually every fast food restaurant. But here's a New Jersey first that puts them all to shame. In 1762, the Seven Stars Tavern in Salem County had what was almost certainly the first "drive-through" window in history. A horseback rider could canter up to the window, order food and drink, get served, and pay the check—all without dismounting from his or her faithful steed.

Although it may sound incredible, considering their popularity, blue-berries owe their broad acceptance and use today entirely to one New Jersey woman, who developed the first cultivated blueberry. The woman was Elizabeth White.

Born in New Lisbon, Burlington County, on October 5, 1871, Elizabeth Coleman White spent virtually her entire life working in the sandy soil of the Pinelands. She wasn't one to sit on the porch drinking tea while others did the work; she personally dug up and transplanted so many blueberry bushes and picked so many blueberries that her hands were permanently stained with dirt and blueberry juice.

In 1910, White and her father, J. J. White, were searching for a companion crop to the cranberry—one that would grow well in the sandy, acidic soil of the Pinelands. In November of that year she read a bulletin about blueberry culture by Dr. Frederick V. Coville, a botanist. Intrigued, she invited Dr. Coville to visit her at Whitesbog. The two hit it off, and White began concentrating on trying to develop the first cultivated blueberry. (Prior to this, the only blueberries on the market were wild ones, which were just as likely to be small and bitter as they were fat and sweet.)

The best way to approach the task, she felt, was to enlist the aid of the Pinelands residents in finding the heartiest wild blueberry bushes. White developed a network of agents and friends who were always scouring the Pinelands for a wild bush with large, tasty berries. She also used handbills to spread the word: "I will pay for Huckleberry Bushes, from one to three dollars a bush, when the largest berries on it will not drop through holes the size of the blue spots [on an accompanying illustration]" read the flyers.

After securing a bush that met her standards, White would cross-pollinate it with others to try to develop the ultimate blueberry plant. Hundreds and thousands of hours of work went into the tedious, time-consuming process of cross-pollination. By 1916, White had successfully marketed the first cultivated blueberry in history.

A generous woman, White was quick to give credit to those who had found the bushes. She dubbed a blueberry developed from a bush found by Ruben Leek the Rubel and called another blueberry the Sam, after Sam Lemon, who had brought her the bush.

White continued working with her blueberry bushes, always seeking the next best bush and berry. Her standards were exacting: between 1912 and 1928 approximately 25,000 plants were sent to Whitesbog. Only fifteen cross-pollinated varieties met White's requirements.

For decades she continued to work with blueberries, developing newer and better varieties. At the age of eighty-three, when most people have long since settled into their easy chairs, Elizabeth White turned over blueberry development to others and began propagating various varieties of holly. By the time she died, on November 27, 1954, this tireless woman had not only left behind a mountain of achievement in the fields of cranberry cultivation and holly propagation but had single-handedly launched the entire domestic blueberry industry.

On the morning of July 17, 1933, two black men boarded a Fairchild 24 monoplane in front of hundreds of cheering spectators at Atlantic City's Bader Field. What they were about to attempt was incredibly risky—and historic.

The men, C. Alfred Anderson and Dr. Albert E. Forsythe, were trying to become the first African Americans to make a transcontinental flight. Their goal was to fly nonstop across the United States to Los Angeles, then fly back to New Jersey.

Even under normal conditions, a nonstop cross-country trip was fraught with risk. However, the two men had decided to make the trip as difficult as possible. Thus the plane carried no parachutes, lights, or even a radio. The only instruments on board were a compass and an altimeter.

"The trip was purposely made to be hazardous and rough," Forsythe later said, "because if it had been an ordinary flight, we wouldn't have attracted attention." What made this decision easier was that both pilots were broke. 'We had no radio, no lights, and no parachutes because we didn't have the money to buy those things," Forsythe said.

Both men deserved credit for even being at Bader Field in the first place. Blacks were not welcomed in aviation during this time, and almost no one would teach a black how to fly a plane. Forsythe, however, didn't let this invisible color barrier stop him. Born in Jamaica, he had always dreamed of flying. After establishing a medical practice in Atlantic City, Forsythe began turning his dreams into reality. Discovering that Anderson had gotten his pilot's license at a flight school outside Philadelphia, he headed there himself.

However, getting a license and flying were two different things. Even with his license, Anderson had been unable to find work, and Forsythe knew that opportunities for blacks in the air were minuscule at best. He hoped that a successful transcontinental flight would prove that African Americans could compete with whites in aviation.

Thus, when Anderson and Forsythe boarded their plane, called the *Pride of Atlantic City*, at Bader Field, they were carrying not only their own hopes but the hopes of an entire race with them.

Without instruments of any kind, the men used a Rand McNally road map as their guide. This worked fine—until it blew away. From then on, for the rest of the 2,500-mile trip, they were on their own. Losing the map, however, was the least of their problems. On their journey, the plane was buffeted by high winds, heavy rain, and hail, the engine overheated over the Mojave Desert, and the craft had barely enough power to scale the Rocky Mountains. Just to make things interesting, at night they were forced to use flashlights to help guide them along.

But they made it.

Two thousand people greeted the pioneer pilots when they landed in Los Angeles two and a half days later. However, when they returned to Atlantic City, their accomplishment was barely noted by the *New York Times,* which ran a small story, well off the front page, headed "Negroes End Flight." This was despite the fact that Wiley Post's attempt to set a new record for around-the-world flying was plastered all over the front page. "First of Race to Span Nation Land at Atlantic City," read a secondary headline above the three-paragraph story, which noted that it was the "first airplane flight to the Pacific Coast and back ever undertaken by two Negro flyers" but carried no details about the trip itself.

New Jersey, however, made up for the newspaper's excuse-me story. A cheering crowd of one thousand greeted the pioneer pilots on their return to Atlantic City. A few days later, fifteen thousand exuberant people lined the streets of Newark for a parade in the two men's honor. Forsythe and Anderson were not only heroes and the owners of another New Jersey first, but they had delivered another stinging blow to that destroyer of dreams known as prejudice.

DID YOU KNOW?

And now, for something completely different, here's a New Jersey first that is not really a New Jersey first,

New Jersey is often credited with having the first brewery in America. Some-time around 1640, so the story goes, a man named Aert Teunissen Van Putten established a brewery in Hoboquin (Hoboken), which was in an area known as Pavonia, named after Michael Pauw, who owned the land. An industrious man, Van Putten cleared the land, started a farm, planted fruit trees, and also built a brewhouse.

However, while Hoboken has been quite prominent in New Jersey history, and owns a distinguished first as far as being the true birthplace of baseball, this seems like one of those instances in which legend has replaced fact. Several sources point to a brewery in a log house built on Manhattan Island by Adrian Block and Hans Christiansen in 1612 as the actual site of the first brewery in America. Brewing went on here for twenty years, until another brewery was established on the island in 1632 by Peter Minuit—still a decade ahead of Van Putten. In fact, it seems as if there might even have been a brewery at the famous Lost Colony of Virginia as early as 1587.

"God created men, but Colt made them equal."

Since the invention of gunpowder, no single weapon has played such a pivotal role in a nation's history as Samuel Colt's ingenious multiple-shot revolver. It was the gun that won the West; as the opening phrase suggests, it put men of unequal ability on the same terms, enabling the weaker to hold their own against the stronger and allowing men more interested in farming than fighting to establish a foothold on the rugged frontier. It was a weapon, and a concept, that Colt tried desperately but unsuccessfully to sell to the U.S. government for years. It was also a weapon that was first developed and manufactured in New Jersey.

Before Sam Colt, guns were simple. They shot one bullet at a time. After the gun was discharged, the weapon had to be reloaded—a time-consuming process that could seem like an eternity if an enemy was bearing down on you with a loaded weapon of his (or her) own.

But then came young Colt (born in Hartford, Connecticut, on July 19, 1814), who displayed a wooden model of a pistol with a revolving cylinder that fed fresh bullets into the chamber automatically. He had whittled the model when he was sixteen, during an 1830 sea voyage. According to the story, Colt got the idea of the revolving cylinder while watching the ship's wheel spin around and seeing how it could be stopped in any position by means of a clutch.

The voyage had been an early attempt by Colt to seek his fortune. When this didn't work out he organized, upon his return to dry land, a traveling sideshow under the name Dr. Coult, expert on "practical chemistry." His knowledge of chemicals, however, was limited to demonstrating to his audiences how silly people act after inhaling laughing gas.

But underneath Colt's sideshow demeanor there still burned a desire to produce an automatic weapon. He continued to have mechanical models built of his "repeating pistol." Each brought him a little closer to success. Finally, on February 25, 1836, after numerous failures, Colt was granted a United States patent.

Now all that Colt needed was a factory in which to begin production. He turned his attention to Paterson, New Jersey, the nation's first planned industrial city, where other members of the Colt family were in charge of the Society for Useful Manufacturers (SUM), the agency that ran the manufacturing sector. Colt's relatives found financial backers for his factory, and the backers used their influence to steer his request for a charter through the New Jersey legislature. By the summer of 1836, the Patent Arms Manufacturing Company of Paterson was in business.

Colt was never a believer in doing anything halfway, and his four-story resplendent factory had a weathervane shaped like a gun and was surrounded by a white fence with pickets in the form of pistols. Here Colt began producing the first automatic weapons ever built in the United States.

To Colt's way of thinking the game was already won, but in reality his troubles were just beginning. Figuring that the best way to generate business was to impress those with the power to dispense it, he built fancy guns with silver and gold handles and engraved barrels and sent them to world leaders. These were universally ignored. He tried interesting two presidents, Andrew Jackson and Martin Van Buren, in his guns, but they wouldn't listen either. The United States Army, always on top of the latest technical innovations, denounced Colt's revolvers as worthless.

Without orders, Colt had nothing but his dogged belief to sustain him, and soon even that wasn't enough. In 1841 the Patent Arms Manufacturing Company went bankrupt, and the following year it ceased to exist. Colt left Paterson penniless, an apparent failure.

Fortune, however, has a strange way of smiling on a person. Some of Colt's weapons had gotten into the hands of Texans who were fighting for their independence from Mexico. The reputation of the guns began to spread. In 1846, many Texans were serving in the American army with Zachary Taylor during the Mexican War. They still had their Colt revolvers with them—at least as many as were still in service, since Colt had been out of business for several years and the guns were showing their age. Their enthusiastic endorsement of the weapon impressed Taylor, who sent Captain Samuel Walker north to find Colt and get as many more of the guns as possible. Walker negotiated a deal with Colt for one thousand revolvers at twenty-five dollars apiece. (Interestingly enough, after Colt made the agreement with Walker he tried to buy one of his former guns as a model, since he had given all his away. Nobody had one, and Colt was forced to sketch the pistol's design from memory and his patents.) Colt arranged for

Eli Whitney to build these pistols for him and subsequently established a new factory in the town of his birth, Hartford, Connecticut. The rest, as they say, is history.

Because it was the first firearm that could be used effectively by a rider on horseback, Colt's pistols soon spread throughout the land. When he died in 1862, Samuel Colt, the man who had departed from Paterson virtually penniless, left an estate of fifteen million dollars.

The man's name was Alexander Boardman, and he had a problem: How to stop visitors to Atlantic City's beach from tracking sand all through his hotel and the train on which he was a conductor.

As anyone who has ever lived at the Jersey Shore knows all too well, beach sand is nearly impossible to clean up. The insidious little grains seem to hide in every nook and cranny of every chair, sofa, floor, and rug, and even after hours of sweeping and scrubbing, they can still be felt. It's enough to make even Mr. Clean throw in the towel.

As a conductor on the Camden & Atlantic Railroad, Boardman spent a lot of time sweeping out sand tracked into his cars by riders returning from a day of walking on Atlantic City's beaches. If this wasn't bad enough, as the owner of the Ocean House Hotel in Atlantic City he also had to deal with sand tracked all over his fine carpets and left on his furniture by guests and visitors.

Desperate to save both his hotel and his railroad cars, Boardman conceived of the idea of a boardwalk—a wooden walkway of planks over the sand that would enable people to walk on the beach without actually stepping on it.

Another hotel owner in Atlantic City, Jacob Keim, heard about Boardman's idea. The two met, discussed the pros and cons, and decided to present the idea to the other hotel owners in town. At that gathering, held in the spring of 1870, Boardman summed up his and the other owner's predicament: "Our carpets and even stuffed chairs are being ruined by the sand tracked into our places from the beach."

The group liked the idea of a boardwalk and petitioned the city council to build one. Finding no opposition, the council agreed, and, after scrip was issued to finance the project (the city treasury was nearly bare), the first boardwalk was built quickly. It was dedicated on June 26, 1870, with parades, celebrations, and speeches.

This initial boardwalk bore little resemblance to today's Disneyland-like extravaganzas of sight and sound. It was noncommercial, since buildings were not permitted within thirty feet of it; the plank walk itself rose just a foot and a half above the beach. The pathway was constructed of twelve-foot sections of boards one and a half inches thick that were nailed to joists set crosswise under the boardwalk every two feet. Most unusual of all was that the first boardwalk was portable; at the end of the season, each twelve-foot section was removed and stored away in anticipation of the next summer.

The first boardwalk was a rousing success as a tourist attraction, although it hadn't been intended as such. People came to Atlantic City from all over to see this clever innovation, and many of those who came liked what they saw and stayed. During the next five years, the number of new people moving into Atlantic City exceeded the town's total population of the previous sixteen years. The boardwalk had launched Atlantic City on its way to becoming the premier resort town of the entire East Coast.

Thanks to Alexander Boardman's dislike of sweeping up sand, one of the Jersey Shore's most enduring symbols had been born.

(Incidentally, the first boardwalk also had its share of firsts: salt water taffy, picture postcards, and rolling chairs all made their debut on the Atlantic City Boardwalk.)

New Jersey has had many other firsts as well. Although space doesn't permit all their stories to be told, here's a list of some of the others:

- The first baseball game played under modern rules (see the Sporting Life chapter for the full story).
- The first collegiate football game (again, see the Sporting Life chapter).
- Edison's astounding legacy: the first incandescent light bulb, phonograph, commercially viable film projector, and hundreds of other firsts.
- The first log cabin, built in Swedesboro in the 1640s.
- The nation's first planned industrial city: Paterson (see the chapter on town histories).
- The first public library in its own building was in Burlington in 1757.
- The first air conditioner, built by Willis Haviland Carrier in Newark in 1911.
- The first national historic park: Morristown, dedicated in 1933 (see the chapter on day trips for more information).
- The first Episcopal church in the country, built in Perth Amboy in 1698.

- The first frozen food, produced by Charles F. Seabrook in 1933.
- The first Indian reservation, located on a 1,600-acre tract of land in Evesham Township (Burlington County) on August 29, 1758.
- The first United States flag made from an American loom, made by John Rule of Paterson.
- The first transistor, developed by a team of scientists from Bell Laboratories in Murray Hill and patented in 1948.

The Rocks, the Land, and Other Things

Although it is a small state, ranking forty-sixth in the country in terms of size, New Jersey's geologic characteristics are large. In stark contrast to our midwestern cousins, New Jersey has several different geologic regions, plus a wide diversity of rocks and landscapes. New Jersey also has some areas not found anywhere else in the world, such as at Franklin in Sussex County, which contains more than three hundred different types of minerals and is the home of the well-known Franklin marble. Spicing up New Jersey's geologic stew even further are several hidden yet fascinating characteristics of the state's natural makeup, such as the existence of a major earthquake fault line in the north. It seems that, just as in everything else, there's much more to New Jersey's geology and landscape than meets the eye.

To understand New Jersey's geology, you have to go back hundreds of millions of years, when all the continents were attached in one giant land mass with Africa as the approximate center. North America was on the outer fringe of this gigantic conglomeration, with the eastern portion of the United States roughly attached to the upper portion of what is today eastern Africa.

Gradually, the continents separated and drifted apart; as they did, the Atlantic Ocean filled the gap between North America, Europe, and Africa. (However, if you think that by walking on Jersey Shore beaches you're treading on land that was once part of Africa, think again; the actual "connection" is well offshore. Much of present-day Florida was once part of Africa, though, and got carried away by North America during the big breakup.)

During this period the eastern edge of North America was experiencing what geologists call an active continental margin. This is similar to what is happening along the western coast of the United States today, with earthquakes, volcanism, and other upheavals occurring.

To understand just how long ago this was occurring, the Appalachian Mountains—which are today low peaks worn down by erosion and are classified as "old" geologically—were as high and awesome-looking as the Himalayan Mountains are today.

For millions of years, the land that would eventually become New Jersey buckled and bubbled along with the rest of North America, as frequent earthquakes, volcanic eruptions, and other often-violent episodes shaped the landscape. As the continent went through its birthing throes, creatures began to appear, first in the seas and then on land. After many more millions of years had passed, time and evolution produced one of the most spectacular species ever to walk the earth: dinosaurs.

Dinosaurs first appeared on earth at the end of the Triassic period, approximately two hundred million years ago. The great beasts flowered during the Jurassic and Cretaceous periods, then abruptly died out about sixty-five million years ago, for reasons still not understood. They then remained hidden underground for hundreds of millions of years, until a discovery in New Jersey helped bring the age of dinosaurs to light.

One day in 1838, John E. Hopkins was digging marl (a type of soil used for fertilizer) on his farm near Haddonfield. Suddenly his plow struck something large and hard in the ground. Mystified, he dug it up, only to find that what he had uncovered was a giant, ebony-black bone. Plainly, it was too large to be from any animal known in existence at that time. Subsequently, Hopkins found more bones of similar size and appearance.

Word of Hopkins's unusual discovery spread. When people stopped by to marvel at the strange find, Hopkins sometimes gave them pieces of the bones as souvenirs. No one suspected the enormity of the discovery that Hopkins was giving away as casually as Halloween treats.

Two decades passed. Then, in 1858, W. Parker Foulke, a fellow at the Academy of Natural Sciences in Philadelphia, was vacationing in Haddonfield when he heard of the discovery and hurried over to Hopkins's farm. Foulke knew of the controversial theories put forth by British paleontologist Richard Owen some years earlier that an entire race of extinct creatures had ruled the earth for millions of years before humans arrived. After receiving Hopkins's permission to dig for more bones, the Philadelphian came upon a cache of fossils, many of them quite large. Foulke's pulse quickened: he knew that something of immense scientific value had been unearthed.

Assisted by Hopkins, Foulke and Joseph Leidy, the director of the Academy of Natural Sciences and a professor of anatomy at the University of

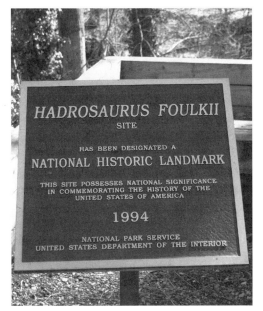

The sign designating the site of the Hadrosaurus discovery as a historic site.

The actual site of the Hadrosaurus discovery.

Pennsylvania, continued the excavation and found many more of the odd-looking bones. The two scientists brought them back to the Philadelphia institute, where Leidy examined them. Finally he announced that Foulke had indeed discovered what Owen had called Dinosauria, or "terrible lizards." Then Leidy, Foulke, and others painstakingly assembled the bones into a dinosaur skeleton that the director called *Hadrosaurus foulkii*, after the town and the discoverer. The creature was twelve-feet high and thirty-feet long, and probably had to eat 200 pounds of plant material per day to sustain its body weight.

Hadrosaurus was the first complete dinosaur skeleton discovered in the United States. Of equal significance was that Leidy concluded that the creature was bipedal, because the hind limbs were larger than the forelimbs. Indeed, when he constructed the skeleton he showed the dinosaur standing

The statue celebrating the discovery of the Hadrosaurus, located in the middle of Haddonfield.

on its hind legs only. This was a clear contradiction of popular theories of the time, which had dinosaurs plodding about on all fours.

The unearthing of Hadrosaurus opened the door for a frenzy of dinosaur discoveries in the later half of the nineteenth century (two scientists were such bitter rivals that their competition was dubbed the "bone wars") and went a long way toward improving the understanding of these strange and fascinating creatures. Today a replica of the skeleton of the "original" Hadrosaurus is still on display at the Academy of Natural Sciences in Philadelphia.

Hadrosaurus is not the only dinosaur discovered in New Jersey. Another is Deinosuchus, a gigantic, meat-eating fifty-foot-long crocodile-like creature guaranteed to be no day at the beach. Dryptosaurus, whose bones have also turned up in the state, was another nasty-looking meat eater with dagger-like teeth and eight-inch foot claws. By contrast, Nodosaurus, a relatively peaceful plant eater, and Quetzalcoatlus, the largest of all the Pterosaurs (its wing span was between forty and fifty feet), seem tame.

One of the most fascinating things about dinosaurs is that new discoveries occur constantly. Will the next big dinosaur "event" happen in New Jersey? It's entirely possible.

Although New Jersey is a relatively small state in area, it boasts several different geologic provinces, or regions, whose natural formations are markedly different from each other.

In the northwestern part of the state (mainly Sussex and Warren Counties, although parts of Passaic and Morris are also included) is the Valley and Ridge Province. This region takes up approximately one-twelfth of the state's area. New Jerseyans call the ridges mountains, although time and erosion have worn them down to little more than humps on the face of the earth. The Wallpack and Kittatinny Mountains, part of the Appalachian chain, are typical New Jersey ridges—or "mountains" if you prefer. One of the most famous natural landmarks in this province is the Delaware Water Gap. Another is in High Point State Park, which, as its name suggests, is the site of the highest elevation in New Jersey, 1,496 feet above sea level; High Point Monument on Kittatinny Mountain raises this to over 1,800 feet.

Moving south, the second geologic province in the state is the New Jersey Highlands. Approximately forty miles long and taking up about one-eighth of the state, the Highlands extend across northwestern Passaic, Morris, and Hunterdon Counties, and southeast along Sussex and Warren Counties.

The Highlands contain the oldest rocks in the state—some are over a billion years old—as well as the mineral deposits at Franklin, which most geologists consider one of the most spectacular concentrations of minerals in the entire world.

Franklin's geologic fame began early in the nineteenth century when Dr. Samuel Fowler discovered zinc ore deposits on his land. Fowler subsequently developed a process for making zinc-based paint, and for years Franklin provided zinc oxide for use as a paint additive. After Fowler's death the New Jersey Zinc Company ran the mine for over a century, mining five hundred thousand tons of zinc ore annually until the mineral was finally exhausted in 1954. (The Franklin Mineral Museum now sits on the site of the former zinc mine.)

Today Franklin is known more for its incredible variations of minerals than for its proclivity with zinc. Some of the more than three hundred different minerals uncovered at Franklin are found nowhere else in the world, and geologists seem to be constantly discovering new ones to add to the list.

The Highlands have played a major role in the history of New Jersey, as well as that of the United States. The ridges are a continuation of the famed Green Mountains of Vermont, and this is appropriate indeed. During the Revolutionary War, Ethan Allen's Green Mountain Boys gave the American cause for independence a lift by capturing Fort Ticonderoga. In New Jersey, the Highlands provided Washington's often outnumbered forces with a perfect defensive position from which to observe and harass the British during much of the war. The valleys paralleling the ridges acted as ideal supply lines for the Continental troops during the cold winters at Valley Forge and Morristown.

A bit further down the state is the third geologic province, known as the Newark Basin (also called the Piedmont Lowlands). This region extends across New Jersey in a broad fifteen-hundred-mile swath (constituting approximately one-fifth of the state in area). All of Union, Essex, Hudson, and Bergen Counties are in this region, as are large chunks of Mercer, Somerset, and Middlesex and portions of Hunterdon, Morris, and Passaic. Towns in the Newark Basin differ widely in appearance, such as Princeton, Newark, New Brunswick, Lambertville, Frenchtown, and Morristown, yet are alike in geologic characteristics.

The Newark Basin has an extremely diverse geography. The Watchung Mountains, which extend from Bound Brook to Passaic, are one of the most distinguishing features of this region. ("Watchung" comes from the Native American words *Wath Unks,* which means "high hills.") The Palisades Sill, part of which are those large rock outcroppings covered with graffiti that everyone stares at as they travel on major highways in northern New Jersey, are also part of the Newark Basin. However, the soft, marshy area of the Hackensack Meadowlands, home to the Meadowlands Sports Complex among other things, is also part of the Newark Basin.

In geologic terms, the remaining portion of the state (everything southeast of a line running from New Brunswick to Trenton, and south along the Delaware River to the Atlantic Ocean) is considered the Coastal Plain. This is indeed surprising news to people who live in Chatsworth, New Egypt, Vineland, and other towns far away from the coast, but the soil and rock that underlie their communities are the same as those that are underneath Atlantic City, Wildwood, Point Pleasant, and other shore-based towns.

The Coastal Plain is divided into two areas: the Inner Coastal Plain, which is a thin strip from approximately Perth Amboy down to Freehold, and then in a swath across the state to just above Salem, and the Outer Coastal Plain, which constitutes the rest of the region. One of the characteristics that distinguishes the two "plains" is that the Inner Coastal region has much more fertile soil than its counterpart, whose soil is mainly sand and gravel.

The entire Coastal Plain province is a low-lying region, without the hills and mountains of northern New Jersey. There are exceptions, such as Crawfords Hill in Monmouth County, which rises almost 400 feet into the air, and the Navesink Highlands, whose peak elevation is 276 feet.

The Pinelands are in the Outer Coastal Plain, which helps explain much about the unique characteristics of the region. The principal geologic formation found at the surface throughout most of the Pinelands is known as Cohansey Sand. The composition of a soil determines how many nutrients and water it can hold; soils that have a relatively equal mixture of sand, clay, and gravel are much more fertile than those composed primarily of coarse particles such as gravel and sand. Since soil in the Pinelands primarily developed from the Cohansey Sand, it was sandy soil and thus unable to retain moisture and nutrients. This poor soil inhibited plant growth, which lead to the region being dubbed the Pine Barrens by frustrated farmers who tried to grow crops there and failed.

Obviously, since it constitutes such a huge chunk of the state—three-fifths (forty-five hundred square miles) of territory—the Coastal Plain is the largest geologic region in New Jersey. Amazingly, the Coastal Plain was once more than double its present size.

Approximately eighteen thousand years ago, the last great Ice Age, known as the Wisconsin glaciation, was at its peak. (In New Jersey, the ice came down as far south as Newark.) The presence of these large sheets of ice over large sections of the earth drew so much water from the world's oceans that sea level ultimately dropped a staggering 425 feet. Since the reduced water level meant that more land was exposed, New Jersey's shoreline was more than eighty miles farther east than it is today, stretching well out into the Atlantic Ocean, and the land behind it was all part of the Coastal Plain.

When the glaciers began melting and retreating northward, the water released flowed back into the oceans, which caused sea levels to rise. From around seven thousand years ago to twenty-five hundred years ago, the oceans rose at an extraordinarily rapid rate of around 2 millimeters per year. Even when the increase slowed to a more modest .75 millimeters per year, land—such as New Jersey's Coastal Plain—was still being drowned at a steady pace.

Although it may seem as if the Wisconsin glaciation happened a long time ago, in geologic terms eighteen thousand years is barely a speck on the great clock of the earth. To get a better idea of how quickly rising sea levels are impacting New Jersey, consider that in the seventeenth century—just a few hundred years ago—deeds were issued for land that is today underwater, almost a mile off the coast. Sea level is rising today at a rate of about 4 millimeters per year (twice as fast as during the conclusion of the Wisconsin glaciation). Some scientists estimate that this rate will more than double to 8.5 millimeters per year by the year 2100. Considering all this, one has to wonder what New Jersey's Coastal Plain will look like in another geologic wink of an eye.

The glacial ice also affected New Jersey's geology in other ways. In some northern regions, the advancing ice scraped off the cover of soil, exposing the bedrock underneath. As the ice retreated, it formed large glacial lakes in areas like Passaic and Hackensack. (The modern-day Hackensack Meadowlands owe their existence to the presence of these glacial lakes.) Unless they were maintained by sediment dams, most of these lakes did not survive the ice's retreat. The Great Swamp is an example of a glacial lake that has survived until modern times, although on a much smaller scale.

Indeed, one of the things that attracts geologists and other scientists to New Jersey is the fact that ancient lake deposits in the state exhibit some of the best recorded evidence of global climate changes, dating back two hundred million years, of anyplace in the world. A two-year, multimillion-dollar effort to retrieve rocks exhibiting climate change from the Newark Basin concluded in 1993. New Brunswick, Princeton, and Pennington were three of the sites where drilling took place. Certain areas along the Delaware River, such as near Lambertville, also show evidence of climate alteration. As might be expected, during the last great Ice Age, New Jersey experienced great changes in climate and vegetation. In marked contrast to the dinosaur era, when warm temperatures and abundant plant life were the rule, the time of the Wisconsin glaciation was like one long, silent winter. Many scientists believe that the region of the state not covered by ice— primarily the Coastal Plain—was a windswept, treeless landmass much like modern-day Siberia.

Across this desolate, snow-covered land roamed a variety of animals (the dinosaurs, of course, had died out millions of years before). Chief among them in this era (known as the Pleistocene epoch in scientific terms) were the great woolly mammoths and the large mastodons.

The woolly mammoths were truly impressive creatures, with their shaggy coats of fur and large, curving tusks that resembled huge fishhooks. These great beasts were about fourteen feet tall and had tusks more than fifteen feet in length. Mastodons, which were much more common in New Jersey, were somewhat smaller, averaging between eight and ten feet tall.

A superb fossil find of the Pleistocene epoch was made in Hackensack in 1962. Two high school students exploring an area where a road was being built found three mastodon teeth. Subsequent excavation by scientists unearthed almost an entire mastodon skeleton, which was promptly christened the "Hackensack Mastodon."

Like the dinosaurs before them, the woolly mammoths and the mastodons would not last. Extinction claimed them along with other Pleistocene creatures, opening the way for the arrival of yet another species to claim dominance of the earth: human beings. Their history is still being written.

What does New Jersey's geologic future hold? Some geologists consider that what goes around comes around, and that the state will once again enter an active phase. This means earthquakes, volcanoes, and other natural occurrences that will make things in the state much more unpredictable than they are today. (Don't start planning a move to Kansas, however; this isn't going to happen in our lifetime.)

If earthquakes do become more common in New Jersey in the future, one triggering mechanism will likely be the ancient Ramapo Fault. This one-billion-year-old major fault line in the northern part of the state was once quite active but has been relatively quiet for many millions of years. (Part of I-287 lies almost directly on the Ramapo Fault.) The fault extends southwesterly from New York State, running through parts of Passaic, Bergen, Morris, and Somerset Counties.

Although most of the quakes that emanate from the Ramapo Fault are relatively minor, there have occasionally been some larger jolts. On August 10, 1884, an earthquake measuring five on the Richter scale occurred along the fault. The Ramapo Fault was also responsible for a three-magnitude quake in July 1978.

However, even though the Ramapo Fault does kick up its heels every now and then, the magnitude of the earthquakes that this activity produces is barely enough to register on extremely sensitive seismographs, never mind turn the entire state into a mini-California. We can all hope that the Ramapo Fault will continue to be just a source of study for geologists, and not a source of concern for New Jerseyans.

Human beings are relatively recent arrivals on this planet. Geologic time, on the other hand, is measured in the millions and billions of years. Despite this disparity, the future of both is now intermixed: human activity affects the state's geology, while any geologic activity affects people. Whether the next change is measured in millions of years, or thousands of years—or even hundreds of years—it's obvious that the geologic history of New Jersey is still being written.

DID YOU KNOW?

One of the best places in the entire state to learn about New Jersey's geology is at the Rutgers University Geology Museum. Located in Geology Hall on the Cook College campus in New Brunswick, the museum was built in 1872 by George Cook, founder of Cook College, who raised the entire seventy-thousand-dollar cost. For more than one hundred years the building was used for the whole geology department, until rocks, professors, and students were transferred to the Busch Campus in 1976. Currently the museum is used as a research and teaching facility and hosts school groups and other organizations. Besides a wide assortment of New Jersey rocks and minerals, the museum also contains a mastodon skeleton, Indian artifacts, seashell fossils, and even an Egyptian mummy.

Interesting People

Although you'd never get a comedian to admit it, New Jersey's history is filled with an incredible array of fascinating men and women. People, of course, see only what they want to see, so to someone who thinks of New Jersey as nothing more than turnpikes and toxic waste dumps, the idea that the state boasts a roster of interesting and noteworthy people is akin to trying to make four-year-olds eat their vegetables: no way, no how.

Yet the fact is that New Jersey has always played an important role in the history of the United States. Although Benjamin Franklin was being coy when he described New Jersey as "a barrel tapped at both ends" because of its proximity to New York City and Philadelphia, it is precisely this nearness to these major urban centers that has drawn the rich, famous, and just downright interesting here. The result is a historical pedigree that New Jersey can match against any other state in the union.

So throw out those Turnpike jokes. It's time to meet some of the most interesting people in New Jersey's history.

The Battle of Waterloo in 1815 not only destroyed the last hopes of Napoleon for European domination, it also sent members of the Bonaparte family scurrying out of France to seek asylum and escape the wrath of the allies. Many stayed in Europe; others, however, sought to put as much distance between themselves and their conquerors as possible, so naturally they looked to the United States, separated by an entire ocean from the reach of European vengeance. One of those who sought refuge in the United States was Joseph Bonaparte, Napoleon's older brother, and he found it in Bordentown, New Jersey.

Today Bordentown is a small community nestled along the Delaware River just south of Trenton. Little in the town's typical small-town appearance suggests its former heavyweight status as an important link in the chain of travel between New York City and Philadelphia from the mid-eighteenth through the early nineteenth centuries. The town is virtually equidistant between the two major cities, and both stage and boat passengers frequently used Bordentown as a rest stop before continuing their journey. The town has had its share of famous residents, including Thomas Paine, Francis Hopkinson (a signer of the Declaration of Independence), and Commodore Charles Stewart, of "Old Ironsides" fame. (See chapter 10 for more about Bordentown.)

Nothing, however, could have prepared Bordentown residents for the adventure that began on June 16, 1816, when Dr. William Burns of Bordentown encountered two men approaching the town in a carriage. The pair asked whether there were any properties for sale in the area. Burns led the two men—one of whom was Joseph Bonaparte, and the other his American interpreter, James Carret—to the Point Breeze estate, which was currently on the market. Two months later Bonaparte "owned" the huge estate. (A law at that time forbade aliens to own property in New Jersey, so title to Point Breeze was actually in the name of George Reinholdt, an American friend.)

How did the older brother of Napoleon Bonaparte wind up in quiet little Bordentown? According to one story, during the waning days of his empire Napoleon took out a map of America and said to Joseph: "If I am ever forced to fly to America, I shall settle somewhere between Philadelphia and New York, where I can receive the earliest intelligence from France from ships that arrive at either point." Joseph supposedly selected Bordentown on the basis of that conversation.

A more likely reason, however, is that Joseph was seeking privacy. Before buying Point Breeze, he had lived in New York City and Philadelphia and had tried unsuccessfully in both places to blend into the crowd. He was, after all, a fugitive from the European allies and as such a marked man; he never knew whether the next knock on his door would be that of foreign agents, ready to drag him back across the water. Perhaps it was an incident on Broadway, when in full view of hundreds of people a Frenchman dropped to his knees in front of Joseph and sobbed out his devotion to the Bonaparte family, that convinced Joseph he could not hide in a city of thousands.

Who was this mild-mannered, aristocratic Frenchman? At the time he bought Point Breeze for $17,500, he was forty-eight years old, one year older than Napoleon. Lacking his brother's thirst for power, Joseph might have used his considerable financial acumen to enjoy a quiet life as a successful businessman. But you can hardly run a dry goods store when your brother wants to be King of the World. Napoleon thrust Joseph into a series of military and political jobs for which the elder Bonaparte was badly suited, including reigns as the king of Naples (1806–1808) and king of Spain (1808–1813).

After Waterloo, both Napoleon and Joseph prepared to flee to the United States. Napoleon changed his mind at the last moment, leaving Joseph to sail alone for the United States on July 29, 1815, aboard the *Commerce*. Napoleon was captured and exiled to St. Helena. The two brothers never saw each other again.

Joseph's Point Breeze estate initially consisted of a house and 211 acres. After the New Jersey legislature repealed its objections to aliens owning property in January 1817, Joseph went on a buying spree that eventually enlarged his holdings to approximately 1,000 acres.

The land that Joseph purchased was pure wilderness, shot through with marshes, thorn bushes, and ravines. He quickly turned the land into an estate fit for a former king. In a biographical sketch of Joseph in *Frank Leslie's Popular Monthly* of February 1894 (in which Bordentown was called "The American St. Helena"), the transformation of Point Breeze was described as follows: "A tract of marshy land . . . [was] turned into an artificial lake; the forest was intersected with walks and drives; open spaces here and there were cleared for lawns; rustic bridges were thrown over rocky-sided ravines, summerhouses were erected in sequestered spots, flowers bloomed in the parterres and rare exotics in the conservatories."

The house also reflected Bonaparte's fondness for things regal. Described by *Leslie's* as "a palace," it was built of brick and covered with white plaster. Inside, said the magazine, "was a grand staircase, flanked by great reception and dining rooms. The huge fireplaces had marble mantels with marvelous bas-reliefs. The bedchambers were hung with rare tapestry. The walls were decorated with still rarer paintings, more or less dishonestly acquired, and statuary of similar beauty."

It took Joseph several years, and much money, to finish both the grounds and the house—one contemporary account said that the house alone cost him $20,000—but by January 1, 1820, the French exile could look forward to the coming year with the knowledge that the work was finally done.

Two days later, the entire house burned to the ground.

Joseph was in Trenton on business on the afternoon of January 3 when word of the fire came. He rushed back to find his home a blazing inferno. Despite the best efforts of the citizens of Bordentown—including the ladies, who formed a bucket brigade—the home was destroyed.

The people of Bordentown did manage to save many precious statues, paintings, books, and papers from the flames. Joseph, used to the pillaging and looting that routinely occurred during European wars, was astonished when the residents returned these valuable items to him. In gratitude, he addressed a letter to them, saying that the incident showed him that "Americans are, without contradiction, the most happy people I have known."

Undeterred by this disaster, Joseph quickly converted his stable into a new home. Soon this house too was filled with paintings, sculptures, gold tapestries, chandeliers, and other objects of nobility. Upon his arrival in America he had adopted the name the Count de Survilliers (the name of a village on his estate in France), and he continued to use this title at Point Breeze.

Despite his obvious wealth, lofty title, and aristocratic manner, Bonaparte was clearly liked by his Bordentown neighbors. He used local labor in every endeavor he undertook, such as clearing his land and building his house. When there was no work to do, Joseph often invented jobs for residents who wanted to earn some money. In the book *Bonaparte's Park and the Murats,* written in 1879 when the memory of Joseph was still fresh, author E. M. Woodward said: "The count was a great benefit to Bordentown . . . besides liberally patronizing the shops, he gave employment to all who asked for it. He always paid most liberal wages; cash each day, and in hard money."

Bonaparte let the locals wander freely over his vast estate, where peacocks strutted across immaculate lawns, swans glided over the lake, and deer gamboled in the thicket. In the winter Bonaparte allowed ice skating on the lake, and he would often go down and watch the action, frequently rolling apples and oranges onto the ice for the skaters. On the day before Christmas, Joseph's daughter Zenaide would drive along the length of the lake in a sleigh made in the shape of a swan, throwing out sugarplums and toys as holiday treats.

Visitors to his home were always warmly welcomed and given a tour that highlighted the many *objets. d'art*. Joseph particularly enjoyed showing his strait-laced American visitors his many nude and semi-nude female paintings and sculptures, and watching his guests' "blushes and giggles." The April 1845 edition of *Godey's Lady's Book,* described the walls of Bonaparte's sleeping quarters as being covered with oil paintings of young women "with less clothing about them than they or you would have found comfortable in our cold climate."

Although Joseph's wife remained in Italy and never joined him at Point Breeze, claiming she was too ill for the ocean voyage, he did have the company of many friends and relatives, including his daughters Zenaide and

Charlotte, his devoted secretary Louis Maillard, and others. A steady stream of famous personages also came to Bordentown, including Henry Clay, Daniel Webster, John Quincy Adams, and the Marquis de Lafayette.

The many French expatriates who came to Point Breeze gave rise to tales that Joseph was plotting a revolution that would once again place a Bonaparte on the throne of France. On the surface, these rumors seem unfounded; Joseph, finally free from his brother's ambition, seems to have genuinely enjoyed playing country squire. In 1820, when Mexico revolted against Spanish rule and Joseph was offered the Mexican crown, he turned it down with the comment: "I have worn two crowns. I would not take a step to wear a third."

Yet, suspicions still linger about Joseph's true intentions at Bordentown. Was Point Breeze supposed to be the site of a government in exile for the Bonapartes, while they plotted their return to power in France? The French considered the Mexican offer as part of a plot to help Napoleon escape. Indeed, reports of plots to free Napoleon from his St. Helena exile were as numerous then as JFK assassination conspiracy theories are today.

What gives these theories an extra pinch of intrigue is the network of underground tunnels that Joseph built at Point Breeze. One led directly to the Delaware River and was wide enough to allow a boat with an eighteen-foot sweep of oars to be rowed from the river directly to the basement of Joseph's home. Other tunnels led from nearby Crosswicks Creek to the house, while still others connected different buildings on the estate.

The "official" version is that the tunnels allowed family members to pass from one building to another during bad weather. Adolph Maillard, son of Joseph's trusted secretary, wrote that "when Joseph built the lakehouse for his daughter Zenaide and her household, he connected it by an underground gallery, with the main house, for the facility of service, and for her own use in bad weather."

In 1914, *The World Magazine* came up with the best tunnel theory yet: the real Napoleon, it said, did not die at St. Helena in 1821 but escaped his rocky exile and wound up in New Jersey.

"And if Napoleon did get away from St. Helena, where did he go?" the magazine asked. "There is but one reasonable answer . . . Bordentown, N.J. He could have been rowed from the Delaware River directly into his brother's house. And during the years that he was watching for a chance to return to power, he could have had the freedom, through a labyrinth of secret underground passages, of one of the most beautiful estates in America."

These gates mark what was once the entrance
to Joseph Bonaparte's home at Point Breeze.

Was this pure fantasy, or did one of the world's most notorious men once
live in New Jersey, emerging from his hiding place only in the darkest hours
of the night to walk the deserted streets of Bordentown and dream of glo-
ries past? We'll never know for sure.

By the 1830s the European political climate had changed, and Joseph was
able to travel to England in 1832, where he stayed for five years. He returned
to the United States in 1837, but just to settle his affairs. He left for Europe
again in 1839 and was finally reunited with his wife in Italy. It was there, in
Florence, that he died on July 28, 1844, at age seventy-six.

In March 1847, a correspondent for the Massachusetts newspaper *Daily
Herald* visited Point Breeze and found the "broad roads covered with
weeds . . . the deer all departed . . . the once favorite home a dreary, tenant-
less pile of bricks and mortar."

The days of royalty in Bordentown were over.

They called James Still the "Black Doctor of the Pines." He was more than a country doctor with an encyclopedic knowledge of herbs and plants; in an age when the shackles of slavery had given way to the bonds of uncertainty for blacks, James Still was a symbol of hope to African Americans everywhere.

"I was born in Washington Township (now Shamong), Burlington County, State of New Jersey, April ninth, one thousand eight hundred and twelve, at what was called the Indian Mill," writes Still in his 1877 autobiography, *Early Recollections and Life of Dr. James Still.* His parents were Levin and Charity Still, former slaves in Maryland who bought their freedom and came north to live.

At the age of three, Still had a moment of epiphany: a doctor came to his home to vaccinate the children. Still was deeply impressed by the doctor's mastery of the healing powers.

"From that moment I was inspired with a desire to be a doctor," Still wrote. "It took deep root in me, so deep that all the drought of poverty or lack of education could not destroy the desire."

Still began playing doctor, using a thin piece of pine bark for a needle. His thoughts were always of the time when he too could travel around, "healing the sick and doing great miracles."

It is fortunate that Still's desire to be a doctor ran so strong, because it was sorely tested in his early life. The family experienced bouts of extreme poverty, times when things were so desperate that Still had to wrestle a piece of meat out of the mouth of the family cat in order to have something to eat.

Education was a hit-or-miss proposition for the young boy. Still went to school only in bad weather, because on good days he had to work around the house. Even when he did go to school, the teacher was so poorly trained that the students were taught incorrect grammar and pronunciation. Sometimes Still would contemplate the enormity of the obstacles standing in the way of his becoming a doctor: There were no black doctors, no white doctor would teach him, and he couldn't afford to go to college. But the dream did not die.

When he was eighteen years old James was farmed out for by his father to Amos Wilkins for one hundred dollars for three years. As part of the agreement, James received one month's schooling each year.

Although Still worked at the Wilkins farm without complaint, he had attacks of extreme loneliness. These were moments when his hope of becoming a doctor seemed nothing more than a cruel joke. "I had no books, no money or friends, no one with whom to keep company," he wrote. "I often thought myself the most desolate person in the State—no one with whom to commune of my future hopes."

When his servitude expired, Still, now twenty-one, packed his meager belongings into two handkerchiefs, collected $9.50 from Wilkins, and prepared to face the world. He walked to Philadelphia—fearful that he would be picked up as a runaway slave along the way—to visit his sister Keturah, and promptly got a job in a glue factory.

For the next several years Still experienced life's typical ebb and flow. He worked a succession of jobs that ranged from good to awful. He married Angelina Willow in 1835 and had a daughter named Beulah, only to lose both wife and child to illness within a year of each other, in 1838 and 1839 respectively.

In 1843, after remarrying, James bought a small still. With this he began distilling sassafras roots and various herbs and selling the mixtures to druggists in Philadelphia. The old dream of becoming a doctor, which had retreated to the back of his mind, now came to the fore once again. Obtaining some books on medical botany, he began making medicines from the plants that he found in Burlington County. He used one of these mixtures to cure his neighbor's daughter of scrofula (a form of tuberculosis). Unknown to Still, he had begun fulfilling his long-cherished dream.

"I thought it [curing the girl] no great thing, for it always seemed to me that all diseases were curable, and I wondered why the doctors did not cure them," he wrote.

Word of Still's medical expertise spread, and soon so many people were coming to see him that he had to hire someone to dig and distill roots and herbs, which remained his only source of income. Then Still took the case of a young girl who was so severely ill with scrofula that all the doctors had given up on her. In ten weeks time she was nearly well, and Still's reputation as a healer took a giant leap. People began calling him "Doctor" Still.

Giving up his distilling business to concentrate full time on his practice, Still built a small wagon out of pine. Using a cigar box as a medicine chest, he traveled around the area, dispensing his homemade medicines. Physicians laughed at the uneducated black man driving around in his homemade wagon, derisively calling him "Black Jim," but his patients never laughed at the results.

"My calls were many, and I rode continually," Still said. "The cases under my care I cured."

Although his usual charge was just one dollar for medicine and advice, Still and his family soon grew prosperous. The man who once had to wrestle a cat for supper acquired property at the old Cross Roads section of present-day Medford, built a large home there, and was able to keep his growing family (eventually numbering seven children) properly fed and clothed. Yet he changed little; he still traveled great distances to visit patients and took a keen interest in all his cases. On Sunday he tried to rest, but so many people would come to his office then that he didn't even have time to eat.

Still practiced under difficult circumstances. Often he took so-called hopeless cases, knowing that if the patient died under his care he would be blamed by prejudiced people just waiting for this successful black man to stumble. Since he was not a licensed physician, he had to tread carefully. He learned that if he sold his homemade medicines, instead of giving prescriptions and charging for medical services, that he could continue his practice without obtaining a license.

As might be expected, the medical community was not fond of Still's success. "Oh, they will soon be well now; Black Jim has been there!" was the contemptuous cry often hurled at those Still treated. Families were pressured by doctors to ignore Still's advice—sometimes with disastrous results. Once Still advised a girl that he was treating for cancer not to have the tumor cut out, or she would die. But upon hearing that, a physician assailed the girl's father: "Why are you taking your daughter to Medford, to that old nigger?" He told the father to have the tumor surgically removed. The man did just that, and his daughter was dead within two weeks.

Still was supremely confident of his healing powers. "I can say assuredly that I have found no disease but that I have also found a remedy for it in some stage of it."

Besides medicine, Still also gave his patients the power of positive thinking. Often he would visit the bedside of someone seriously ill and give them what amounted to a pep talk that seemed to have amazing results.

One such case was that of a girl named Mary Sooy. When he arrived at the girl's home, it was filled with grieving men and women on a deathwatch. Undaunted, Still went to the girl, took her hand, and said: "Miss Sooy, you are not dying, and will not die this time. I know that you and everyone must die sometime, but you will not die now." The girl recovered completely under Still's care.

In 1872, Still's rigorous schedule finally caught up with him, and he became seriously ill. Although he recovered, in the next year he suffered a slight stroke. This made him stop traveling, and he could treat only patients who came to his Medford office. But this didn't stop the flood of patients, and he remained busy up to the day he died. On March 9, 1882, James Still died, one month short of his seventieth birthday.

Still was survived by his wife, Henrietta, three sons, and four daughters. Though he had at one time wrapped all his worldly belongings into two handkerchiefs, Still left an estate valued at $19,921.

He also left, in his autobiography, his philosophy, which stands as a lasting tribute to this decent, humble man:

> Be kind to all. Do not speak disparagingly of your neighbors. Treat your enemies with all the courteousness you can command. Let not wordly riches be your chiefest goal, for you cannot take them with you when you exchange time for eternity. The race is not to the swift or the battle to the strong, but to those who honestly contend until the warfare is ended.
>
> Aspire to greatness.

DID YOU KNOW?

Medical advice from Dr. Still:

For fevers [at a time when most physicians did nothing for fevers, preferring to let them run their course]: "Moderate the violence of the arterial excitement and prevent local inflammation and congestion. Support the powers of the system, relieve urgent symptoms, and restore the suppressed evacuations."

For rheumatism [arthritis]: "By giving sudorific medicine to promote perspiration, and bathing the feet in tepid water with ashes added at night before retiring to bed, drinking freely of catnip or other herb tea, and applying stimulating liniment to the affected parts, relief is obtained by the sufferer."

For coughs: Eight ounces of spikenard root, comfrey root, horehound tops, elecampane root, bloodroot, skunk-cabbage root, and pleurisy root. All bruised. Boil in two gallons of soft water down to one gallon. Express and strain the liquid, until you have one gallon. Add ten pounds of white sugar, and boil to form a syrup. Strain again. When nearly cool take two drachms oil anise and four ounces alcohol, mix and pour into the balsam. Also one pint tincture of lobelia. Let the whole stand twenty-four hours. Dose: one teaspoon three, four, or five times a day.

Antibilious Powder: Take four ounces of pulverized jalap root, eight ounces of pulverized alexandria senna, three drs. of pulverized cloves, and 1/2 ounce of cream of tartar. Mix and rub well in a mortar. Dose: one teaspoonful in warm water, sweetened, on an empty stomach.

Emetic Powder: Take four ounces of ipecac, four ounces of lobelia, and two ounces of bloodroot. Pulverize separately, mix, and rub well with a mortar. Dose: teaspoonsful given every thirty minutes in warm boneset tea.

Artist John Frederick Peto found nothing in New Jersey but heartbreak and frustration. Yet today he is recognized as one of the finest still-life painters in American history. The story of Peto's posthumous rise to greatness is a tale of detective work that unearthed the secrets buried in a small Ocean County town.

Peto was born in Philadelphia on May 21, 1854. As a boy he sketched pictures of local scenes, animals, birds, and flowers. By the time he was twenty, Peto had decided to become an artist; his first known picture is dated 1875. Besides painting, his creativity found outlets in photography and cornet playing.

For over a decade Peto worked as an artist in Philadelphia. Then, in 1887, two important things happened to him: he married Christine Pearl Smith from Ohio, and he began visiting Island Heights, New Jersey.

Located just outside Toms River in Ocean County, Island Heights today still displays the charm and serenity it had in the 1870s, when it was founded as a Methodist camp meeting town. As a cornet player, Peto was in great demand at the camp meetings, and the young painter found himself spending more and more time there. For a few years he continued working in Philadelphia, but Peto had fallen under the spell of the raw natural beauty that the Jersey Shore possessed at that time. In 1889 he decided to move to Island Heights.

Peto built a sweeping Victorian house at 102 Cedar Avenue, in what was then an open field. The home commanded an unobstructed view of the broad Toms River, less than half a mile away. At the rear of the house was a two-story art studio. Into this large but cozy room Peto crammed his canvases, paints, piano, and the countless objects that he loved to depict in his still-life paintings, such as books, envelopes, photographs, candles, lanterns, knives, musical instruments, and door hinges.

Peto's still-life paintings are examples of the trompe-l'oeil school of painting, which means, literally, "trick the eye." His paintings are so realistic that, for example, a picture of a wall, with playing cards and pictures pinned to it, looks so real that one is tempted to reach out and pluck the items off. Peto's uncanny ability to alter perspective make his paintings some of the finest examples of trompe-l'oeil ever produced.

In 1888 Peto's only child, Helen, was born. The artist seemingly had it all: a beautiful home, lovely wife, adorable child, and monumental talent.

But appearances can often be deceiving. Although his home was indeed gorgeous, moving to Island Heights removed him from Philadelphia's mainstream art world. The difficulty of any creative person trying to support him- or herself solely through his or her work has been a recurring theme since prehistoric man first scratched a picture on the cave wall, for centuries, and Peto was no different. Without any standing in the art world, he was forced to sell his paintings for whatever money they would bring, usually a few dollars at most.

As the economic pressures grew, his home life became more turbulent. Peto had been brought up by his maternal grandmother and her four unmarried daughters. When he moved to Island Heights, two of his aunts came to live with him. One was extremely demanding, causing tension between Peto and his wife. In her later years, this woman became senile and had to be locked in her room. There she spent hours rattling the doorknob, while below, in earshot, Peto tried desperately to concentrate on his painting.

Peto also suffered from Bright's disease, a painful condition of the kidneys. His daughter remembered being sent out of the house when the doctor came to examine her father. Often Peto would cry out in anguish as the doctor performed some type of treatment. There was also a long legal battle over the estate of one of his great-aunts that further spent Peto's time and emotional resources.

Because of his mounting troubles, the paintings that Peto produced during his final years, while some of his best work, have been described by art historian John Wilmerding as being "tinged by an air of sad exhaustion."

In November 1907, Peto went to see a doctor in New York City, possibly to get treatment for his kidney ailment. After the procedure, however, he fell ill and was feverish when he arrived at his sister's apartment in the city. A few days later, John F. Peto died at age fifty-three.

Normally, this would be the end of the story. Instead, it's just the beginning.

Living in Philadelphia at the same time as Peto was a still-life painter named William Harnett. Peto was a friend and admirer of the slightly older artist, and paintings by the two are often remarkably similar. Unlike Peto, however, Harnett remained in Philadelphia throughout his career, and his body of work became well-known, unlike Peto's.

Perhaps inevitably, the work of the two became intertwined, and the more famous Harnett was credited with many Peto paintings. This confusion was helped along by an unscrupulous Philadelphia art dealer, who forged Harnett's name on some of Peto's works. Thus, Peto suffered the indignity of being obscure not only in life, but in death as well.

This was the situation for decades, even though paintings credited to Harnett were wildly divergent in style: one style was tight, jewel-like, and rational, the other softer and more romantic. This was chalked up to different "periods" that Harnett had gone through. Of Peto there was nary a thought.

Then, on July 21, 1947, an art expert named Alfred Frankenstein left New York for a trip to Philadelphia. On the way he intended to stop for a few minutes at Island Heights to see Peto's daughter, Helen, who had converted the family home into a boardinghouse. Frankenstein, who had been researching United States still-life painters, was troubled by the stylistic differences in Harnett's work. But he wasn't looking for the answers in Island Heights. He wanted only to gather some biographical information about the forgotten Peto from the artist's daughter.

As Frankenstein wrote in his 1953 book *After the Hunt:* "Nothing was known about John Frederick Peto beyond the fact that a number of still lifes bearing his name had for some years been kicking around the galleries of various New York dealers. Peto was . . . one of a large, completely unexplored group of painters whom the art world casually accepted and casually dismissed as "Harnett imitators."

After locating Helen, Frankenstein explained his purpose. Helen agreeably led him into her father's former studio. Frankenstein described what happened next: "Up to this point, it was clear that she thought me rather strange; as soon as I stepped into Peto's painting room, however, she must have thought me violently insane. For on ledges, shelves, and wall brackets in Peto's workshop were the very candlesticks, pistols, lamps and other objects represented, over and over again, in paintings by William Michael Harnett."

The secret had been discovered. Intending to stay in Island Heights only a few hours, Frankenstein remained there for the next five days, questioning Helen and her husband and examining Pew's models, photographs, and other evidence. At last, he could arrive at only one conclusion: "The 'hard' style, and the 'hard' style alone, was Harnett; the 'soft' style was Peto concealed under forged Harnett signatures." Frankenstein also noted that the Petos with Harnett's signature were very popular and were in some of the country's most important public and private collections. Forty years after his death, John Frederick Peto had finally been vindicated.

Today, Peto's studio, called, appropriately enough, The Studio, still exists in Island Heights. The walls are still adorned with some of the objects he used in his paintings, and when you look at them, you get a feel for Peto the artist. But to discover something of Peto the man, you need look no further than two iron hooks sunk into a ceiling beam. From these Peto, the devoted father, hung a swing for his daughter Helen. This is how they would spend hours together, she swinging, he painting, and neither one of them ever dreaming that one day the work he was creating in a tiny studio in New Jersey would be considered genius.

Today she's not very well known. No one speaks of her in the same breath as Eleanor Roosevelt, Amelia Earhart, or other famous women. Even though there's a hospital named in her honor in Belleville, many are unaware of who the name refers to.

At the beginning of the twentieth century, however, millions of people in the United States knew the name Clara Louise Maass. She was a genuine hero; people everywhere praised her courage and selflessness.

Born in East Orange on June 28, 1876, Clara was the oldest child of German immigrants Robert E. and Hedwig Maass. After emigrating from Germany the Maasses, like so many others, found that the streets of the New World were paved not with gold but with sheer hard work. Without skills, Robert Maass was forced to toil in the local hat mills. His tiny wage was barely adequate for the needs of his growing family, which soon numbered nine children.

Because money was tight, Clara began working while still in grammar school. This helped her mature emotionally at an early age. At fourteen, she was an intelligent-looking girl, with honey-blonde hair hanging in bangs over her forehead and eyes already filled with the burdens of adulthood.

Two years later, after leaving school for a full-time job, Clara's appearance had changed even more. Now her hair was bound in a tight knot atop her head, and her expression was thoughtful and serious. Clara Maass had left childhood behind forever.

In 1893, at age seventeen, Maass took a step that would change her life, and ultimately the lives of millions of people. She enrolled in the nursing school of Newark German Hospital.

Built in 1870 to ensure that the city's large German population received proper medical care, Newark German Hospital had been advertising for nursing candidates between the ages of twenty and forty. But the years of responsibility had paid off for Clara; she looked and sounded much older than her seventeen years. Hospital officials could tell that she was a woman used to hard, thankless work and long hours, which was what nursing offered back then. (Nursing was so difficult that the hospital would graduate just one nurse from its program in 1894—everyone else dropped out.) Maass was accepted into the nursing program.

Hard work was no stranger to Clara. She threw herself into her studies with her customary determination, and was rewarded in 1895 when she, along with three other girls, received their nursing caps and pins. Just three years later, Clara was named head nurse at German Hospital. The young girl with the serious smile was rising rapidly in her profession.

Then, abruptly, Clara took a detour off the straight-ahead road of job, home, and family that she had been expected to travel: She applied to become a "contract nurse" for the United States Army in the Spanish-American War.

Viewed today through the prism of history, it's easy to recognize the Spanish-American War as a jingoistic exercise forced upon an unsuspecting populace by the patriotic exhortations of William Randolph Hearst and other newspaper publishers. But back then, the war was very simple: Spain was the bad guy that was bullying her Cuban colony, and the United States was the good guy, riding to the rescue of our small southern neighbor.

As wars go, the Spanish-American War was more period than paragraph; the fighting, which took place entirely in Cuba and the Philippines (another Spanish territory), was over in less than four months, with the United States victorious. Seven hundred U.S. soldiers died in battle.

But the United States was fighting two enemies during that war: Spanish soldiers and the deadly disease yellow fever—called "Yellow Jack" by sailors (because when it struck a port city a yellow quarantine flag was flown alerting incoming ships to avoid the area) and *el vomito negro* (the black vomit) by the Spanish.

Of all the diseases to plague humanity throughout the ages, yellow fever was one of the worst. Between 1668 and 1893 there were 135 major yellow fever epidemics in United States port cities, including one terrible bout in Philadelphia in 1793 that killed one out of every ten citizens. Yellow fever's symptoms—headaches, backaches, chills, nausea, fever, swollen lips, inflamed eyes, discoloration of the tongue, and dark vomit colored by blood—were among the most terrible of any disease. Worst of all, no one knew what caused yellow fever.

Then, in the mid-1890s, British Army surgeon Sir Ronald Ross discovered that the *Anopheles* mosquito was the carrier of malaria. Medical researchers began to consider insect hosts as the cause for other diseases, including yellow fever. As more and more soldiers on both sides died of yellow fever during the Spanish-American War, the idea of an insect host gained momentum.

This was how things stood when Clara Maass volunteered for duty as a contract nurse for the army. However, by the time her offer was accepted, the brief war was over. Instead of Cuba, Clara was ordered to the field hospital of the Seventh U.S. Army Corps at Jacksonville, Florida, to help nurse soldiers suffering from typhoid, malaria, and other diseases. From there she was sent to Savannah, Georgia, and then to Santiago, Cuba. On February 5, 1899, her contract with the army expired, and Clara returned to the United States and the German Hospital.

She would not remain there long, however. When U.S. troops were sent to the Philippine Islands to put down a revolt, Clara again volunteered her services.

"I am in excellent health and I have a good constitution, and am accustomed to the hardships of field service," she wrote the surgeon general on November 9, 1899.

Her answer arrived quickly. On November 20, she received a telegram ordering her to board the U.S. Army transport *Logan* for the trip to Manila, the capital of the Philippines.

She arrived at Manila in the midst of a yellow fever epidemic. For the first time. Clara saw the terrifying speed and destructive force of Yellow Jack as infected soldiers rolled violently back and forth in their cots and the doctors looked on helplessly.

After seven months of nursing the sick, Clara was stricken with dengue, an illness that produces severe pain in the joints and muscles. When she took a long time to recover, the army sent her home in the summer of 1900.

By then, a team of physicians in Cuba led by Dr. Walter Reade were zeroing in on the cause of yellow fever. In August 1900, the doctors had targeted the *Aedes aegypti* mosquito as a likely carrier of the disease. They began experiments to see if people bitten by the insect would catch yellow fever.

At the same time, Havana was in the grip of a horrifying yellow fever epidemic. A new wave of Spanish immigrants had provided *el vomito negro* with fresh victims, and dozens were dying every day. Dr. William Gorgas, one of the team involved in the mosquito experiments, issued a call for nurses to administer to Havana's sick. One of those who answered was Clara Maass.

By then—the autumn of 1900—the life of the twenty-four-year-old nurse was settling into a more typical pattern. She was engaged to be married to a New York businessman (who has never been identified). Yet she immediately responded to Gorgas's call. By November she was in Havana, and working at a tree-shaded hospital called Las Animas.

At the hospital, Clara learned from Doctor Juan Guiteras about the yellow fever research going on. Still searching for definitive proof that the *Aedes aegypti* mosquito was to blame for the disease, the United States Army in the spring of 1901 offered one hundred dollars to anyone who volunteered to be bitten by a mosquito suspected of carrying yellow fever, and two hundred dollars if the person got the disease. Six Spanish immigrants submitted to the test; two died.

These were the odds facing Clara early in 1901, when she volunteered for the experiment. At first the doctors resisted her offer, but Maass quietly and firmly insisted. Finally she was accepted into the program, the only woman and only American among nineteen participants.

Maybe she volunteered for the dangerous experiment because she believed herself immune after having worked with so many yellow fever victims, or possibly she did it for the money. Most likely, however, is that Clara Maass saw an opportunity to serve yet again, and in the spirit of nurses everywhere, could not refuse.

Maass was bitten by ten mosquitoes on five different occasions between March and June 1901. The results were negative. She insisted that the doctors try again. They did—at nine A.M. on August 14 with two mosquitoes already suspected of having caused the disease.

The suspicions were correct. Yellow fever ripped through the young woman's body, battering her with violent headaches, extreme muscle pain, intense vomiting, and a high fever. This time there would be no escape.

As Yellow Jack closed in on her, Clara wrote a final letter home: "Goodbye, Mother," it said. "Don't worry, God will care for me." In a line that summed up the brave young woman's life, she said: "You know I am the man of the family but do pray for me."

On August 24, 1901, Clara Maass died of yellow fever.

Her death ended the yellow fever experiments. She was the only American, and the only woman, to die in the research. Her death proved that the bite of an infected mosquito could not be used to provide immunity from the disease, and also showed that the mosquito was the carrier. Dr. Gorgas began a swift, systematic extermination of the insect. His success was nothing short of spectacular: not a single case of yellow fever was reported in Havana from October 1901 to June of the following year. This was after a period of 140 years—from 1762 to 1901—when not a single day had gone by without at least one case of yellow fever being reported.

As for Clara, her death was widely reported in the New York City newspapers. "Trained Nurse, Sacrifice to Duty, Dies from Yellow Fever In Cuba," said the *New York Herald,* which featured a picture of Clara with the story. The *New York Times* carried the story on the front page. Two days later, the *Times* eulogized the brave young woman under the heading "The Martyrs of Science": "Miss Maass was willing to incur the risk of infection if thereby she might assist in establishing a scientific hypothesis of first importance," the paper said. "The annals of medicine are full of the records of the noblest and most disinterested self-sacrifice for the sake of truth. No soldier in the late war placed his life in peril for better reasons than those which prompted this faithful nurse to risk hers."

In time, the story of Clara Maass was forgotten. A burst of publicity occurred in the early 1950s, but that too faded away. In 1976, the United States issued a thirteen-cent stamp with Clara Maass's picture to commemorate the one hundredth anniversary of her birth. What made this action significant was that it took place during the nation's bicentennial year, when names like Washington and Jefferson were on everyone's lips. A nurse from New Jersey had upstaged the Founding Fathers.

Today, the former Newark German Hospital is named in her honor. And even though not many people know her name, or what she did, the supreme sacrifice of Clara Maass will always stand tall in the annals of humanity.

On October 17, 1933, the ocean liner *Westmoreland* docked in New York Harbor. Waiting at the Twenty-third Street pier was an official delegation all ready to welcome the famous German scientist Albert Einstein to America and, more specifically, to Princeton, New Jersey, where the fifty-four-year old physicist had decided to live. Included among the people in the delegation was a group of cheerleaders, anxiously waiting for the famous man to come off the boat so they could begin the parade that was designed to accompany him to Princeton.

Everyone strained to catch a glimpse of the famous face framed by its thatch of wild hair that had never met a comb it liked. There was only one problem: Einstein was not aboard the ship. The director of Princeton's Institute for Advanced Studies, Einstein's employer in his new country, had slipped him off the liner via a tugboat to avoid all the publicity.

Thus began Albert Einstein's stay in America. Although New Jersey has been the home of many a famous person throughout its history, perhaps no one has had as many stories told about them while in residence as Albert Einstein in Princeton.

Many of the stories concern his love of music, particularly his playing of the violin. As soon as he and his wife, Elsa, found a house to rent in Princeton, Einstein celebrated by hosting a small musical recital with the famous Russian violinist Toscha Seidel playing lead. Who played second? Einstein, of course.

Happily, many of the stories about Einstein's violin playing were true, such as how he unexpectedly serenaded a bunch of Halloween pranksters and how he accompanied a group of Christmas carolers. Einstein dearly loved expressing himself through music, and the violin was the instrument of his self-expression. An article in *Time* magazine described him at one musical performance as becoming so deeply absorbed in playing the violin that "he was still plucking at the strings when the performance was all over."

In the summer of 1935 he and Elsa bought a house at 112 Mercer Street in Princeton, and it was here that Einstein would live for the remainder of his life. The house was typically Einstein—unpretentious, yet charming—and he and his wife were soon quite at home in the famous university town.

"The whole of Princeton is one great park with wonderful trees," Elsa gushed to a friend.

Einstein was joined at the Mercer Street home by a variety of pets, including Bibo the parrot, Tiger the cat, and Chico the dog. Chico and the mailman occasionally had issues, but Einstein had a ready explanation. "He [Chico] feels sorry for me because I receive so much mail. That's why he tried to bite the mailman."

Like the man himself, Einstein's routine was simple and uncomplicated. He would have a morning bubble bath, a big breakfast with at least two eggs sunny-side up, and then walk to the Institute. (Driving was "too complicated" for Einstein, explained his wife.) He walked home for lunch, then went upstairs for a nap, after which he dived into his huge allotment of daily mail and then tackled more work until dinner.

Bust of Einstein put on display in 2005 in Princeton.

Einstein enjoyed Princeton's tree-lined streets and university campus.

Throughout the years, the legend has come down of a distracted Einstein, deep in thought, wandering up and down the streets of Princeton in his rumpled clothing. Indeed, there was a ring of truth about these stories, for Einstein could get so deep in thought that the mundane dropped out of his memory: once he called the Institute posing as someone else and asked for the home address of Dr. Einstein. When told that that information was private, he sheepishly explained that he was Dr. Einstein and had forgotten where his house was located. At times he would walk to his home from work, stop outside the front door and furiously think for a time, then turn around and begin heading back to the Institute. Someone usually had to run outside from his home and gently guide him inside.

Besides the absent-minded professor figure, another of the enduring images of Einstein in Princeton is of him helping children with their homework, such as the little girl down the street who bribed him with fudge. Another time, a girl and her friend showed up at his door, and Einstein offered them lunch, which turned out to be beans in the can heated on a Sterno stove.

Although of his many Princeton personas the sweetly absent-minded rumpled professor may have been his favorite, Einstein could play other roles just as well, such as when he was the conscience of the community when African American singer Marian Anderson was denied a hotel room in town and he let her stay at his house.

This was Albert Einstein in Princeton. Unfortunately, his wife Elsa did not get to enjoy the college town atmosphere for long. She died on December 20, 1936, just a few years after the couple had come to town. Yet after this Einstein was usually not alone, and was almost always surrounded by visitors, housekeepers, and other people.

On Monday, April 18, 1955, Albert Einstein died at Princeton Hospital. "It is tasteless to prolong life artificially," he had once said. "I have done my share, it is time to go." When he did, the United States—not to mention the entire world—lost one of its most interesting human beings, and New Jersey had lost the adopted son who had made a tree-lined university town his home.

So far, this chapter has dealt with topics of considerable weight. Thus it seems only fitting that we conclude on a lighter note—a considerably lighter note—with the story of Sam Patch.

Who was Sam Patch? He was a celebrity of the type later perfected by Evel Knievel, Bobby Riggs, and others of that type, people who achieve notoriety by making up in hustle, guts, and showmanship what they lack in ability. Sam blazed the trail for all the P. T. Barnums who were to follow—and he did it "merely" by jumping over waterfalls.

Sam Patch was born in 1807 in Rhode Island. After a few years spent at sea, he found work at the Hamilton Mills cotton works in Paterson. Since his wages supported both himself and his widowed mother, it seemed likely that Patch would spend his life as so many others did then, toiling long, hard hours in industrial obscurity.

But Sam Patch had other ideas.

In 1827, near his twentieth birthday, Sam announced that he was going to jump over the Passaic Falls. Upon hearing this, his coworkers undoubtedly laughed; the falls, while no Niagara, were still extremely dangerous. A person would have to be crazy to willingly jump into those swirling waters.

Patch, however, persisted in his claim, and set September 29 as the date, the same day that a new span of the Chasm Bridge was going to be dropped across the falls.

On that Saturday, a large crowd, including Sam, gathered to watch the new bridge being installed. Having heard what Patch intended to do, the police followed him around most of the day, until he gave them the slip.

When he reappeared, Patch was on a precipice eighty feet above the falls. After a brief speech about how the bridge engineer, Mr. Crane, had done a great thing, and how he was about to do another, Sam launched himself into the air.

The stunned crowd watched as the young man disappeared into the foaming water. Seconds later a thunderous cheer arose when Sam poked his head up and swam to shore. He had proved the naysayers wrong.

Patch's leap was considered so momentous that the *Saturday Evening Post*, one of the country's leading periodicals, carried the following item about it on Saturday, October 6, 1827: "It is stated that on Saturday last a man by the name of Samuel Patch leaped from a rock at Patterson's [sic] Falls, New Jersey, which is from seventy to eighty feet high, into the water, merely for the vanity of performing a surprising feat. He escaped unharmed."

Thus was born "Jumping" Sam Patch.

First Patch solidified his national fame by jumping over the Passaic Falls a few more times. Before he jumped, according to one local report, he would remove his coat, vest, and shoes, and "lay them carefully by, as if debating the question whether he should want them again." Then, after a brief speech in which either one or both of his favorite expressions were used ("Some things can be done as well as others" and "There's no mistake in Sam Patch"), Sam would dash forward and leap over the falls.

Although spectators thrilled to Jumping Sam's exploits, others were not so easily impressed. The *Providence Cadet* sniffed that "water passing down the falls accumulates a large quantity of air and renders it almost impossible for a person to sink to any considerable depth." The paper likened the water at the bottom of the falls to landing on "an ocean of feathers."

The *Elizabeth Town Journal* was even more cold-hearted: "Our informant states that Patch is a mechanic connected with one of the factories in Patterson [sic]—that he is perfectly sane and that his object in the hazardous enterprise is gain."

Patch didn't argue with that last remark. The money was indeed good; at one jump he had cleared thirteen dollars, and at another fifteen dollars, primarily by passing the hat among spectators.

People didn't care why he was doing it; they just wanted him to continue doing it. Thus Sam began what would today be called "The Jumping Tour." His wanderings took him all over the eastern part of the United States. He jumped from cliffs, bridges, masts, and virtually any other object high enough to look dangerous. As Patch's fame grew so did the crowds, and so did his income. Somewhere along the way he picked up a fox and a small bear. Occasionally, he was able to persuade the bear to jump with him.

For an opera singer, the ultimate is performing at the New York Metropolitan Opera. For a waterfall jumper, the ultimate could only be Niagara Falls. In October 1829, the now-famous Sam Patch was invited to Niagara Falls by a committee that was planning to make a day of it at the falls by also blowing up part of a huge rock that had become unsafe. Patch obligingly showed up on the big day, October 6, but after inspecting the preparations and realizing that he would have to share top billing with the explosion, announced that he would not jump. Come back tomorrow, he advised everyone.

They did—and on October 7, 1829, Sam became the first person ever to jump over Niagara Falls. The *Colonial Advocate* filed this enthusiastic report of the event: "The celebrated Sam Patch actually leaped over the Falls of Niagara into the vast abyss below. A ladder was projected from Goat Island about 40 feet down, on which Sam walked out clad in white, and with great deliberation put his hands close to his sides and jumped from the platform. . . . While the boats below were on the look-out for him, he had in one minute reached the shore unnoticed and unhurt, and was heard on the beach singing as merrily as if altogether unconscious of having performed an act so extraordinary as almost to appear an incredible fable. Sam Patch has immortalised himself."

These words were heady praise indeed for the former Paterson mill-worker. Just to prove that his feat was no fluke, Patch did it again, jumping over Niagara Falls a second time on October 17.

By now Sam had no detractors, only supporters. His jumping exploits had captured the country's attention, and made him a star. On November 14, 1829, the *Saturday Evening Post* raved about the Jersey Jumper: "The now distinguished name of Samuel Patch, which erst had never been pronounced out of the little town of Patterson [sic], is rapidly running the honorable circle of newspaper eulogy, from Maine to Georgia. Wherever Sam goes, he meets with welcome! The good people of every town anticipate his arrival, and not a man, woman, or child, are content, till they hear from his own lips that *there is no mistake.*" In closing, the paper offered this poem:

Hail to the hero, Samuel Patch!
Who knows not any equal—
In jumping, Sam can find no match
Among ten million people.

Little did the *Post's* editor know that by the time he printed that glowing tribute, Sam Patch was dead.

The events leading up to Sam's demise were innocent enough. After his triumphant return from Niagara Falls, Sam announced that he would "astonish the natives of the west before returning to the Jerseys" by jumping over Genesee Falls at Rochester, New York. In a newspaper ad, Sam said that he was "determined to convince the citizens of Rochester that he is the real 'Simon Pure' . . . by jumping off the falls . . . from the rocky point in the middle of the Genesee River into the gulph [sic] below, a distance of 100 feet!"

On Friday, November 6, with ten thousand people looking on, Sam dove off the falls. An eyewitness wrote that Sam, after gravely examining the "abyss below him," suddenly "sprang from the cliff . . . and . . . descended like an arrow." Upon surfacing, he was "received with exultation by the crowd." It was, said the witness, an "imposing spectacle."

Perhaps it was the warmth and affection of the Rochester crowd that made Sam declare he would jump the Genesee Falls again on the following Friday—Friday the thirteenth.

Whether you're superstitious or not, it's never a good idea to knowingly tweak the nose of Fate. Yet that was precisely what Sam was doing when he arrived at the falls on that unlucky Friday. At first when he jumped, everything seemed fine; he "descended about one-third of the distance, as handsomely as ever." But then, without warning, his body began to droop. With arms extended and legs separated, he hit the water with a loud smack and immediately sank. "Sam Patch is no more!" said the *Post*.

Although it has been erroneously reported throughout the years that Sam's body was not recovered until several months later, "frozen in a cake of ice" like some long-lost cave man, in reality Sam's body was found two days later. According to the *Post* of December 5, 1829, "it floated ashore a few rods below the spot where he came in contact with the water." After several surgeons examined the Jersey Jumper's corpse, it was found that Sam had suffered "the rupture of a blood-vessel, caused by the sudden chill of the atmosphere through which he passed to the water." Another report said that both of Sam's shoulders were dislocated.

Death, however, could not erase the memory of Sam Patch. For years afterward, two plays—*Sam Patch* and *Sam Patch in France*—toured in the United States, with an actor named Danforth Marble in the title role. By coming such a long way in a short time, and by doing exactly what he had said he would do despite the odds and the dangers, the former millworker from Paterson had proven that there was, indeed, "no mistake in Sam Patch."

4 The Sporting Life

Sports have always played an important role in New Jersey. The history of athletic competition in the Garden State is a long and proud one, filled with many memorable events, including the extraordinary fact that both the first baseball game and the first college football game were played in New Jersey.

There was little in New Jersey's early history to indicate that it would become a sportsperson's paradise. In fact, the state frowned on virtually every type of sporting activity. Card playing and shooting dice were declared public nuisances in New Jersey by virtue of a 1748 law. In 1787, the faculty at the College of New Jersey, as Princeton was then known, prohibited play in which balls and sticks were used because they thought it unbecoming for gentlemen to behave in such an outlandish manner.

But people's craving for sports remained unabated. "Training Days," featuring local troops performing military maneuvers in front of the public, were popular New Jersey events in the early nineteenth century. Gradually, Training Days became like holidays, and other events, such as horse racing, gambling, and games of chance, were held in conjunction with the military exercises.

DID YOU KNOW?

Another popular public activity of the early nineteenth century was inhaling nitrous oxide. On October 24, 1809, at the Academy in Newark, twenty gallons of "exhilarating gas" was prepared for public consumption. The most common effects of this rather unusual "sport" were giddiness, sudden bursts of inspiration, and a sudden desire for physical activity. Similar exhibitions were later held in New York and Philadelphia.

Before too long, sports were booming in New Jersey. Cricket matches were popular in the mid-nineteenth century; the Philadelphia Cricket Club played its matches in Camden, and Hoboken's Elysian Fields was the site of an international contest between the United States and Canada in 1856. It would be another sport, however, that would capture the public's fancy at Hoboken.

The sport was baseball, and it was born right on the Elysian Fields. Unfortunately, due to the international baseball conspiracy—a cover-up rivaling any political-military intrigue of modern times—any link between baseball's birth and Hoboken is purely coincidental.

To find out if you've been a victim of the international baseball conspiracy, ask yourself: Who invented organized baseball? If your answer is Abner Doubleday, then you too have been hoodwinked.

According to the "official" version of baseball's birth, Doubleday conceived of the game in 1839, in Elihu Phinney's cow pasture in Cooperstown, New York. In reality, in 1839 Abner Doubleday was a second-year cadet at West Point; his family had moved out of Cooperstown two years before. When he graduated in 1842, Doubleday said that he was opposed to outdoor exercise and that his favorite sport was chess. And, despite having "invented" the famous game, not once in his life, *never* in a distinguished career as a soldier, writer, and public speaker—did Doubleday publicly mention baseball.

Indeed, the Doubleday story has been thoroughly discredited by baseball historians and sportswriters. For the real story of baseball's birth, think not of Cooperstown, but of Hoboken.

By 1845, the once tree-filled and gloriously green city of New York was growing up fast. Buildings, sidewalks, and streets were rapidly replacing the thigh-high fields of rye and barley and glades of blossoming trees laden with sweet-smelling flowers that had characterized New York in its infancy. As urbanization swept inexorably across Manhattan Island, it destroyed many of the recreation areas that New Yorkers enjoyed. For some this was just an inconvenience; others, such as the New York Knickerbockers baseball club, were deprived of a place to play their game. Fortunately, someone thought of Hoboken.

Although its name comes from the Indian words "Hoboran-Hackingh" (meaning "land of the tobacco pipe," from the time when the Indians would make bowls for their pipes out of stones found at Hoboken), by 1845 Native Americans had vanished from Hoboken. The pleasant small town, consisting of just one square mile of land then just as it does now, was known primarily as a recreation center.

Hoboken's chief relaxation attraction was the sprawling greenbelt called Elysian Fields, named for the place of paradise and forgetting in Greek mythology. And a paradise is what it truly was: shade trees lined the walkways, flower gardens bloomed with eye-popping color, and refreshing breezes from the nearby Hudson River wafted throughout. On Sundays, hundreds of people, including many New Yorkers, would pack this pastoral place, picnicking, drinking the cool spring waters that flowed from the earth, and watching cricket matches, foot races, and the miniature railroad that rambled over the green fields.

So it was to Hoboken that the Knickerbockers came, in the early autumn of 1845, to play the first game of modern baseball, which they had adapted from the older and more common game of town ball. On the ferry with them from New York was Alexander Cartwright—the real "Father of Baseball."

When Abner Doubleday was proclaimed the founder of baseball, it effectively buried the pivotal role that Alexander Joy Cartwright had played in the formation of the game. Born on April 17, 1820, in New York City, Cartwright in 1845 was a twenty-five-year-old teller at the Union Bank who was married to the former Eliza Ann Gerrits Van Wie and living at the fashionable address of 76 Eighth Street. Cartwright, a black-whiskered, burly volunteer fireman, was forced to change professions in July 1845, when a fire at the bank he worked at forced him to become a bookseller. Nothing, however, could quench his passion for playing town ball with his friends.

But as much as Cartwright enjoyed town ball, he knew it needed refinement. After all, being struck by a thrown ball in order to be put out while running the bases was certainly no fun, nor was it very exciting to stand in the field with dozens of other players and fight for the right to catch the occasional ball that came your way. Cartwright's orderly, analytical mind began devising new rules for town ball, rules that would make the game faster and more exciting for both players and spectators. By mid-summer 1845, he had shown some of his fellow players his ideas, which they enthusiastically accepted. They began recruiting members for a new club called the New York Knickerbockers, which was the name of Cartwright's volunteer fire-fighting organization.

DID YOU KNOW?

Cartwright devised twenty rules for his version of baseball. Among the most significant were:

- Limiting a team to three outs per inning, rather than allowing an entire team to bat.
- Throwing to bases to make outs, rather than throwing the ball at runners.

- Stationing the bases ninety feet apart.
- Limiting the number of outfielders to only three, instead of the unlimited number that used to be allowed.
- Inventing the new position of short stop.
- Establishing fair territory and foul lines.
- Restricting teams to nine men on each side, instead of an unlimited number.

It has long been thought that the first game of organized baseball was played on June 19, 1846. However, as James M. DiClerico and Barry J. Pavelec, reveal in their book *The Jersey Game*, the first game was actually an intrasquad contest between members of the Knickerbockers in late September or early October 1845, at Elysian Fields.

On that historic day, the Knickerbockers rode the Hoboken ferry from New York to New Jersey. Once the boat docked in Hoboken, the team walked up Hudson Street and along the river, past the famous rendezvous spot for lovers known as Sybil's Cave, until they came to Elysian Fields. There, at what is today the approximate intersection of Twelfth and Hudson Streets, they found a large, grassy field and immediately began laying out what Cartwright called a "diamond." Before long, the game was underway.

No one knows the particulars of this game, since no scorebook was kept. It has been reported that forty-two runs were scored, although this was a recollection reported years after the fact. The most important thing was that the new rules worked fine. On October 6, armed with a scorebook, the Knickerbockers split into two teams and played the first recorded modern baseball game. The score was 11–8, with Cartwright's team losing.

During the next few weeks, the Knickerbockers played several more games at Elysian Fields. Then, flushed with success, and excited by the brisk pacing and new excitement of their game, the Knickerbockers challenged the Brooklyn Base Ball Club to a match. The game was set for two in the afternoon on Tuesday, October 21, 1845, at Elysian Fields.

On that day, the *New York Herald* carried this day-late notice: "The New York Baseball Club will play a match of baseball against the Brooklyn Club tomorrow afternoon [actually, that same day] at 2 o'clock, at the Elysian Field, Hoboken."

No one knows how many spectators were there to see this historic contest, the first game between two teams using modern baseball rules. What is certain, however, is that while Cooperstown and Abner Doubleday were doing whatever it is they were doing on that October day, baseball history was being made in New Jersey. The Knickerbockers won the game, although the score is unknown.

By now there should be little doubt that Hoboken's Elysian Fields was the place where a game remarkably similar to modern-day baseball was first played. From these contests there exists such tangible evidence as newspaper accounts and schoolbooks; from Cooperstown there is . . . nothing. But Cooperstown and Doubleday have been appointed the home and creator of the game, and the legend is too stubborn to repudiate. Thus today Cooperstown reaps the benefits of the glory that should have been Hoboken's.

On March 1, 1849, Cartwright, lured by the discovery of gold in California, headed west. Along the way, he sowed the seeds of the game that he and the Knickerbockers had played in New York like a baseball Johnny Appleseed, still using the original ball that had begun it all at Elysian Fields. According to one source, he taught the game to "enthusiastic saloonkeepers and miners, to Indians and white settlers along the way," and at "nearly every frontier town and Army post where his wagon train visited."

Improbably, Cartwright wound up in Hawaii, where he died on July 13, 1892. Before he went to the great stadium in the sky, however, Cartwright spread baseball throughout the Hawaiian Islands. In 1939, when organized baseball celebrated its "centennial" with much hoopla about Doubleday, Hawaii indignantly struck off a plaque honoring Cartwright and sent it to Cooperstown, demanding that it be placed in the Hall of Fame.

The Knickerbockers played baseball until the early 1870s, when they built a clubhouse at Elysian Fields. Then they vanished into history, drowned by a burgeoning tide of baseball clubs that played the game for money, not sport.

Sadly, Elysian Fields are also no more. Thanks to urbanization, all that remains of this once-glorious greenbelt is a tiny park where children play and parents gather in the shadow of New York City's imposing skyline, which looms within shouting distance just across the river. Rows of brownstone apartment buildings and an abandoned coffee factory occupy the ground where a group of men changed the face of organized sports throughout the world.

Hoboken has tried valiantly to stake its claim for baseball immortality, but the Doubleday legend is strong, and the name of Cooperstown deeply ingrained in the public consciousness. Except for a plaque at the intersection of Eleventh and Washington Streets, there's nothing in Hoboken to commemorate the city's historic role in the creation of our national pastime. Like Alexander Cartwright, Hoboken's place in baseball history seems destined to be forgotten.

New Jersey is the only state in the union that can say "Here's Mud in Your Eye" to organized baseball—and mean it! For over half a century, mud from the Pennsauken Creek (or somewhere close by) has been used by all major league baseball teams to remove the shine from new baseballs before they're put into play. The product is called Lena Blackburne's Baseball Rubbing Mud, and fifteen pounds' worth is sent in a single coffee can to each team before the start of the season. As far as where the company is located, who owns and operates it (although there once was a Lena Blackburne, who introduced the mud to the game and died in 1968 in Riverside, New Jersey), and, especially, where the mystery mud comes from, no one in major league baseball is telling. (This isn't just some dirty story either: a can of Lena Blackburne mud is on display in the Baseball Hall of Fame.)

On a cold Saturday afternoon in November 1869, passersby near a large field in New Brunswick were shocked to see a large group of male college students from the colleges of Princeton and Rutgers engaged in what appeared to be a massive and often violent free-for-all that had no purpose other than to kick a small rubber ball through a couple of upright poles. As the people watched the young men rolling, jumping, and running about, they must have shaken their heads in bewilderment, thinking: What was the younger generation coming to these days?

What those people didn't know, however, was that they were witnessing the birth of college football.

Today, college football is an immensely popular sport in the United States. Not only bragging rights but millions of dollars go hand-in-hand with having a top collegiate team.

But dreams of charting the future of college football weren't the motivation that brought students from both schools together on that November afternoon in 1869. The reason was far more basic: revenge.

During the War of 1812, Princeton had lent the town of New Brunswick a cannon for protection against a possible British invasion. In 1859, obviously figuring that since the war had been over for four decades the cannon had served its purpose, a Princeton militia company reclaimed—or stole, depending on whose side you're on—the cannon and gave it to Princeton students. Then, in May 1866, the men from Nassau Hall added insult to injury by shellacking Rutgers 40–2 in baseball. Stung by these setbacks, Rutgers cast about for a means of revenge. What they came up with was football.

It was an unusual choice. In those days, football wasn't exactly a national institution. More of an organized brawl than a sport, the game had been banned by some colleges because upper classmen used it as a way of kicking hapless newcomers around the field. By the 1860s, the game was being played sporadically by groups of college students among themselves, using a round rubber ball that resembled a miniature basketball. To advance the ball, the teams—with as many as twenty-five players per side—kicked and dribbled it with their feet, much as in soccer. The object was to get the ball through the opponent's goal, usually by kicking.

This was the game that Rutgers challenged Nassau Hall to, a challenge that was immediately accepted by the Princetonians. A series of three matches were agreed upon: the first and third at New Brunswick, the second at Princeton. The first game was set for Saturday, November 6.

Rutgers's new student newspaper, *The Targum,* described the morning of that fateful day: "The strangers came up in the 10 o'clock train, and brought a good number of hackers with them. After dinner, and a stroll around the town, during which . . . billiards received a good deal of attention, the crowds began to assemble at the ball ground, which . . . is a lot about a hundred yards wide, extending from College Avenue to Sicard Street."

Prior to the game, team captain William J. Leggett of Rutgers (history's first intercollegiate football captain) had corresponded with his opposite number at Princeton, William S. Gummere, in order to agree upon the rules. Now, as their colleagues roamed New Brunswick, Leggett and Gummere got together again. Although the two teams used different rules, courtesy prevailed over competition; Gummere agreed to abide by his host's rules. (This stunned *The Targum,* which wrote: "The Princeton captain, for some reason or other, gave up every point to our men without contesting one.")

It was now nearly three o'clock in the afternoon. The time for socializing was over; the time for settling matters on the field had arrived. "Grim-looking players were silently stripping, each one surrounded by sympathizing friends," reported *The Targum,* "while around each of the captains was a little crowd, intent upon giving advice, and saving as much as possible."

In "stripping," the players removed their hats, coats, and vests, and rolled up their pants. There were no uniforms; to distinguish the teams, Rutgers players wore hats or turbans made of scarlet, while the Princetonians played bareheaded. (One Rutgers player, D. D. Williamson, misunderstood the instructions, and wore both a turban and shirt made of bright scarlet.)

In 1930, Rutgers's John W. Herbert, one of the last surviving participants in that historic contest sixty-one years earlier, wrote in the *Sunday World Magazine*: "To this day I remember the moment that preceded the whistle. Each team had two 'captains of the enemy's goal,' who took and more or less kept posts directly before their opponents' goal. The rest of each team was divided into two parts, one of eleven and the other of twelve men. The players in one were assigned to cover their own section of the field . . . they were called fielders. The men in the other section of each team were rovers [also called bulldogs], their assignment being to rush up and down the whole field, kicking the ball toward the enemy's goal."

As the players lined up, approximately one hundred spectators craned forward anxiously. Those who had arrived early were perched on top of a wooden fence that enclosed part of the lot; the rest sat on the ground or watched from horse-drawn buckboards pulled along the dirt roads alongside the field.

The winner would be the first team to score six goals. Princeton, which had the bigger and stronger players, kicked first, but the ball went wide, and Rutgers pounced on it. Immediately the New Brunswick players surrounded the ball, blocking any Nassau Hall student from touching it. Then they began moving the ball down the field via a series of quick kicks and dribbles. This primitive version of the flying wedge was highly successful; within minutes the ball was kicked through Princeton's goal. Rutgers had scored the first point in intercollegiate football history.

But if the New Brunswick students thought that they were in for a quick victory, they were mistaken. Seeing the effectiveness of the flying wedge, Gummere quickly whispered instructions to a "veritable Goliath of a man" on the Princeton team named Jacob E. "Big Mike" Michael. When Rutgers received the ball again, they formed its wedge, hoping to duplicate its first success. However, they had reckoned without Big Mike; ignoring the ball, the young giant plowed into the players, scattering them like bowling pins. "Time and again Rutgers formed the wedge and charged," wrote Herbert. "As often, Big Mike broke it up." Spurred on by Michael's efforts, Princeton scored the next goal to tie the game.

This is how it went all afternoon: Rutgers would pull ahead, only to have its rivals come storming back. "Every game was like the one before," said *The Targum*. "There was the same headlong running, wild shouting, and frantic kicking." Herbert remembered that "[i]t was difficult to distinguish . . . between friend and foe in the ever shifting change of players on the field of battle."

At one point during play, the Princeton rooters began yelling "Sis Boom Ah!" Startled, the Rutgers spectators asked what that meant. It was explained that the Seventh Regiment of the New York National Guard had shouted this out as they marched through Princeton during the Civil War. The Princetonians liked the sound of it, and adopted it as their own. Thus was the first college cheer born.

Not all the shouting, however, was positive. During the action, an elderly Rutgers professor pedaled up on his bicycle. After watching fifty college students pushing, pulling, mauling, kicking, and tackling one another, the professor became college football's first heckler by yelling in disgust: "You men will come to no Christian end."

The old man's words went unheeded, however, as the competition rose to white-hot intensity. At one point, the ball was kicked toward the wooden fence that served as the first grandstand. Streaking after the ball went George H. Large of Rutgers and the freight train–like Big Mike. All at once, it became apparent that the players could not stop in time; the audience tried to scramble off the fence, but they were too slow. Both players smashed into the fence, knocking it to the ground and spilling the spectators into a "seething mass" on the ground.

Eventually both players and nonparticipants sorted themselves out, and the game resumed. With the contest knotted at four goals each, Rutgers's Leggett instructed his team to use low, short kicks to get the ball past the taller Princetonians. The strategy worked; Rutgers scored the next two goals and won the game six goals to four.

After the game, the combatants resumed their cordial ways. *The Targum* reported that "the players had an amicable 'feed' together," and Herbert recalled it as "an epicurean feast. Stories were told, songs sang, and good fellowship abounded."

The game did not exactly garner rave reviews in the press. The November 9, 1869, edition of the *New York Times* carried the following laconic lines: "A picked twenty-five of the students of Rutgers College played the same number of Princeton a game of foot ball, on Saturday. After an exciting contest of one hour, the Rutgers were declared the winners, the score standing six to four. On returning from the ball ground the Princeton boys partook of the hospitalities of tile Rutgers."

The editor of the *Bergen County Gazette* was much harsher, terming the game a "jackass performance." Sounding a theme that still echoes on college campuses, the editor called for the students to "construe correctly a page of Homer or of Virgil [rather than] be able to kick a football powerfully."

The next Saturday, November 13, 1869, the two teams met again, this time on a Princeton field near where Palmer Stadium stands today. Unlike the first game, this contest was all Princeton; the Nassau Hall students swamped Rutgers 8–0. Enthusiasm for the rubber match ran at a fever pitch on both campuses, but the contest never took place. Fearful that things were getting out of hand, administrators from both schools banned the game.

It didn't matter. The two schools had begun something that couldn't be stopped. As word of the game spread to other campuses, other schools began playing each other, and rules became more standardized. Just seven years after Rutgers and Princeton met, representatives of Yale and Harvard formed the first Intercollegiate Football Association. The game was on its way.

After its initial victory, it would take Rutgers almost three-quarters of a century to enjoy another triumph over its archrival. On November 5, 1938, sixty-nine years after its win in the first game ever, Rutgers beat Princeton 20–18 at the dedication of the new Rutgers Stadium. Ironically, that same day, Colonel William Preston Lane, the last survivor of Princeton's first team, died at Hagerstown, Maryland. He was to have been a guest of honor at the stadium dedication.

DID YOU KNOW?

Football was not exactly an immediate hit. Many decried the brutality and violence of the game, such as in this poem, entitled "The Noble Game," authorship of which was credited only to "J." It appeared in the Rutgers *Targum* in November 1870:

In the Name of the Prophet—Football.

Heaven have mercy—what do I hear?
Is a civil war in progress here?
A dusty field before me lies,
From which come shrieks and groans and cries.
As if some folks from a "warmer clime"
Were bent on having a jolly good time.
Fifty young men—with lives to lose—
Fifty young men—with canvas shoes—are lustily kicking a rubber ball
And sometimes kicking each other; that's all.

And though some are half and others are lame,
They all agree—it's a "noble game."

Here comes a victim: What's the matter?
What occasions this horrible clatter?
Football, my boys, is making the row.
The noblest game on earth, I vow.
And really, there's nothing the matter with me,
Only broken my arm and strained my knee;
My churn got kicked in the abdomen,
And hasn't been out of his bed since then.
Two of our class have gone home to die,
And five are under the doctor's eye.
But doctor or not—it's all the same;
I tell you, sir, it's a "noble game."

See how the dust their faces begrimes
Look at that mass of writhing limbs.
Really, I think, if they come this way,
'Twould be highly impolitic here to stay.
Oh, murder! They're here! I'm down and alack,
The football is lying upon my back.
Kick after kick is all I can feel,
My neck bears the weight of one big villain's heel.
Get off! Let me up! Don't you hear me shout?
Let me up! Let me up! Let me out! Let me out!
My soul is quitting its earthly frame,
I'll be choked if I think it's a noble game.

This is a story of baseball—baseball that some pretended did not exist. Back when Jim Crow racism was riding high in the United States, some excellent baseball was being played right under the prejudiced nose of the professional game. Because of the racist attitudes of those running pro baseball, everyone pretended that Negro League baseball, and its African American players, did not exist. That did not stop some of the teams from being exceptionally good, however. One of those teams was based right here in New Jersey, in the proud city of Newark: the Newark Eagles.

To baseball fans today, the idea of the Negro Leagues is incongruous. Black ballplayers have long been such an integral part of the game that if they suddenly went and played in a league of their own, baseball would be a far poorer game. But for years, that was exactly what black players had to do, thanks to a "gentleman's agreement" among the owners of professional baseball clubs that barred African Americans from the game. This meant that men like Josh Gibson, LeRoy "Satchel" Paige, Smokey Joe Williams, and Oscar Charleston, all prodigiously talented, were denied access to major league baseball solely because of their skin color.

Negro League ballplayers lived on a scale far below their major league counterparts. They rode buses instead of trains, played as many as four games in one day, and had to use equipment and play in ballparks that would be considered substandard in the majors.

It also meant sometimes witnessing acts of extreme human cruelty. Once, in Alabama, the Eagles' team bus stopped at a roadside cafe so the hot, thirsty players could get something to drink. But no sooner did the players approach the cafe then the owner came out and started shaking her head.

"Why are you saving no," asked Eagles star Monte Irvin, "when you don't even know what we want?"

"Whatever it is, we don't have any," said the woman.

Finally, she agreed to let them use the drinking well out back. But after the players had all drunk and the team bus was pulling away, the players saw the woman methodically smash the drinking gourd to pieces.

To their credit, the Eagles did not let this type of episode affect their play on the field. The team was a powerhouse in the Negro National League, finishing no lower than third for eleven of its thirteen years in the league, winning the pennant twice, and the Negro World Series once.

Formed in 1935, the Eagles spent their maiden season in Brooklyn before moving to Newark the following year. The city was a logical choice; approximately 39,000 blacks—nearly one-fifth of New Jersey's African American population—lived in Newark in 1930. Despite ongoing discrimination (blacks were forced to take out food from restaurants rather than eat it there and were barred from the city's municipal hospital), Newark was still a good home for African Americans. It was a "small" big city, with neighborhoods full of people who looked out for one another, and groups and organizations that helped promote family life and togetherness. Those familiar with Newark during this time, such as Monte Irvin, remember it fondly as "just a wonderful city." In 1936, the Eagles landed in this wonderful city.

The Eagles were the dream of Abe Manley, a numbers boss in Newark. A lifelong baseball fan, Manley sat in the Eagles' dugout during home games, often traveled with them on the road, and was happy just to be near the diamond.

Manley could afford to indulge his passion for the Eagles because of his wife, Effa. It was she who actually ran the ball club, keeping one eye on the bottom line and the other on the team's performance. In the man's world of Negro League baseball, Effa was an original.

Effa was born around 1900 to a multiracial Philadelphia family that contained a white mother, black father, and mulatto children. As she freely admitted, she was white—"I was this little, blond, hazel-eyed white girl always with these Negro children"—but that didn't stop her from falling in love with the African American Manley when the two baseball fanatics met at the 1932 World Series, nor did it prevent her from quickly assuming a leadership role in the Negro League. The other owners respected her business acumen.

Effa brooked no interference with her team. Once she stopped talk of a players' strike in its tracks by announcing to the militant players that "no Newark Eagle was gonna strike, period." Former players remember her "suggestions" to the manager during games. "She was loud, and if the pitcher was going bad you could hear 'Get him out of there,'" said former first baseman Francis Matthews. "She wanted everyone in Newark to know she was in charge."

It was this potent combination—Abe the benevolent sugar daddy, Effa the hard-nosed number cruncher—that made the Eagles soar. The Manleys built the Eagles not only into a sports powerhouse but into a potent social force as well. White politicians soon found that they had to attend Eagles' games. The Eagles became a social institution in Newark, appearing at functions in the black community and holding clinics for kids.

The two greatest Eagle players were Monte Irvin and Larry Doby. Irvin was a phenomenal New Jersey high school athlete (All-State in football, basketball, baseball, and track for three straight years) who joined the Eagles at age nineteen in 1938 and finally broke into the major leagues with the New York Giants in 1949. Doby had a superb high school career in Paterson before landing with the Eagles. In 1947 he became the first black player in the American League when he signed with the Cleveland Indians.

The pinnacle for the Eagles came in 1946. With World War II over, the Negro Leagues were flourishing, and so were the Eagles. The team finished the season with a record of 47–16, with Irvin hitting .395 and Doby .348. In the Negro World Series that year, the Eagles' foes were the powerful, Yankee-like Kansas City Monarchs. In a classic seven-game series, the Eagles defeated the Monarchs to win the championship.

As they celebrated their team's triumph, little did Abe and Effa know that it was the Eagles' last hurrah. Once the Brooklyn Dodgers broke baseball's color line in October 1945 by signing Jackie Robinson (who, incidentally, played his first professional game at Jersey City on April 18, 1946), other teams began following suit. As black stars went to the majors, they took Negro League fans with them, and attendance plummeted. In 1947, just one year after being crowned the kings of black baseball, the Eagles lost $22,000.

Further hurting the Eagles was the tendency of major league owners to either pay Negro League owners nothing—as in the case of Jackie Robinson—or a pittance for signing their stars. In 1947, Effa negotiated the sale of superstar Monte Irvin to the New York Giants for a paltry $5,000. "If he'd have been white they'd have given me $100,000," she remarked bitterly.

By 1949 the Newark Eagles were gone, along with most of Negro League baseball. All that was left for Newark was the memories.

DID YOU KNOW?

The Newark Eagles weren't the only successful New Jersey–based African American team. Two decades earlier, the Atlantic City Bacharachs (named after the town's mayor, Harry Bacharach) were one of the top teams of several different blackball leagues. In 1926 and 1927 the Bacharachs played in that era's version of the Negro World Series, only to lose both times to the Chicago American Giants. The man considered by many to be the greatest black player of all time, John Henry "Pop" Lloyd played several seasons with the Bacharachs.

DID YOU KNOW?

New Jersey has a long and proud history of minor league baseball. Match these cities with their team nicknames.

Camden	Skeeters
Trenton	Atlantics
Jersey City	Giants
Paterson	Merritt
Newark	Resolutes
Elizabeth	Indians

Answers: Paterson Atlantics, Camden Merritt, Newark Indians, Elizabeth Resolutes, Trenton Giants, Jersey City Skeeters

It was Saturday, July 2, 1921, and the biggest fight in the history of boxing was about to take place between scowling Jack Dempsey, "the Manassa Mauler," and handsome Georges Carpentier, an urbane Frenchman. As more than ninety thousand people roared, Dempsey and Carpentier stepped into the ring—a ring located not in the boxing world's most spectacular venue, New York's Madison Square Garden, but on a patch of land called Boyle's Thirty Acres across the Hudson River in Jersey City.

If Babe Ruth put baseball on the map and the Baltimore Colts–New York Giants' overtime struggle in the 1958 NFL title game opened the door for mass acceptance of pro football, then the 1921 bout between Dempsey and Carpentier was the match that made boxing legitimate. Long accustomed to being run out of cities and states because of public displeasure over a sport in which two grown men tried to beat each other's brains out, boxing by 1921 had at least gotten to the point where the local sheriff didn't come down and arrest the participants of every match. Still, it was because some of those old-fashioned prejudices against boxing still lingered that Jersey City was able to become for a moment the center of the sporting universe.

New York Governor Nathan L. Miller was a man who held firmly to his convictions, and one of those was that professional prizefighting was disgusting. Lost in the nineteenth century dream world of amateur athletics, when men competed just for the sport of it, he waged a vigorous campaign against professional boxing in his state despite a law that had made prizefights legal in New York.

Miller's steadfast but naive convictions threatened the plans of George L. "Tex" Rickard, the first true genius at boxing promotion. To build up interest in a fight, Rickard would pull stunts like letting the prize money remain on public display for weeks, so that even those people who didn't like boxing would finally buy a ticket just to satisfy their natural curiosity and find out who was going to win that money they'd been staring at for so long. Rickard didn't have to go to those lengths to publicize the Dempsey-Carpentier fight; public interest in the bout had been sky-high even before the two fighters signed the contract. It was a match made in promotional heaven.

In July 1921, at the age of twenty-six, Jack Dempsey was at the peak of his power. Born William Harrison Dempsey on June 24, 1895, in Manassa, Colorado, Jack Dempsey by 1921 had brawled and bludgeoned his way to boxing's top prize, the heavyweight championship. Back then boxing was much more violent than it is today, and Dempsey's savage fury was usually given full vent by referees, who normally only stopped a bout if blood made the ring too slippery. Already a forbidding-looking man, the black-haired Dempsey added to his arsenal of fear by not shaving before a fight. Opponents took one look at the stubble-bearded wild man across from them and began wondering what fool notion could have possessed them to step into a ring with such a creature. Usually the next thing they remembered was waking up in the trainer's room.

Georges Carpentier, on the other hand, was the perfect antithesis of Dempsey. Urbane, cultured, witty, and handsome, the erudite Frenchman had won the hearts of millions by serving with distinction in World War I (a war Dempsey avoided serving in). Then, in one of the biggest upsets at the time in boxing history, Carpentier had knocked out English champion Joe Beckett, a strapping two-hundred-pounder who looked as if he could snap Carpentier in two. Ever since that victory Carpentier had been regarded as the "class" of boxing, and a match between him and Dempsey set up a classic Beauty and the Beast confrontation. As Randy Roberts wrote in *Jack Dempsey—The Manassa Mauler*: "Give the masses of people some rosy-checked, clear complexioned Lancelot to cheer and some thick-bearded, Simon Legree to boo and jeer, and the money would roll in in waves."

Getting the fight wasn't a problem for Rickard; finding a place to hold it was another matter. Miller was firmly against having it in New York, which ruled out Madison Square Garden and the Polo Grounds, the two most desirable sites. Other cities were ruled out because Rickard wanted to be close to New York City, then the publicity capital of the world.

Then in April 1921, New Jersey Governor Edward I. Edwards stepped in and offered his state as host for the bout. Rickard dove for the offer like a drowning man for a life preserver. Quickly the sites were narrowed down to a precious few: Newark, Jersey City, and Atlantic City. For reasons that probably had a lot to do with political boss, mayor, and boxing enthusiast Frank Hague, Jersey City was the winner.

The only problem with Jersey City was that it didn't have a place big enough to hold the bout in. Rickard didn't let that stop him, however. Within days hundreds of workers were swarming all over the patch of ground called Boyle's Thirty Acres. The pinewood arena that was frantically constructed was first planned to seat 50,000. As fight fever rose, the capacity of the oval, saucer-shaped arena was increased to 70,000, then 90,000. Unfortunately, time (the workers had just over thirty days) and the repeated changes to the design to accommodate more fans made the final structure incredibly shaky. Those who sat in the expensive seats near ringside had no worries. For those in the hastily improvised wooden seats on the outskirts, it was like sitting on the raised section of a seesaw; whenever those on the bottom (near the ring) made noise or stamped their feet, the vibrations raced through the stands and made the top of the seesaw shake like a leaf in the hurricane.

The two fighters trained in very different ways for their upcoming clash. Carpentier set up camp in Manhasset, Long Island, an area of ritzy estates. The press and public were barred from his workouts. (Ring Lardner believed the reason for this was that he knew be was going to get killed, so he hardly bothered to train.) Dempsey, on the other hand, trained in Atlantic City. Everyone was invited to come and see the champ, who, when he wasn't sparring or engaged in rigorous runs up and down the beach, would often talk to anyone who happened to be around.

As the fight date grew closer, groups protesting the bout grew louder. The Clergymen's Community Club of Jersey City sent an official letter of protest to Mayor Hague, claiming that the fight would corrupt the moral standards of the city. Other organizations made similar pronouncements, but they were merely fanning the breeze. It would have been easier to try and stop Halley's Comet.

By the end of June the fight was making international news. In fact, a Swiss newspaper complained that "one-tenth of the press-power concentrated upon [the fight] would have put the United States into the League of Nations." Every scrap of information about the fight was plastered over the front pages of newspapers around the world.

Naturally, local newspaper tripped all over themselves in covering the contest. Typical of the breathless coverage was this lead paragraph from a June 30, 1921, *Newark Evening News* story: "When Jack Dempsey and Georges Carpentier face each other for the world's heavyweight boxing championship in Jersey City Saturday afternoon there will he present a greater number of persons prominent in national and international life than ever before attended a pugilistic contest in the history of the sport."

Despite its florid tone, the story was correct. Among those notables going to the fight were J. P. Morgan, Henry Ford, Vincent Astor, Payne Whitney, Al Jolson, John D. Rockefeller, Douglas Fairbanks, members of the Theodore Roosevelt family, and George M. Cohan. Even more remarkable was the number of women who bought tickets. Drawn by the dashing

Carpentier, thousands of females came to see a sport that they had virtually ignored before.

Fight day—July 2—dawned hazy and humid, with a threat of rain. In fact, just before one in the afternoon it did sprinkle a little, nearly giving Rickard a heart attack. Thousands of people had camped overnight in the field surrounding the stadium, hoping to buy a ticket at the gate, but these were gone quickly. At nine A.M. the gates opened, and the crowd started to file in. They wouldn't stop until a record 91,163 seats had been filled. According to one contemporary source, by the time of the fight, the boxing ring looked like a small, square lump of sugar at the bottom of a bowl covered with ten thousand black flies.

The spotlight was on Jersey City that day, and the city was ready. To guard against the risk of fire in the wooden arena, barbecue equipment, old newspapers, and other inflammables were left outside the gates, and four hundred firemen were on duty. For medical care, an emergency hospital was set up near the arena. Police had taken every precaution against crooks and pickpockets sneaking into the stadium; over three thousand officers and detectives patrolled the inside and outside of the arena.

As Dempsey later wrote, promoter Rickard was so overcome with the grandeur and spectacle of it all that he rushed into the champ's dressing room, crying: "Jack! Jack! You never seen anything like it. We got a million dollars in already and they're still coming! And the people, Jack! I never seen anything like the people we got at this fight. High-class society folk—you name 'em, they're here. And dames! I mean classy dames, thousands of them!"

Those "classy dames," "high-class society folk," and everyone else got what they came for just after three o'clock that afternoon, when first Carpentier, then Dempsey, climbed into the ring. By then, the heat and humidity had caused many men in the crowd to shed clothing. (The women resisted this temptation.) Dempsey looked so menacing, and Carpentier so frail, that the wife of one sportswriter gasped and said "It's over."

The first round was tame, as each man felt the other out. The few punches Carpentier landed on Dempsey had as much effect as gnats landing on the champion's skin. The Manassa Mauler's punches, however, were more devastating; one bloodied the Frenchman's nose.

In the second round Carpentier bore in more aggressively, and hit Dempsey with a solid right on the chin. The crowd roared, feeling that Georges might have a chance to win after all, and many sportswriters later wrote that Dempsey was in danger of being knocked out at that point. The truth is, however, that the blow did little more than annoy Dempsey. "Dempsey was never in any more danger of being knocked out than I was," cracked H. L. Mencken.

By the third round Dempsey was through fooling around. Punches rained in on Carpentier from all angles, and the Frenchman wobbled back to his corner. Less than a minute into the fourth round, Carpentier lay prone on the canvas, with blood flowing from his nose and mouth. The Battle of the Century was over.

"Dempsey Knocks Out Carpentier in Fourth Round of Title Bout," screamed the front page of the *Newark Evening News* in an extra July 2 edition. "Dempsey gave Carpentier an unmerciful beating," reported the paper. "He opened up a cut under the Frenchman's eye and batted him so viciously around the head with vicious rights and lefts until Carpentier's face was swollen and bleeding."

Although the fight was not that good, everyone connected with it had reason to smile. It was the first sports event ever to be broadcast on radio, and the first to gross over a million dollars. Sports history had been made again in New Jersey.

DID YOU KNOW?

On the same day as the Dempsey-Carpentier fight, a historic event occurred in New Jersey that should have been plastered across the front page of newspapers all over the world: the signing of the treaty formally ending World War I. Because of all the fight hoopla, however, the occasion passed virtually unnoticed.

Because of partisan politics, the United States never signed the Treaty of Versailles, which formally ended the war for the European allies. Technically, the United States remained at war with Germany long after the guns had stopped. Finally, after Warren G. Harding was elected president in 1920, a compromise resolution was crafted and passed by Congress on July 1, 1921. Harding had left Washington for a relaxing Independence Day weekend at the Somerset County home of his friend, Senator Joseph Frelinghuysen. On Saturday, July 2, Harding interrupted a golf game to return to the Frelinghuysen home and sign the resolution that officially ended the Great War. Just thirty people witnessed the event, and newspapers, dominated by stories of the great fight, gave the news short shrift. Even the staid *New York Times* played down the signing, putting it in a one-column story entitled "Harding Ends War" and splashing the Dempsey-Carpentier bout all over the front page. Clearly, the Great War had been superseded by the Battle of the Century.

Canning, Building, Riding, and Other Fascinating Things About New Jersey

In trying to come up with a title for this chapter, I tried to figure out a theme for it. Eventually, I realized the problem: There is no theme. (Poke me long enough with a sharp stick and eventually I'll say ouch.) This chapter is a hodgepodge of things that are relatively unknown about New Jersey but fit no definite theme. Above all, I find them incredibly interesting. My writing teacher back in the day would be aghast; chapters need to have themes, he taught, and for the most part I've tried to stick with that in this book and throughout my writing career. But hey, you can't win them all.

So, ultimately, I decided to follow the advice of a baseball umpire I knew: "I call them as I see them" he used to say whenever he called a pitch fifty feet outside the plate a strike. (I used to wonder just what he was seeing.) So that's how I came up with the title.

As we all know (or should all know) New Jersey's nickname is the Garden State, and anybody who doubts it has only to drive down a county highway in the summer and see the host of delicious produce offered for sale by the many farm stands that dot the roadside—especially the world-famous Jersey Tomato.

Of course, unless you're going to eat every one of those tomatoes the moment you acquire them (tempting, I know, but not very practical), you have to be able to preserve them. That, often, calls for canning them, and it just so happens that the first person to successfully can tomatoes comes from New Jersey. Destiny? Dumb luck? Divine intervention?

The fact of the matter is, New Jersey has always been concerned about food preservation. In 1676, a century before the American Revolution was even a gleam in the Founding Fathers' eyes, the New Jersey Assembly passed a measure that stated, in part that "there shall be in every Town, a Packer chosen by the Freeholders, to see that all Meat in Barrels for Sale be good and merchantable, and well Packed and Salted." Lawmakers knew that food packaging was one area that it was important to get right, and they wasted little time trying to do just that.

Fast forward to the 1820s. The food preservation industry had been given a giant boost by Nicholas Appert, often called the "Father of Canning." Appert developed a new method of canning foods in response to the needs of Napoleon's army, which was busy conquering much of the world and couldn't do it on an empty stomach.

However, despite its obvious deliciousness, the Jersey tomato had a hard time being accepted as the wonderful food it is. It was something about tomatoes being thought of as poisonous, according to legend.

Well, one good legend deserves another. One day in the 1820s, Colonel Robert Gibbon Johnson strode up the courthouse steps in Salem, New Jersey. With a confident smile at the huge crowd that had gathered around, Johnson reached down into a basket at his feet and picked up something that everyone agreed was poisonous. As people in the audience watched in disbelief, Johnson proceeded to eat first one "poisonous" object, then a second, and, incredibly, even a third, and was still very much alive when he finished.

The crowd gasped in disbelief. How could Johnson have done it? How could he have eaten those things and survived? Finally, someone said aloud what was on everyone's minds: "Colonel Johnson is the first person to eat a tomato and live!"

A tomato? Poisonous? Indeed, according to local legend, in the early days of the United States, tomatoes were considered quite harmful. Just one bite would make a person sick, while eating a whole one was tantamount to calling the undertaker. Johnson, a farmer and learned man who knew better, finally decided that drastic action was the only way to disprove the "killer tomato" theory.

Unfortunately, even though this story has a long and glorious history in New Jersey (supposedly it was even dramatized on a radio broadcast), it's probably not true. After all, Spanish colonists in the New World were eating tomatoes for many years before Johnson's supposed demonstration on the courthouse steps. Still, it's a great story.

Whether the Johnson story is true or not, the Jersey tomato was off and running. So it was in 1845 that Harrison Woodhull Crosby (1814–1892) of Jamesburg was one of the first (if not the first, but again, that's open to debate) to successfully put tomatoes in a can for commercial purposes. Crosby was the assistant steward and chief gardener at Lafayette College in Easton, Pennsylvania, from 1845 to 1849, and it was during these years that he worked his magic with the tomato.

According to an account related by Lafayette's president, Dr. Ralph Cooper Hutchison, in September 1847, Crosby got six little tin pails similar to what kids nowadays use on the beach. He made a lid with a hole in the center for each, then soldered the lids onto the pails. He stewed tomatoes, then placed the tomatoes into the pails through the lid hole and soldered the opening shut with a piece of tin.

The following winter Crosby opened the containers, and the tomatoes were "fresh and delicious." Excited by his results, and certain that he could sell them, Crosby packed one thousand cans of stewed tomatoes. Unfortunately, asking someone to buy tomatoes in a can at that time was like asking them to purchase cooked stinkweed; tomatoes were still not a popular treat, and sales languished.

Undaunted, Crosby decided to send the tomatoes to newspapers and famous people both in the United States and throughout the world. Queen Victoria got one, as did President James K. Polk. So it was, as Mary B. Sim relates in her book *Commercial Canning in New Jersey History and Development,* that the *New York Tribune* printed the following notice: "Mr. Crosby of Middlesex, New Jersey, has sent us some fresh tomatoes preserved in tin cans. Whatever the secret of their preparation, we are bound to acknowledge that their preservation has not impaired their flavor. They taste as they would have tasted when plucked from the vines."

(Even though this commercial venture was unsuccessful, this did not end Crosby's involvement with tomatoes. After this he went to Staten Island and managed a factory that made tomato sauce. He then went to Middlebury and Plymouth, Connecticut, and at each place he canned tomatoes. He returned to New Jersey, where he managed a New Brunswick factory that canned—you guessed it—tomatoes. Eventually he took over the factory and produced numerous tomato-based products, such as Crosby Celebrated Ketchup. His tomato career came to a close in 1877, when he was appointed postmaster at Jamesburg.)

However, as successful as Crosby was in canning tomatoes, he did not have the first commercial canning facility in New Jersey. That honor may well belong to that grand experiment in communal living, the North American Phalanx.

The Phalanx set up operations on nearly seven hundred acres of land about four miles from Red Bank in September 1843. Since farming was to be the primary economic engine of the Phalanx, the group's members planted two orchards of numerous varieties of fruit, as well as many types of vegetables. The Phalanx was the first to supply the New York City–area marketplace with okra. Indeed, products produced by the Phalanx with the legend N.A.P. quickly came to mean items of the highest quality.

The commercial canning factory was built at the Phalanx in 1847. This puts the Phalanx in the running for the first commercial canning operation in the state. After a fire caused the Phalanx to dissolve in 1855, John Bucklin, who had been a member of the group, bought the canning facility, which fortunately the fire had spared. He began canning products under his own name. When he took his son Charles into the business in 1862, he changed the company's name to J. & C. S. Bucklin.

The Bucklin name is a famous one in the history of New Jersey canning operations. Besides his roots at the North American Phalanx, Charles Bucklin was quite inventive and produced several different products that pushed the entire canning industry forward, such as machines for filling and a steam cooker.

The North American Phalanx cannery was located near the coast slightly north of the state's midpoint, and the industry had many successful canneries in the central part of the state. However, it was Cumberland County in South Jersey, with its abundance of fertile agricultural fields and large farms, where the canning industry really prospered. From 1840 to 1942, nearly thirty canneries existed at some point or other in Cumberland County.

Yet even Cumberland County had to take a back seat to the mighty Canton Canning Factory in Salem Township. Opened in 1881, Canton Canning was the largest canning operation in the United States at the time. It packed forty thousand cans per day, with a majority of those being filled with— what else?—tomatoes.

Of course, all those South Jersey farms chock-full of delicious produce— including the world-famous Jersey tomato—had to go someplace, and more often than not that someplace was the Campbell's Soup Company in Camden.

Starting in the later stages of summer, and going through approximately Halloween, lines of wagons (and later trucks) jammed full of produce— especially tomatoes—began forming before the sun rose along Second Street in Camden. Sometimes the line stretched as long as nine miles. That time of year, as all home gardeners know, is tomato-ripening season, the moment when all that effort you put into your plants at the beginning of the season pays off in (you hope) giant, juicy tomatoes. And what better place for these tomatoes to wind up than Campbell's? The trucks, usually loaded with between three and four tons of tomatoes, would inch along the road as they slowly moved up toward the factory, and sometimes some of the thin wooden and metal baskets with the tomatoes in them would tumble off the back of the wagon or truck and fall to the ground, dyeing the street red with tomato juice.

As anyone knows who has fought the tomato wars in his or her own backyard, tomatoes are not the easiest things in the world to grow. The plant can get a variety of illnesses that turn its leaves droopy yellow, or dotted with black spots. And if that doesn't happen, insects can invade, strip off the leaves before you can blink, and make a tomato plant look like a green pencil. Then there are always rabbits, deer, skunks, and other wandering wildlife who decide to make your tomato garden their own personal restaurant.

If you can avoid all that, the reward of juicy red Jersey tomatoes is well worth the effort. Campbell's knew that, and so it would hold meetings with growers and share growing tips and information with them. As agricultural expert Harry Hall related once: "One or more meetings are held each year, usually at Campbell's Soup Farms, where prominent speakers discuss the most approved methods of crop production. At these meetings liberal prizes are awarded for the best baskets of tomatoes, thus providing the opportunity to impress upon them our standards of perfection."

Campbell's usually contracted with around two thousand farmers for the vegetables they needed. Most of them were near Camden, thus saving shipping costs. Although all vegetable growers received help and advice from Campbell's, it was the tomato growers on whom they especially concentrated. Hall was constantly trying to breed the ideal tomato for making soup, and he would provide the growers with seeds from his efforts.

Of course, all those tomatoes and vegetables were turned into Campbell's products, and in the days before motorized transport, the items would be delivered by horse-drawn wagons. Sturdy Belgian and Percheron horses were used to pull these wagons, which could hold up to 304 cases of metal cans and containers, and were thus just a tad heavy to pull.

As long as we're on the subject of Camden, there's a subject that not too many people are aware of, and that's Camden's unique role in at one time being the home of the largest private ship-building companies in the entire world.

Indeed, there was once a time when the industries of Camden kept the city alive and working all day. So it was with the New York Shipbuilding Corporation in Camden, the colossal city-within-a-city.

To say that New York Ship (as it was usually referred to) was big is to say that a blue whale is kind of large. During its World War II heyday, the company employed more than thirty-five thousand people and was the economic colossus of the area, a sprawling giant that attracted workers from everywhere. It was truly a massive establishment whose key role in turning out ships during both world wars cannot be overemphasized.

The company was established in 1898 by Henry G. Morse, who had been the president of the shipbuilding company Harlan and Hollingsworth. Morse carried with him the financial backing of wealthy tycoons Andrew Mellon and Henry Frick, so he wasn't going to be shy of money anytime soon. His goal was to establish a new shipyard in Staten Island, but he wound up instead at Camden, drawn by the availability of land, plus the presence of a vast transportation network and a ready workforce. Morse established his new company north of where the Walt Whitman Bridge stands today.

Of course, Mellon and Frick didn't get rich tossing away their money on silly ideas, and with Morse they had backed a winner. He originated the idea of applying the same mass production techniques used by makers of other things to shipbuilding.

We've all seen pictures of large ships being built outside, in the open air, but at New York Ship there areas were covered, so that work could continue in all kinds of weather. The yard had a system of gigantic cranes that acted as conveyor belts, quickly moving the manufactured sections around the yard. Thanks to these and other techniques, New York Ship cranked out destroyers, battle cruisers, P.T. boats and other vessels for the United States Navy. As the service rapidly built up because of the demands of World War I, New York Ship answered the call.

As the shipyard turned out more and more ships, it naturally needed more and more workers. The work demanded long hours, so the company began building communities nearby for its workers to live in.

After the war shipbuilding demand slacked off, and the yard went through some fallow years. However, it did not take long for the war drums to start beating again, and as World War II approached and then became a reality for the United States, New York Ship once again became a very busy place. The yard turned out light aircraft carriers, many heavy and light cruisers, dozens of landing craft, and many other different types of vessels.

The work was difficult and dangerous. Period photos show workers dwarfed by the things they were building, such as ship's propellers. It is no exaggeration to say that ships turned out in Camden helped the United States win the war; New York Ship–built ships saw action in such war theaters as northern Africa, Normandy, and the Philippines.

After the war New York Ship continued turning out ships, such as attack submarines, guided missile cruisers and destroyers, and others. As military contracts dried up the yard slowed up. Finally, in 1967, New York Ship closed for good.

Yet the legacy of New York Ship—and by extension, Camden, a New Jersey city with a proud history—lives on every day, in the form of a free United States.

DID YOU KNOW?

Despite what you've seen on television and at the movies, writing is not a particularly lucrative profession. No one proves this better than Walt Whitman, who struggled financially throughout his life and lived in Camden on Mickle Boulevard for the last eight years of his life (1884–1892).

Whitman's poems were condemned by many in the straitlaced United States (Europe was much more understanding), and he always seemed to be living with friends or relatives because he was losing jobs and didn't have any money. Even his landmark work, *Leaves of Grass*, was not highly thought of in the United States throughout most of his lifetime.

(There seems to be no truth, however, to stories that have the aged Whitman selling copies of *Leaves of Grass* and other works door-to-door to scrounge up a few bucks. Several biographers, as well as the guide at the Whitman House, have cast doubt on the tale.)

Finally, in the twilight of his life, Whitman managed to sock away enough money to buy a small house in Camden for $1,750. Legend has it that the house was only worth $900, but the poet was in the midst of a heated argument with his brother, with whom he lived, when he excused himself, walked around the corner, and bought the house in a fit of I'll-show-you temper.

Whitman was a likable, if somewhat eccentric, figure in Camden. With his flowing white hair, long white beard, and plain attire (usually he dressed all in gray, although he sometimes wore blue), the poet stood out on the street. Although he was pleasant to those he met, nodding and smiling in response to greetings, he almost never spoke; when he did, it was in a soft and deliberate manner.

The house is packed with Whitman memorabilia. The reason there is so much material is that Whitman was very concerned with self-promotion (that's why he had more than 150 photographs of himself taken throughout his life) and saved many items for the posterity he was certain would be interested. He also had a devoted group of followers who swooped down on the house immediately following the poet's death and kept it, essentially, as a shrine to him.

Whitman didn't care much for the house, calling it a "shanty" in one letter. Indeed, those who first visit the poet's impressive tomb in nearby Harleigh Cemetery assume that his home will be just as imposing and thus drive right by the tiny row home without even a sideways glance. This probably gives Whitman, looking down from poets' heaven, quite a few chuckles. (See chapter 15 for more information about Whitman and his tomb.)

For most of his tenure in the house, Whitman, crippled by illness, was cared for by Mary Davis, a sea captain's widow. Much of the furniture there is hers. As for the Good Gray Poet, there are photos, articles of clothing, personal effects, and many other items to make him come alive.

New York Ship made ships, a conventional mode of transportation. For a rather unusual mode of transportation, we turn to the Bicycle Railroad of Smithville in Burlington County.

On paper it was a great idea: build a rail track, fit specially made bicycles to it, and use it for commuting back and forth to work. The idea was sound, and in 1892 Arthur Hotchkiss received a patent for it (not H. B. Smith, as is often erroneously listed). Hotchkiss then approached the Smith Machine Company to build it.

By September 1892, this unique cross-breeding between the horseless carriage and pedal power was completed. The track ran a distance of about 1.8 miles, from Smithville to Pine Street in Mount Holly. The track crossed the Rancocas Creek ten times. A monthly user pass cost two dollars.

The idea of the Bicycle Railroad was that it would allow employees of the factory at Smithville who lived in Mount Holly to commute to work quickly and easily. In that respect the bike track lived up to its potential; the trip took six or seven minutes. The invention was considered so forward-thinking that it was exhibited at that repository of fantastic futuristic things, the 1893 World's Columbian Exposition.

The Bicycle Railroad was initially popular, but after several years ridership tailed off. There was a major flaw in the Bicycle Railroad that ultimately doomed it. There was just one track, so if a rider met someone coming the opposite way, one or the other had to pull off the main track onto a siding. You can see how this would get tedious after a while. Anyway, by 1898 the

Bicycle Railroad was in need of repairs, and with ridership dropping, the decision was made to discontinue it.

DID YOU KNOW?

Back when horses were the sole mode of transportation, the Wick House, located in Jockey Hollow in Morristown, was the site of one of the most amazing—albeit undocumented—stories of the Revolutionary War.

One day, twenty-one-year-old Temperance Wick was out riding her horse when she was accosted by several Continental soldiers who were quartered nearby. When the soldiers saw the good horse Tempe was riding, they told her that the army needed such fine animals, and that they were going to take hers. But Tempe—an experienced rider—dug her heels into the horse's flanks and raced away from the men.

Arriving home just ahead of the pursuing soldiers, Tempe led the horse into the house, through the kitchen and parlor, and then into a guest bedroom. The soldiers searched the barn, the outbuildings, and all the other logical places for a horse to be, but never thought of the house. According to the legend, Tempe kept the animal hidden in the bedroom for three weeks, until the army left Morristown. Only then did she bring the horse back to the barn (which, for the horse, must have been quite a letdown).

6
Celebrated Sons and Distinguished Daughters

The people in this chapter have two things in common. The first is that they're all famous. The second thing they share is a link with New Jersey. Some, like Paul Robeson, were born in New Jersey but made their mark outside the state. Others, such as Clara Barton, came here and made a significant contribution to the history and heritage of the state. Either way, they are celebrated sons and distinguished daughters of New Jersey, and their stories are now to be told.

Clara Barton

The immediate reaction to that name is *the Red Cross*. And indeed, Barton's establishment of the famous relief agency is clearly her most important work in a lifetime filled with achievement.

Less well known, however, is that in the decade before the Civil War, Clara Barton made another very important contribution to society in New Jersey—a contribution that saved lives as surely as did her later work with the Red Cross. The only difference is that in New Jersey, these lives were being threatened not by bullets but by ignorance.

In the spring of 1852, Clara Barton was a thirty-year-old woman besieged by self-doubt and bouts of depression. In March of that year, she had written in her journal that she was "badly organized to live in the world or among society" and that she had grown "weary of life at an age when other people are enjoying it most."

"I contribute to the happiness of not a single object and often to the unhappiness of many and always my own, for I am never happy," she wrote. "How long I am to or can endure such a life I do not know."

Contributing to her frequent dark moods was the fact that she was an ambitious, intelligent, resourceful woman in an age when it was virtually useless for a woman to be any of those things. Her burning desire to accomplish something helped propel her into what has been called "the first ambitious project" of her life, the establishment of a free public school in Bordentown, New Jersey.

In the autumn of 1851, possibly to alleviate her gloom, Barton had journeyed to New Jersey to visit Mary Norton, a friend who taught school in Hightstown, near Bordentown. A teacher herself, Barton had taught in Massachusetts and Washington, D.C., for more than a decade but was seeking new horizons by the time she came to New Jersey. When after a few weeks Barton became restless and wanted to leave, Norton begged her to teach winter school—a feat never before undertaken by a woman—in Hightstown. Eagerly accepting, Barton taught a class of forty farm boys for several months.

What bothered her about the job, however, was that her students came only from families who could afford to pay for the privilege of education; in essence, the school was a private one, although the term was not then in vogue. The children of those who could not afford school were simply left to their own devices, because they were not considered worthy of education.

Although the New Jersey legislature had passed a bill designed to spread public schools throughout the state, widespread opposition to the measure had made it a paper law without hope of enforcement. This bothered Barton, who longed for the true public education system she had experienced in Massachusetts.

While at Hightstown, Barton heard about the deplorable state of education in nearby Bordentown; gangs of boys, it was said, were lolling about the streets with nothing to do. Going there, she saw the rumors were true: "I found them [the boys] on all sides of me. Every street corner had little knots of them idle, listless, as if to say, what shall one do, when one has nothing to do?"

Talking to the boys, Barton found that they, far from being gleeful at escaping the classroom, were actually unhappy about it. "Lady, there is no school for us," said a fourteen year old. "We would be glad to go if there was one."

With her reforming spirit thus stoked, she marched up to Peter Suydam, chairman of the local school board, and demanded to know why there wasn't a free public school in Bordentown.

Calling the boys "renegades," Suydam explained politely to the tiny but determined Barton that they were more fit for the penitentiary than school.

"They wouldn't go to school if they had a chance," he said, adding that a female schoolteacher could do nothing with them.

Suydam's words were like a red flag waved in front of a bull. Barton offered to open a school for them and to teach without pay, as long as the school board backed her efforts.

Suydam had more objections: The boys' parents would never send their kids to a "pauper school"; the entire town would be up in arms at the idea; and, the ladies who taught private schools in the town would be Barton's enemies.

But Suydam had reckoned without Barton's persistence. Eventually, she won him over. On July 1, 1852, the school board issued her a teacher's certificate and established a small, shabby schoolhouse for her. Notices a foot square "advertising" the school were posted throughout the town.

On the first morning of school, Barton, with "a few books and a desk outfit," walked to the building. There she found six boys, ranging in age from six to fourteen, sitting on the rail fence waiting for her. With a confident smile she led them into the long-abandoned building.

"I recall at this day," she later wrote, "the combination of odors that greeted the olfactories. The old musty smell of a long shut untidy house, the pungent flavor of freshly cut southern pitch pine, and the bitter soot of the long iron stove pipe rusting for years."

She and her six charges devoted the morning to cleaning the schoolroom. In the afternoon Barton led her students on a geographical trip around the world, so that by the end of the day, "We were travelers and really knew more about the world and its ways than we ever had before in our lives."

When she arrived at school the next morning Barton got a shock; her class of six had more than doubled in size, to sixteen. By that afternoon it had become twenty, and by the end of the week forty boys were in attendance. On the Monday morning of her second full week fifty-five boys jammed into the little schoolhouse, forcing Barton to give up her desk and chair. In the third week a breakthrough occurred when girls began showing up as well. The larger boys squeezed smaller ones beside them to make room for the new arrivals.

As classes continued to grow, Barton recruited several assistants and expanded her "classroom" into a hallway above a tailor's shop. Many people began taking their children out of the private schools and sending them to Barton.

Clara Barton schoolhouse in Bordentown.

Barton enjoyed living in Bordentown. She loved taking long walks through the woods, with the "silver flow of the Delaware [River] below [the] rocky bluffs." She also enjoyed tramping through Point Breeze, the former estate of Napoleon Bonaparte's elder brother, Joseph. Although Joseph had been gone from Bordentown for twenty years, the grounds were much as he had left them. Barton considered the "miles of shrubs and flowers, its walks, its rests, the ripple of brooks, and the unceasing song of birds—the repose of nature—a home fit for a King."

Barton's roommate for much of her time in Bordentown was Frances Childs, who Barton had recruited to become her first assistant teacher. The two teachers got along famously.

"She said to me once," Childs wrote, "that of all the qualities she possessed, that for which she felt most thankful was her sense of humor. She said it helped her over many hard places."

Yet even at the height of her triumph, Barton was haunted by doubt. At a time when most people embraced a career for life, Barton continued to smolder with new ideas and attitudes. "Had ever one poor girl so many strange wild thoughts, and no one to listen or share one of them or ever realize that my head contains an idea beyond the present foolish moment," she wrote.

One thing she did not have to worry about was the success of her school. By the end of the first year, enrollment was a building-bulging six hundred students, and the town had to build a new four-thousand-dollar schoolhouse. This might have been the thing to keep Barton in Bordentown, and history would have been very different indeed. However, along with the new building, the school board created the position of principal. Then, in a scenario all too familiar today, the school board gave the job to a man, despite Barton's overwhelming qualifications.

Grievously disappointed, Barton tried to continue teaching. But after a few months, a persecution campaign organized by her new boss and her own mental anguish caused Barton to suffer from a severe case of laryngitis. Citing this as the reason, she resigned her position.

"I could bear the ingratitude, but not the pettiness and jealousy of this principal," she later wrote.

Early in February 1854, Barton left for Washington, D.C., where the clouds of civil war were already gathering. Although she couldn't know it at the time, Barton's teaching career was over. Ahead lay the Red Cross.

In later years Clara Barton would be credited with starting the first public school in New Jersey. While this may or may not be true—there seem to have been some small steps toward public education in a few large cities in the state earlier than this—there is no doubt that the success of Barton's school, and the notoriety it received, set the wheels of New Jersey public education firmly in motion. No longer could elitists claim that education should be just for those who could afford it. Clara Barton had shattered the lies and the excuses, and in so doing opened the school door for all children in New Jersey.

Who was the first president of the United States?

If you're like 99.99 percent of the people in New Jersey (as well as the rest of the country), your answer is "George Washington." That would be a good answer, too—except that it's wrong.

In actuality, the first president of the United States was Elias Boudinot of New Jersey.

Don't begin throwing out your vast collection of Washington's Birthday decorations; the Father of Our Country is still the first president of the

United States as we know it. It's actually just some historical hair-splitting, not significant enough to change all the textbooks, that designates Boudinot as the first president. Still, it's appropriate that Elias Boudinot is denied his rightful place in history, for no other figure from this era of independence is so important, and yet so obscure, as this eminent New Jerseyan.

Elias Boudinot was born on May 2, 1740, in Philadelphia. Around 1750 Boudinot's father, a silversmith, moved first to Rocky Hill and then to Princeton, in order to be closer to a copper mine in which he held an interest. Thus New Jersey became young Elias's home; it would remain so for the rest of his life.

Although he wanted to be a minister, because of his family's feeble financial state young Boudinot had to choose a career that did not require college, and so he became a lawyer (and isn't that a switch!). After he married Hannah Stockton in 1765, it seemed as if Boudinot was ready to follow a familiar path in colonial times: establish a career, marry, have children, and work at becoming prosperous.

But big changes were in store for everyone in the colonies, including Boudinot. Perhaps he should have seen it coming when his nine-year-old daughter, Susan, during tea at the home of Royal Governor William Franklin (son of Benjamin) of New Jersey, walked to the window and deliberately dumped the drink onto some nearby bushes.

Shortly thereafter, a group of colonists protesting the high tax on tea re-enacted Susan's action on a larger scale by throwing chests of tea into Boston Harbor. The Boston Tea Party set the colonies on a collision course with Great Britain that finally erupted into war at Lexington and Concord in April 1775. Although at first Boudinot hoped for reconciliation with the mother country, by early 1777 he was firmly on the side of independence. Soon he would be in the midst of the revolution he had once opposed.

Boudinot plunged headfirst into the conflict in April 1777, when George Washington asked him to become the commissary general of prisoners for the Continental Army. Although Washington's letter arrived on April Fool's Day, the job was no joke; the commissary general was responsible for taking care of British prisoners of war, arranging prisoner transfers, making sure that American prisoners were being treated right, and a variety of other delicate tasks. Although constantly hampered by a lack of funds with which to buy American prisoners food, clothing, and other necessities, Boudinot greatly improved conditions for the captive Continentals. A compassionate man, Boudinot could not bear to see or hear of Americans suffering; many times, when money was tight, he used his own. Boudinot wound up spending forty-five thousand dollars of his own funds to buy supplies and other items for the Continental prisoners.

Boudinot worked as the commissary general of prisoners for over a year. Upon resigning the often-frustrating post in May of 1778, he served as a New Jersey delegate to the Continental Congress. Following the completion of his term, he returned home and tried to pick up the pieces of his family and professional life, which had largely been ignored during his time in public service.

For three years Boudinot remained a private citizen. He obviously worked overtime at building up the family fortune, for within a few years he had large land holdings in New Jersey, Ohio, Pennsylvania, North Carolina, and New York. Then, in July 1781, the nation came calling again; the New Jersey legislature elected him to the Congress to fill an unexpired term. Somewhat reluctantly, Boudinot went back into public life.

By the summer of 1781, the assistance of the French had helped swing the war pendulum in favor of the United States. When Washington trapped Cornwallis at Yorktown in October of that same year, everyone thought that the war was over and that a peace treaty with Great Britain was imminent. The war was over, all right—but peace remained as elusive as ever.

Meanwhile, Boudinot continued to be reelected to Congress by the New Jersey legislature. Although a patriot, his vast land holdings made him favor the aristocracy and all the privileges that went with being a member of that class. This got him into several spirited scraps with a young Virginian named James Madison, a vociferous champion of the common man.

At this point the former colonies were operating under the Articles of Confederation, the forerunner to the Constitution. This document elevated the states to supreme sovereignty over the union, so much so, in fact, that the country was referred to as the "united States," the unusual capitalization being used to distinguish the superiority of each individual member over the union of the whole.

The Articles of Confederation did not provide for a president of the nation as we know the office today; the closest thing was the president of Congress. It had been the practice to rotate the office yearly among the states, and when the new session of Congress opened in November 1782, New Jersey had yet to contribute a president. Thus it didn't take too many people by surprise when Boudinot was tapped for the post. Apparently, however, the election threw Boudinot's plans into disarray, as he indicated in a November 4 letter to his wife:

The things of this World are as uncertain as the Wind. . . . This moment I have accepted the President's chair of Congress, not without a trembling hand. . . . The confusion of my affairs and the total derangement of all my Plans and indeed the great loss & Expense that must ensue to me in my circumstances with the difficulties that will necessarily devolve on you, have not been unthought of by me. . . . But these reflections even are now in vain . . . the ways of Providence are in the great Deep.

Some of those difficulties quickly became apparent to Hannah Boudinot, when her husband followed with another letter two days later that basically told her to pack up everything, scrape together every cent she could, wind up his affairs, and get to Philadelphia without delay. Such were the woes of the patriot's wife.

Boudinot's presidency came at a critical time for the young republic. Although the Yorktown victory had ended the fighting, negotiations with Great Britain had not yet produced a peace treaty. Not only did Boudinot have to continually monitor the negotiations, he also had to deal with several crises that revealed how weak the Articles of Confederation were as a governmental framework. One flaw was that nothing compelled the states to participate in Congress, and several times Boudinot had to beg states (Delaware, Maryland, and Georgia were prime offenders) to send delegates to Philadelphia so that the government could function.

Another problem was that there was no revenue-raising mechanism in place, and the government was always down to its last dollar. This brought the country to the brink of anarchy when several hundred soldiers demanding back pay marched on Philadelphia and surrounded the building where Congress was meeting. Finances were so bleak that when peace negotiations with England faltered and it looked as if the war might be renewed, Congress had to tell Washington he couldn't plan any military activities because the government couldn't afford it.

However, it wasn't all bad for the man from New Jersey. On September 3, 1783, came the event that the entire nation had been waiting for, and the occasion that made Boudinot the answer to the trivia question: "Who was the first president of the United States?" On that date, Great Britain signed the Treaty of Paris, formally ending the state of war between the two countries. Before this, the states had technically still been colonies; this document formally recognized, for the first time anywhere, their existence as a free and sovereign nation. Since the treaty was signed during Boudinot's term as president of Congress, Elias Boudinot became the first president of the new nation of the United States of America.

Another happy occasion during Boudinot's term was the issuance of the first national Thanksgiving Day Proclamation. Although the document was drafted by a congressional committee, the language is very reminiscent of Boudinot, and it would not be surprising to someday discover that he had a hand in the writing.

As the end of his term as president drew near, Boudinot requested that he be allowed to return to his home in Elizabeth as a private citizen, and not be reelected to the Congress. This wish was granted, and once more Boudinot picked up the pieces of his life.

But the United States simply could not afford to let a man of Boudinot's talents go. He served six more years in Congress, and ten years as director of the fledgling United States Mint. After retiring to Burlington in 1805, in a magnificent home at the corner of Broad and Talbot Streets, he returned to his first love, religion, and helped to found the American Bible Society in 1816.

Elias Boudinot died on October 24, 1821, at age eighty-one. He was buried in Burlington next to his wife, who had died thirteen years earlier. A true giant of the tumultuous era of independence, he has been overshadowed by the greatness of contemporaries such as Washington, Hamilton, and Jefferson. Yet even if the memories have faded, the result of Boudinot's many years of public service live on in the great monument to liberty and freedom that he helped to create called the United States of America.

DID YOU KNOW?

When the army demanded back pay and accosted the Congress in Philadelphia, it made many members fearful that the city was unsafe. Boudinot adjourned the body and reconvened it in Princeton, thereby making the college town the official capital of the United States. At first Congress met at the home of Colonel George Morgan; subsequent meetings were held in Nassau Hall on the college campus. The sudden notoriety turned the sleepy little village upside down. The formerly quiet streets were suddenly filled with the hustle and bustle of clattering carriages, people constantly coming and going, and merchants hawking all manner of goods and services at all hours of the day and night. It was a distinctive time for the little town—especially when men such as George Washington, John Paul Jones, and Thomas Jefferson could be seen walking the streets—but also a riotous one.

Paul Robeson was a keen observer of the world around him. The internationally renowned African American singer, actor, and social activist used the spoken and sung word rather than the written to tell people exactly what he thought of that world. The tragedy of Paul Robeson was that he lived in a time when it was dangerous to speak your mind.

Paul Leroy Robeson was born in Princeton on April 9, 1898. His father was the Reverend William Drew Robeson, who had been a slave in North Carolina until age fifteen, when he escaped to the North via the Underground Railroad. Maria Louisa Bustill Robeson, Paul's mother, burned to death when he was six years old when hot coals from the household stove fell onto her dress and ignited it.

A few months after his wife's death, Reverend Robeson moved the family first to Westfield and then Somerville. One of only two black children in Somerville High School, young Paul graduated with honors.

In 1915 the seventeen-year-old Robeson entered Rutgers University, only the third black student ever to attend the school. Having starred in football at Somerville, Robeson wanted to play on the Rutgers team almost as much as the coach, George Foster Sanford, wanted the big, strapping athlete to play. But this was not a time of racial tolerance. At the first scrimmage, as Robeson later recalled: "One boy slugged me in the face and smashed my nose . . . and then, as I was down, flat on my back, another boy got me with his knee . . . dislocating my right shoulder."

These injuries kept him in bed for ten days. But Paul Robeson was no quitter, as his teammates soon found out. On his first practice back he made tackle after tackle on defense, despite receiving an inordinate amount of punishment from the other players. The crowning blow came when a player stepped on Robeson's outstretched hand and ripped off his fingernails. In a rage, on the next play Robeson shredded the interference, grabbed the ball carrier, and hoisted him over his head. At that moment Sanford yelled out, "Robey, you're on the varsity."

It was one of the best decisions Sanford ever made. Robeson starred in football for Rutgers, twice being named a Walter Camp All-American. He also won letters in baseball, basketball, and track. No slouch in the classroom either, he won Phi Beta Kappa honors and was chosen class valedictorian.

After graduating from Rutgers, Robeson enrolled in Columbia University Law School and settled down to study for what he assumed would be a career as an attorney. But fate had other plans. He began to be drawn toward the theater, appearing in productions like the Harlem YMCA's presentation *Simon the Cyrenian*. Although he continued to pursue his law degree, the acting itch grew steadily stronger. In the summer of 1922 he had a featured role in the play *Voodoo*, which subsequently toured London.

Upon his return to the United States Robeson completed his studies at Columbia and in 1923 received his law degree. "At this time," he remembered, "I was an aspiring lawyer. . . . Theatre and concerts were furthest from my mind." After working for several months at a prestigious law firm in New York City, however, he quit when a white secretary wouldn't take dictation from him. The law's loss was the theater's gain. Eugene O'Neill, whom Robeson had met before, offered him the lead role in *All God's Chillun Got Wings*, and an actor was born. (O'Neill called Robeson "a young fellow with considerable experience, wonderful presence and voice, full of ambition and a damn fine man personally.")

Robeson's work in *Wings* got him the lead in another O'Neill play, *The Emperor Jones*. While the play wasn't a great success, it led to another defining moment in the young man's life. One scene required him to exit while whistling; unable to whistle, Robeson reached back to his roots as a boy in his father's church and sang a spiritual instead. The majesty of his deep bass voice was instantly electrifying. Everyone knew that it was something special indeed.

Robeson couldn't have picked a better time to become an entertainer. This was the era of the legendary Harlem Renaissance, when black performers like Josephine Baker, Eubie Blake, and Claude McKay fostered a growing recognition of African American artists. Black actors, actresses, and singers were in demand on Broadway and in Hollywood to play real roles, not the demeaning, feet-shuffling clowns of years past. Young, talented, and handsome, Paul Robeson was every casting director's dream.

Robeson became known as much for his singing as his acting. One critic wrote that his was a voice in which "deep bells ring." His concert tours both at home and abroad were tremendously successful. Singing mainly spirituals, Robeson poured his heart and soul into each verse, leaving both him and his audience emotionally drained at the conclusion. His performance as Joe in *Show Boat* (both the play and film), in which he sang Jerome Kern's "Ol' Man River," still stands as an entertainment milestone.

Yet something else was happening to Paul Robeson during these years of his growth and maturity as an artist. Always conscious of prejudice—he and his wife, Eslanda, had moved to London in the 1920s to escape the poisonous racial atmosphere in the United States—Robeson began to link the sufferings of blacks with those of other oppressed peoples around the world. Now, instead of singing at opulent concert halls, he began giving concerts in small auditoriums at inexpensive prices so that the less-affluent could attend. Expanding his repertoire to include folk music from other countries (which won him a broad international following), he announced that he would not sing any music that he couldn't feel in his soul.

In December 1934, Robeson went to the Soviet Union to meet filmmaker Sergei Eisenstein. Unaware of his popularity in that country, he was stunned when thousands of Russians roared their approval of "Pavel Robesona." He was also pleasantly surprised by Soviet society. Racial tolerance was taught in the schools, and Russia's numerous ethnic groups were being encouraged to get along. After the bitterness and hatred he had experienced in the United States, Robeson found this atmosphere unbelievably refreshing. "I feel like a human being for the first time since I grew up," he told Eisenstein. "Here I am not a Negro but a human being. . . . Here, for the first time in my life, I walk in full dignity."

This trip began a fascination with Russian life and the Soviet Union for Robeson, an appeal that went so far that he even enrolled his son Paul Jr. in a Russian school in 1936. It was far more the lack of racial prejudice than any infatuation with Communism that led Robeson down this path, and in the 1930s he was not alone. Many people, both in the United States and abroad, were drawn to the Soviet Union because of the country's reputation as a champion of the oppressed.

Things changed quickly, however, once World War II ended. As Stalin inexorably drew the Iron Curtain around Europe, the Soviet Union changed from wartime ally to enemy. Anyone who had ever said anything complimentary about Russia was considered a traitor. The House Un-American Activities Committee bred an attitude of paranoia and suspicion throughout the country by grilling supposed "Communists" and "fellow travelers." It didn't take a genius to know that Robeson's extremely vocal support of Russia in the past was going to come back to haunt him.

The persecution began innocently enough, with a few concerts being canceled. Then the press began to pepper Robeson with questions like "Are you a Communist?" Robeson was hauled before the California Legislative Committee on Un-American Activities, where he was asked if he was or had been a member of the Communist Party—a charge he angrily denied.

Then, in August 1949, a howling mob attacked people leaving a Robeson concert in Peekskill, New York. While the police who were supposed to provide protection stood idly by, dozens of innocent people were beaten by anti-Robeson thugs. When an "investigation" ordered by New York Governor Thomas E. Dewey failed to blame the police or the rioters for the incident, Dewey redirected it to find out whether the concert was "part of the Communist strategy to foment racial and religious hatreds."

Harassment of Robeson steadily increased. The FBI kept him under constant surveillance and work became almost nonexistent, thanks to an entertainment-industry boycott. (Robeson's annual income at one point shrank to six thousand dollars.) Former friends now crossed the street to avoid him. In August 1950, the State Department canceled his passport, a move that one newspaper said would "be acclaimed by every firm-minded American." Throughout it all, Robeson remained defiant. "I will not retreat," he said. "Not even one thousandth part of one inch."

In June 1956 came the confrontation everyone was waiting for: Robeson was called before the House Un-American Activities Committee. Those hoping for a public crucifixion, however, were disappointed. Instead of kowtowing like most other witnesses, Robeson repeatedly attacked the committee, questioning its members' integrity and denouncing them for the witch-hunt mentality they had fostered. "You are the nonpatriots, and you are the un-Americans and you ought to be ashamed of yourselves," Robeson charged, in his memorable bass voice.

As the 1950s ebbed, so did the anti-Communist zeal; Americans began to pull their heads out of the sand and realize what they'd done to many innocent people who had merely expressed a different point of view. For Paul Robeson, however, the regrets came too late. The years of struggle and anguish had taken their toll on his once-powerful body. Beginning in 1958, his health began to fail. In December 1963, besieged by illness, he retired from public life.

After Eslanda died in 1965, the frail Robeson went to live with his sister Marion in Philadelphia, where he died on January 23, 1976. Death had finally done what years of persecution could not—still Paul Robeson's powerful voice.

Robeson's death was reported on page one of the *New York Times,* which devoted a long introspective story to his life. "The tragedy of Paul Robeson, like that of Othello, was stark; virtue and misjudgment were sharply juxtaposed," editorialized the newspaper. "Yet Paul Robeson, like Othello on his deathbed, could honestly say, 'I have done the state some service, and they know 't.'"

DID YOU KNOW?

Known for his lightning-like quickness on the football field, Robeson made perhaps his best play during a scrimmage in the autumn of 1918. After making an acrobatic grab of a pass, wide receiver Jim Burke tumbled fifty feet down an embankment and fell into a canal. Robeson, in full football gear, raced down the bank, dove into the water, and pulled Burke to shore, almost certainly saving his life.

This chapter has already told the story of Elias Boudinot, an important figure in the fight for independence whose story has been obscured by the greatness of his fellow revolutionaries. But there's obscure, and then there's *forgotten*; a case in point is Garrett A. Hobart, the only vice-president of the United States to come from New Jersey.

In fairness, Hobart was a capable man and not the embarrassment that some vice-presidents become. However, the vice-presidency is, by its very nature, an obscure office; if people's lives depended upon naming ten vice-presidents of the United States, we'd have a sparsely populated country. Hobart's misfortune was to be a colorless man in an invisible office.

Garrett Augustus Hobart was born on June 3, 1844, in Long Branch. The son of Addison Willard Hobart and the former Sophia Vanderveer, Hobart graduated from Rutgers in 1863 and embarked upon a highly successful law career. After marrying Jennie Tuttle in 1869, Hobart entered New Jersey politics. He was elected to both the state assembly and the state senate, serving as the speaker and president, respectively, of each body. In his only try for higher office, he lost a race for the United States Senate.

But it is not as a national political figure that Hobart made his mark in the Republican party. He was a money man, plain and simple, good at spending his own funds and getting others to part with theirs. Hobart practically oozed cash; he was the chairman of the board of directors of a mind-boggling sixty corporations and owned banks, railroads, and even a water company.

As chairman of the New Jersey Republican Committee from 1880 through 1891, Hobart had ample opportunity to make friends with the party's kingmakers, especially party chairman Mark Hanna. In 1896 Hanna got his fellow Ohioan, a pleasant, tepid man named William McKinley, the Republican presidential nomination. Hobart was able to secure the second spot on the ticket, thanks to his money, his efforts on behalf of Republicans throughout the country, and his relationship with Hanna. In the election, a national economic recession helped sweep the Republicans into the White House.

Hobart, despite a fear of public speaking (and doesn't that sound like a little slice of heaven!), was a remarkably effective vice-president. As a man used to operating behind the scenes, he knew how to get things done, and he became a successful liaison between the White House and the Senate. Hobart also frequently opened his home to lawmakers, and the gracious hospitality of both him and his wife—cigars and liquor were always in season at the Hobarts' home—helped the administration maintain cordial relations with Congress, which made for an easy ride for McKinley.

Hobart played a crucial role on the major issue of the day, which was war with Spain over the supposed mistreatment of Cubans. McKinley was something of a dove, but Hobart was an outspoken hawk; it is possible that the vice-president's intransigence on the matter swayed McKinley to the war side. (When the president signed the declaration of war with Spain, he used Hobart's pen.) After the brief conflict ended with the United States victorious, the Senate was deadlocked over whether to keep the Philippine Islands or give them their independence. Hobart cast the tie-breaking vote in favor of making the country a U.S. possession.

Unfortunately, Hobart's timing was all wrong. In 1898 he began having respiratory problems, which worsened; on November 21, 1899, he died in Paterson. Two years later, McKinley, after being reelected in 1900, was assassinated. His successor was Vice-President Theodore Roosevelt, who almost certainly would not have been on the ticket had Hobart lived.

Another distinguished New Jerseyan that you've probably never heard of is William F. Allen of South Orange, even though you have him to thank whenever you want to know the time.

No, Allen didn't invent clocks or even the concept of time. He did, however, devise the system of time zones used across the United States today.

Today time is an integral part of our lives. Businesses and people swear by it, and, thanks to digital clocks on everything from smartphones to microwave ovens, it is never difficult to find out precisely what time it is. However, little more than a century ago things were completely different. In the largely agrarian economy of the nineteenth century, the specific time mattered little. People lived by the sun, the seasons, and the almanac; clocks were largely superfluous.

This casual reliance on natural forces to keep time gave rise to what was called "local" time. Local time was whatever it happened to be in your particular town or area; what time it was somewhere else was insignificant, since the time in New Jersey hardly mattered for farmers in Ohio. Thus, there were over seventy different local time zones throughout the United States, virtually none of which agreed with the other.

While this was fine for most people, it drove the railroads crazy. A train traveler could quickly find his or her watch (set to local time) hopelessly wrong and not have a clue when he or she would arrive at the train's destination. Even worse was the havoc that the numerous time zones wreaked on railroad schedules: When people arrived in Columbus, Ohio at 1:30 P.M. New York local time, were they too late, too early, or right on time to catch the train leaving at 1:30 Columbus local time?

Beginning in the early 1870s, the railroads made several attempts to come up with a standardized time system, but to no avail. In 1882 they dumped the problem into Allen's lap.

William Frederick Allen was born on October 9, 1846, in Bordentown, New Jersey. His father, Joseph, an engineer, was killed during the Civil War. After completing his education at the Bordentown Model School and the Protestant Episcopal Academy in Philadelphia, Allen got a job in 1862 with the Camden & Amboy Railroad as a surveyor and engineer.

Ten years later Allen joined the staff of a publication called the *Official Guide of the Railways and Steam Navigation Lines of the United States and Canada*. (Imagine asking for that by name at a newsstand!) This was merely a collection of all the various timetables then used for trains and ships. The next year Allen, an intense man with a close-cropped beard and mustache, became the guide's editor, and so became intimately familiar with the mass confusion generated by the various time zones. Thus, in 1875, he was the logical choice to be named secretary of the General Time Convention/ Southern Railway Time Convention, which met periodically to try to solve the vexing problem of time.

By 1882, however, the conventions had gotten nowhere; time was still a mess. Scientists and businesses favored establishing a standardized time system but hesitated to tamper with such a cherished American tradition as local time. ("If you derange the habits of a people too much they will have none of it," warned a foe of standardized time.) However, Allen doggedly continued working on the problem, evaluating various time standardization schemes and soliciting opinions about how best to accomplish the objective. Impressed by his work, in 1882 the convention asked him to develop a time standardization proposal for its meeting in April 1883.

What the New Jerseyan devised was a model of simplicity and common sense. Borrowing the idea of four time zones from the theorists, he made the divisions across the country—the same ones used today—conform more to existing railroad lines rather than the strict by-meridian designs of the scientists. (This is why the time zones today bend and bulge in spots, rather than divide the country with razor-straight lines.) This gave Allen's plan the benefit of practicality over theory. He also paid close attention to state boundaries, trying whenever possible to keep whole states within a single time zone—again, a crucial distinction between his scheme and previous ones, which usually sliced states right down the middle. This made the time zones easier for people, who would be losing local time as a result, to accept. Once the convention accepted his plan, Allen began lobbying various influential people in cities across the country to accept the new time system.

While today it would take an act of Congress to do something so monumental as merge dozens of different time zones into just four, at this time the railroads were the main economic power in the United States. The Iron Horse usually did what it wanted. So the railroads, with great public fanfare, unilaterally implemented standard time in the United States on Sunday, November 18, 1883. This day would become known as the "Day of Two Noons," because, at 12:28 P.M., all railroad line clocks were turned back to twelve noon to signal the beginning of standard time. Faced with either being totally out of step with the railroads or conforming, the rest of the country began adopting standard time.

Conformity didn't come without a fight. This was especially true where standard time and local time differed by more than a few minutes. "Let us keep our own noon," wailed the *Boston Evening Transcript,* and the *Louisville Courier-Journal* called the concept "a compulsory lie, a monstrous fraud," and "a swindle." Some cities, like Detroit and Cleveland, simply ignored the whole thing and remained on local time. Congress thought about mandating standard time, then, faced with local opposition, decided to do nothing. (It wouldn't be until 1918 that the present system became federal law.)

Even with all the grumbling, Allen could justifiably claim that his new system "now governs the daily and hourly actions of at least fifty million people." The implementation of standard time not only meant new ways of living and working but also influenced how people thought and acted toward each other; suddenly, being "on time" was important and punctuality became a way of judging people. The man from New Jersey had profoundly changed the United States forever.

The next "distinguished daughter" in this chapter is unique in several ways. First of all, she's the only person who wasn't born in the United States. Secondly, while she was well known during her lifetime, her national fame came later, as the result of an epic poem. Yet her story is too important to ignore. That's why this is really the tale of a brave, resourceful, and determined individual, Elizabeth Haddon Estaugh, who came to the New World all by herself and wound up founding a town that to this day, still bears her name—Haddonfield.

Elizabeth Haddon was born in 1680 in the county of Surrey, in England. She and her younger sister Sarah were the only two of seven children born to John and Elizabeth Haddon who survived infancy. Young Elizabeth grew to be a smart, lively, and serious child.

The Haddons were Quakers, a persecuted religious sect at that time in England. One of the Haddons' frequent visitors was fellow Quaker William Penn, who regaled the family with his tales of the New World. Young Elizabeth listened raptly to Penn's stories about the woods, the Indians, the animals, and the way he and others were literally carving a new and tolerant society out of the wilderness.

In 1698 John Haddon bought several thousand acres of land in western New Jersey. It seems clear that he intended to move his family there, yet for some reason he never did. Elizabeth, however, had never forgotten Penn's stories of this exciting region. In the manner of teenagers since time immemorial, she pestered her parents to let her go to America to oversee the family's land holdings. Finally, in the manner of parents since time immemorial, they gave in; in the spring of 1701, Elizabeth Haddon, accompanied by two servants and a document giving her the power to "look after and occupy" her father's lands, set sail from England.

Landing at Philadelphia in June 1701, Elizabeth quickly set out for her family's land. On the way, she saw that all Penn had said was true: compared to the built-up, hustling community of homes and shops that she had come from, New Jersey was a primordial wilderness. What few houses existed were separated by miles of dense woods, from which either friend or foe could pop out at any moment. Roads were virtually nonexistent, as were stores and businesses. If you couldn't make it yourself, you couldn't have it. It was a rough, raw, and untamed land, and quite possibly, dangerous for a young woman on her own.

Elizabeth Haddon, however, couldn't have been happier. Here was a place totally different from her former home; here was a place where the scent of wild roses perfumed the air, where deer and rabbits hopped freely about, and where the only sound was the rustle of leaves in the wind. She moved into a small house built by John Willis, who had surveyed the Haddon lands, called it Haddonfield (it was two miles outside the boundaries of modern Haddonfield), and immediately began expanding it.

Elizabeth's house was on Cooper's Creek, which served as a main transportation artery in the absence of roads. As one of the few outposts of European civilization in the area, the home received frequent visits by travelers looking for a hot meal and a dry place to sleep. In this they were not disappointed; all were welcomed to Haddonfield.

Elizabeth's medical skills were of particular importance in those days. A salve she made was called "the sovereignest thing on earth," and her ability to bandage wounds was a godsend in an area where proper medical services were nonexistent. The Native Americans in the area also depended on Haddon for medicine, much of which she made from herbs she grew. In gratitude for her kindness, they shared with her some of their medical secrets and local cures. Haddon sent medicine to other parts of New Jersey and Pennsylvania, and it was said that never a day went by without a need for her medical knowledge.

In 1702 Haddon married a Quaker minister named John Estaugh. Although her husband's religious work kept him on the road frequently, Haddon was far from idle. She received numerous visitors, her medical skills were always in demand, she was clerk of the Women's Meeting, and she handled her father's business affairs with intelligence and skill.

In 1713 she and Estaugh built a much larger house. This became the first settlement in what is today Haddonfield. Soon a thriving community had sprung up there, with the Estaughs' house at the center of the activity.

Throughout her life Haddon remained a kind, gentle person, as illustrated by a contemporary account of her: "Her heart and house were open to her friends, whom to entertain seemed one of her greatest pleasures; [she] was prudently cheerful, and well knowing the value of friendship was careful not to wound it herself, nor encourage others in whispering and publishing the failings, or supposed weaknesses."

In 1742 John Estaugh died. Childless, Haddon continued her many activities for the betterment of Haddonfield, surrounded by grandnieces and grandnephews. Finally, on March 30, 1762, after a three-month illness, Haddon died at the age of eighty-two, "as one falling asleep, full of days, like unto a shock of corn fully ripe." On her memorial plaque was etched a fitting tribute: "A woman remarkable for resolution, Prudence, Charity."

For the brave Quaker woman, the adventure was over.

DID YOU KNOW?

There are many stories told about Elizabeth Haddon's life in the New World. However, the most famous one concerns her forthrightness. In fact, the tale so impressed Henry Wadsworth Longfellow that he wove part of it into his epic poem "Tales of a Wayside Inn."

Before she was married, Haddon was among a group of Quakers, including John Estaugh, who were traveling by horseback to Salem. At one point, Haddon slowed her horse because the saddle needed adjustment. As the rest of the party rode ahead, Estaugh came to her assistance. Haddon seized the opportunity to tell Estaugh that she thought he had been chosen by God to be her life's partner. In his poem, Longfellow had her say: "I will no longer conceal what is laid upon me to tell thee, I have received from the Lord a charge to love thee, John Estaugh."

Since women generally didn't speak until spoken to during this era, Haddon's bold talk about love and marriage must have sent the shy Estaugh's head reeling. But to his credit, the young minister listened, then told her that while he found Haddon pleasant in many ways, he had had no similar directions from God.

The two did indeed get married, however, and according to all accounts, it was a happy union. "I'll venture to say, few if any, in a married state, ever lived in sweeter harmony than we did," Haddon would later write. Fortunately for John Estaugh, Elizabeth Haddon had spoken before being spoken to.

Thomas Edison at Menlo Park

Thomas Edison was not born in New Jersey, but in Milan, Ohio, in 1847. Yet he is so associated with New Jersey as the Wizard of Menlo Park and later with his facilities in West Orange that, for all intents and purposes, Edison might as well be a native son.

Thanks to a large contract from the Atlantic and Pacific Telegraph Company, young inventor Edison was free in late 1875 to look around for a new site for his laboratory and manufacturing facilities, which up until then had been located in several buildings scattered around the Newark New Jersey area. The site he chose was a place so remote that it had neither town hall, school, or church—Menlo Park, New Jersey.

Menlo Park was part of six neighborhoods that composed Raritan Township. It contained about thirty large homes, spread out and connected by board walkways. Here Edison purchased thirty-four acres of land from the family of William Carman, who had worked for him in Newark. Just a few years earlier, big things had been planned for the new community of Menlo Park. However, those plans never panned out, and until Edison's arrival it seemed that Menlo Park was destined to be just another in a long line of failed communities that would slowly wither and die. Little did the residents of this tiny village, too small to have its own sign at the railroad stop, know that it was destined to become world-famous.

Although Menlo Park seemed a random selection, in reality Edison had several very specific reasons for choosing it. Not only was the land from Carman's family available, but it was priced very cheaply because of an economic recession that had occurred a few years earlier. Although it seemed extremely isolated, Menlo Park was in fact only twenty-five miles south of New York City—close enough that reporters for the city's many newspapers could easily get there and back. As any small business owner knows, favorable publicity reaps enormous benefits for the bottom line, and Edison, with his propensity for coming up with new things, needed favorable publicity more than most. Finally, Menlo Park provided easy access to men and materials without the obtrusiveness and distractions of city life.

Indeed, after Edison moved to Menlo Park in the spring of 1876, the village quickly took on all the aspects of a company town. Many of his workers moved into homes in the community. Edison took the largest home in town, which had formerly been the sales office for the development. Besides the laboratory complex, Edison built other buildings, such as a glass house, a carpenter's shop, and a blacksmith's shop. Edison even prevailed upon a former Newark neighbor, Sarah Jordan, to move to Menlo Park and establish a boardinghouse for his employees. The town being what it was, the boardinghouse was close to Edison's home.

Thus many of the workers were never far out of their boss's sight. The many distractions of the big city were lacking, so the workers could do little except work and go home. For recreation the only thing available was Menlo Park's sole tavern, known as the Lighthouse, where alcohol, food, and billiards were available.

Menlo Park was the world's first research and development facility, and maybe its isolation was good for creative inspiration. Although he was only at Menlo Park a few years, Edison enjoyed a burst of creative fire that stunned the world.

It all started in the summer of 1877, when a simple suggestion from Edison sparked the idea that would ultimately become the phonograph. Once he demonstrated the machine to the editors at *Scientific American* in December 1877, the resultant storm of publicity assured Edison that he would never be an unknown again. Reporters from New York City and other places flooded into Menlo Park, and the stories they produced made both the inventor and the town famous. Readers couldn't get enough of the Wizard of Menlo Park, who even appeared in a drawing on the front of the *Daily Graphic* in wizard's robe and a tall hat to complete the image. Between the phonograph and the electric light bulb, there was no stopping Edison. While working at Menlo Park, Edison applied for patents on more than four hundred inventions. The Wizard of Menlo Park became an indelible American image.

Finally, in the early 1880s, Edison decided that he needed to be closer to New York. That, combined with the fact that he was simply running out of space for all his various enterprises, caused Edison to move to new facilities at West Orange by 1887. The Menlo Park buildings were abandoned and eventually either burned down or fell apart, except for two that Henry Ford rescued and took to Dearborn, Michigan.

Today, the "Wizard of Menlo Park" has entered the Hall of Legendary American Phrases. Edison took an otherwise nondescript New Jersey town and made it world-famous. Because of that, Thomas Edison belongs in this chapter about Famous Sons and Daughters—even if he wasn't born in New Jersey.

Alice Paul

A lot of people don't know the name Alice Paul, or if they do, it's only in a vague, fuzzy way. Mention Susan B. Anthony or Elizabeth Cady Stanton, and you're likely to get a flash of recognition. *Oh yes. They were two of the ladies involved in the women's suffrage movement—the struggle for equal rights for women, particularly when it came to voting.* Sadly, like a lot of things New Jersey, Alice Paul doesn't get the respect that she should, yet she was every bit the equal of Anthony or Stanton—and she was a native New Jerseyan.

Alice Stokes Paul was born on January 11, 1885, on her parents' farm, Paulsdale Farm, in Mt. Laurel. It was 170 acres that her father liked to think of as a gentleman's farm; most of the actual work was done by hired hands.

The Pauls were Quakers, and Alice grew up a firm proponent of the Quaker idea of trying to create a better society. She also attended woman's suffrage meetings at an early age along with her mother, and thus grew up accepting gender equality as a matter of course.

When she was sixteen, and a student at Swarthmore College outside Philadelphia, her father died suddenly, stunning the family. Yet Alice managed to put the tragedy behind her and continued to excel at school. A political science course taken in her senior year sent the formerly rudderless Alice on a new path: social betterment through political action. She continued to maintain a quite demeanor and attitude. It took a trip to England in 1907 to turn Alice from pacifist to activist. One day she had occasion to hear

Paulsdale, Alice Paul's childhood home,
and now home to the Alice Paul Institute.

radical woman's activist Christabel Pankhurst speak. She was a member of a group whose motto was "deeds, not words," and it became a clarion call to action for Alice.

Paul went to speeches by politicians where she shouted out questions about woman's rights until she was hauled away, and she participated in demonstrations that resulted in window-breaking and other physical acts. The British police were determined to put these radical women in their place and continually arrested them. Paul and the others responded to their arrests by staging hunger strikes in prison, and the police responded to that by force-feeding them, a painful and sometimes even dangerous procedure. By the time Paul, age twenty-five, returned home in 1910, she was a changed woman both physically and emotionally. The quiet little Quaker girl was gone. In her place was a full-fledged radical activist.

Paul believed that the Pankhursts and their radicalism offered a way forward to women's suffrage that the more sedate American movement did not. The push by political action for a constitutional amendment in this country for women's suffrage had faltered; actions, not words, were needed to reenergize the movement. Paul spearheaded the organization of a large women's suffrage parade up Pennsylvania Avenue in Washington, D.C., on March 3, 1913—the day of Woodrow Wilson's inauguration. More than eight thousand women participated, but the parade quickly fell apart as males along the route first verbally, then physically, started abusing the marchers. The police stood by and watched, their attitude best summed up by one cop who said to a female marcher who appealed to him for help: "If my wife were where you are, I'd break her head."

Yet the parade served its purpose by getting people in the United States once again talking about women's suffrage. Paul went to the White House, but Wilson hemmed and hawed his way through a discussion of the women's movement, and Paul knew that more work was needed. For the next several years the petite Paul, almost always dressed in purple or lavender and wearing a hat with a shawl wrapped around her as if perpetually cold, picketed Wilson wherever he went and held other public events, demanding equal rights. Once the war started, the American public saw the women's suffragists as unpatriotic, and Paul and her colleagues in the movement were arrested time and again and thrown into prison, where the conditions were, to put it mildly, deplorable. Rats overran the cells, forcing the women to beat them off with whatever they had. The food was awful, and contests were held to see whose bowl contained the most worms. The women were told that African Americans freely roamed their section of the prison, subtly introducing the idea of forcible rape. Paul was thrown into the psychiatric ward, where doctors tried to declare her insane so she could be institutionalized.

Eventually, this treatment turned the public's feelings toward the women's suffrage activities from anger at to outrage for, and support began building for women's right to vote. Wilson, sensing a shift in the wind, announced he'd support a constitutional amendment granting that right as a "war measure." On August 18, 1920, Tennessee ratified the Nineteenth Amendment to the U.S. Constitution, and women throughout the country finally received the right to vote.

For Alice Paul the fight was far from over. She spent the rest of her life fighting for passage of the Equal Rights Amendment and died on July 9, 1977, without seeing it ratified. However, thanks to this brave and resourceful New Jerseyan, who endured difficult conditions because of her beliefs, millions of American women have had much to celebrate over the years. More people should indeed know her name.

Great Storms

Ah, weather! Is there anything more fascinating in life—or more frightening?

Just like the little girl with the curl, when the weather is good, it is very good, offering us gorgeous sunshine, bright blue skies, and refreshing breezes. But when it is bad, weather—in the form of howling blizzards, ferocious hurricanes, raging nor'easters, and the like—can be very bad indeed.

Thanks to its geographic location nearly halfway between the equator and the North Pole, and also because it is a coastal state, New Jersey enjoys (or suffers from, depending upon your perspective) a broad diversity of weather. Hurricanes, nor'easters, heat waves, cold snaps, blizzards, ice storms, tornadoes—we get them all here. And, although we all like nice weather, it is the storms that get our attention, these awesome examples of Nature's fury that make us realize that there are some things that will always be beyond the control of humanity.

"500 Girls Wanted"

No, that isn't a plea from some overzealous Don Juan that was snuck into this book by mistake. It's the beginning of a story about the most fearsome snow storm ever to strike New Jersey: the legendary Great Blizzard of 1888. Rarely has a storm caused such an impression that its memory remains nearly a century and a half later, but such is the legacy of the Blizzard of '88.

(Incidentally, that "500 Girls" line was written on a sign, along with a second line, "To Eat Snow," displayed outside a Newark business practically buried by the big storm. No one knows if the request was fulfilled.)

People expect a noted Arctic explorer to know about snow. So, when Adolphus W. Greely, famous polar investigator and head of the United States War Department's Signal Service, predicted fair weather for the mid-Atlantic states for the first few days of the week beginning on Sunday,

March 11, 1888, people tended to accept the forecast. In fact, there was no reason to doubt it: the winter of 1888 had been the region's mildest in seventeen years. With the middle of March rapidly approaching, spring was just days away. Everyone's thoughts were on flowers blooming, trees budding, and the return of warm weather—anything but snow.

However, on that fateful March 11, a rather innocent-looking low-pressure trough centered near Augusta, Georgia, was about to make a liar out of Greely. During the day, the trough was blocked from its normal course up the East Coast by a large dome of high pressure, which stalled the storm east of Cape May by the morning of Monday, March 12. At the same time, extremely cold winds from Canada were drawn into the storm, where they mixed with warm southerly winds and picked up plenty of Atlantic moisture. The result was a blizzard of epic proportions, a storm so powerful that meteorologists consider it a five-hundred-year event because it will occur only once in a half a millennium.

The storm began innocently enough; a cold, chilly rain fell throughout most of New Jersey on March 11. During the night, the temperature plummeted and the rain changed to snow. Even more ominously, the wind steadily picked up until, as one Egg Harbor City observer recalled, "[It] blew with the force of a hurricane at intervals, doing considerable damage to property."

The Great Blizzard of 1888 had arrived. It would not leave until Wednesday, March 14—a three-day storm destined to go down in weather history.

Although virtually the entire state received snow, the southern counties might be excused for saying, "What blizzard?" Cape May County reported ten inches of snow—a lot, certainly, but not in line with "the greatest storm ever" reputation of the blizzard—and Atlantic City recorded a mere seven inches of the white stuff.

The central and northern portions of New Jersey got hammered. Snowfall totals in some towns and counties more than doubled those in South Jersey: Toms River, 24 inches; New Brunswick, 24 inches; Rahway, 25 inches; Warren County, 24 inches; Morris County, 20 inches; Union County, 25 inches. (These, in turn, were more than doubled by the totals of some towns in eastern New York State: Saratoga, 50 inches, Albany, 47 inches, and Troy, 55 inches.)

The storm hit suddenly. The Toms River newspaper *New Jersey Courier* reported that the temperature dropped thirty degrees in forty-eight hours, from forty-four degrees Fahrenheit to fourteen. In Newton, the thermometer plunged from above freezing to a bone-chilling one degree above zero in approximately thirty hours.

The arrival of the storm was terrifying to behold. The *New Jersey Courier* of March 14, 1888, reported the blizzard's beginnings: "On Sunday afternoon a rain storm from the southeast, accompanied by high winds, set in, and continued without intermission until about two or half past two o'clock on Monday morning, when the wind, increasing to a gale, shifted to the northwest. The first blast of the storm, after the shift of the wind, was terrific, and most of our residents were aroused by the rocking of their houses upon their foundations. With the wind came snow, flying, swirling, drifting before the blast, and by seven o'clock fully one foot of snow had fallen, which, however, was piled up in drifts some of which attained the height of five or six feet."

The paper also described the effects of the storm: "Fences were obliterated, doors and windows shut in, and business was entirely suspended. All communication with the outside world was cut off, no mails have arrived at the time of writing, and the telegraph wires beyond the station at Long Branch are down. Attempts were made on Monday [the 12th] to get two trains through, but neither succeeded." Noted the paper, in an obvious understatement: "We are snowed up."

The big cities didn't fare much better. Trenton was cut off from the outside world for sixty hours. Trains stopped running on Monday and didn't begin operating again until Thursday. Every hotel in the city was jammed to capacity with stranded rail passengers; many travelers sought refuge in private homes.

A more serious consequence of the paralyzed transportation system was that no food could be brought into the capital city. Many grocery stores ran out of everything and had no way to get more. On top of that, work simply ceased in the city, so that even if there had been food, many people didn't have money to buy it. "No money and no work and depleted provisions have undoubtedly made a thousand people in this city suffer terribly," said the *New York Times* of March 15.

In Newark things weren't much better. All the telegraph and telephone wires were either down or crossed, and just a single train was able to struggle out of the city on March 12. Despite the post office's "rain, snow," pledge, only one small mail pouch from nearby Elizabeth made it into the city. Businessmen desperate to get to New York City offered sleigh drivers up to one hundred dollars to take them to the Hudson River. This was a futile gesture, however, since most streets were clogged with waist-high drifts.

The threat of famine also stalked the Newark streets. As the *Newark Evening News* of March 14, 1888, reported: "Unless the railroads are cleaned and trains are running by Friday many Newarkers will go hungry for nearly every kind of food, except that made with flour." The storm had hit on Monday, the usual stocking-up day for city butcher shops, cutting off the supply of fresh meat into the city as completely as if a spigot had been twisted shut. Poultry dealers and fish sellers were in the same snow-filled boat. Coffee, sugar, eggs, and milk were also in short supply.

Even the dead were impacted by the storm. Bodies stacked up in funeral homes, with no prospect of being buried soon. People who died at home were simply left where they were.

Jersey City was even cut off from its neighboring suburbs. According to the *New York Times* of March 12, 1888, "It was worth a man's life to venture from Bergen Heights across these meadows to the city." Calls for ambulances went unanswered, as did cries for milk by hungry infants; dozens of milk delivery wagons were abandoned on the streets by their drivers. Although schools tried to open, they soon realized their folly and closed. Unfortunately, some people didn't get the message. One plucky child tried to reach school but was overcome by the blizzard and collapsed into a snow bank, where she lay helpless until fortunately rescued by a passerby. ("It took a long time to thaw her out and prepare her for the rest of her homeward journey," said the *Times*.) A policeman named Longe, going above and beyond the call of duty, carried three schoolteachers from the No. 12 school home on his back!

Sadly, not all of the snow stories were so cheerful. At noon on Monday, March 12, the Singer factory in Elizabeth decided to close, and send the 1,800 employees (out of 3,200) who had struggled through the storm back home. Many women refused to brave the blizzard a second time, but most men decided to risk the quarter-mile walk to the railway station. The men left the factory in groups of twenty, hoping that there was strength in numbers. But nothing could match the awesome power of Nature, as one man recalled:

> We meant to keep together, but the storm was so terrible that before we were halfway we were hopelessly separated. As I went on, I met other men who had gone before. Some were helpless. The face of one was a perfect glare of ice. His eyelids were frozen fast and he was groping blindly along . . . as I came up he fell into a drift. At last . . . I reached the station. Six men had been terribly frozen on the way. The hands of some of them, the ears of others and even portions of their

bodies were frozen. A man named Sherwood had both of his hands frozen to the wrists. A man named Ellis was picked up out of the snow . . . and died soon afterwards. Two other men were missing from our party. I do not doubt that they are buried in the drifts.

There were other deaths as well. A schooner cook named Beach froze to death in the rigging of his ship. A New Brunswick farmer out shoveling found the body of a woman who had collapsed on his property and frozen to death. In Raritan Township, Henry Henrithan left Milltown in a "somewhat intoxicated" state, and got lost in the snow. When neighbors went to his home to tell his wife, they found Mrs. Henrithan dead in bed from cold and hunger, and the children half-starved and frozen.

Even remaining indoors did not guarantee safety. The storm with winds so fierce that their icy effects were felt six hundred miles away in Bermuda sought out people wherever they were, as this account by Laura Gwinnup of Blairstown (Warren County) illustrates: "We cannot keep warm in the room, and nearly freeze when we come in the kitchen, the snow blowes in the doors so that we have to shovel it out in large quantities."

In Camden there was a different problem. Between the blizzard winds and low tide, the water was literally blown out of the Delaware River. Ferries and other boats scraped bottom and could not carry either cargo or passengers into port on either side. The water level dropped so low that Camden's water pumps would not work, and the city was gripped by a severe water shortage.

The winds also wreaked havoc in many other New Jersey communities. Winds of ninety miles an hour and more at Sandy Hook piled snowdrifts up to fifteen feet high all across the peninsula. In Burlington the winds crushed the sturdy Burlington Thread Mill as if it were made of papier-mâché, not brick, and in Cape May, the howling gale destroyed numerous oceanfront homes.

Faced with devastation, some businesses tried to cope with humor. Several merchants offered one thousand pounds of free snow with every dollar purchase. Outside a Newark saloon, a sign proclaimed: "Any man who relates any snow reminiscences here will be compelled to treat the house."

Undoubtedly there were many snow tales being told during those days. One of the most remarkable was that of Samuel Decker of Newark. After visiting Midvale (five miles from Pompton Junction) on Sunday, March 11, he arose on the following morning to find a thick curtain of white outside, and no prospect of returning home. Finally, after he had waited two days with no letup in the storm's fury, his patience gave out. Borrowing a pair of boots, he set out on foot for Pompton Junction, despite the unanimous opinion of everyone in the house he was leaving that the next time they would see him would be in a coffin. Although he had to fight his way through snowdrifts up to his armpits, Decker arrived at Pompton Junction only to find that there hadn't been a train there for days. Incredibly, he decided to plunge on to Paterson, a "mere" fifteen miles away. Even more incredibly, he made it, despite not eating anything for eighteen hours and only taking one five-minute break during the entire trip.

Stories with happy endings like this were few and far between. More often, the tales were of incredible hardship, frozen extremities, lack of food, and countless other problems caused by the Great Blizzard. People were exhausted from dealing with the snow and the mess it made of everyone's lives. "Winter has 'lingered' in the lap of Spring. It should now March on," sighed the *Newark Evening News* on March 14.

Finally, after battering the state for three straight days, the storm moved out to sea. On Thursday, March 15, people ventured out of their homes, some for the first time in days, and looked at what the storm had wrought.

This was indeed a phenomenal weather event. The storm intensified as it roared across the Atlantic, and on March 19 it slammed into Berlin, whipping the city with heavy snow and high winds. Still farther east, the floods brought about by the storm wiped out nearly three dozen Hungarian villages.

DID YOU KNOW?

One of the major casualties of the Great Blizzard of 1888 was the reputation of a poet named John Whitaker Watson, who had had the misfortune of writing a popular ode called "Beautiful Snow" just a few years before. A Connecticut newspaper offered a five-cent reward for Watson's arrest and conviction, and a group of citizens in Hartford hung the beleaguered poet in effigy. In New Jersey, when a man stood up among a group of stranded train passengers and offered to recite "Beautiful Snow" as a means of entertainment, a collection was quickly taken up to buy his silence.

Of all the types of storms that strike New Jersey, none is more vicious or deadly than a major hurricane. To be struck by one of these Atlantic behemoths is like being attacked by a mindless monster with unlimited destructive power; just when you think it can't get any worse, it does. The memories of a major hurricane linger long after the storm itself has gone—as in the case of the Great Atlantic Hurricane (the naming of hurricanes was still nine years in the future) of 1944.

That storm formed on September 9, six hundred miles east-northeast of Puerto Rico and quickly grew in strength and intensity. Just four days later, the *Philadelphia Inquirer* warned of "a great hurricane fraught with peril for life and property . . . bearing down on the North Carolina coast."

The storm banged into North Carolina early in the morning on September 14, then set its sights on New Jersey. As it barreled toward the state, the barometric pressure plummeted to 27.97 inches and the winds increased to 134 miles per hour, with gusts to 150. Clearly, this was going to be a storm that New Jerseyans would long remember.

Being farthest south, Cape May was the first to feel the storm's fury. Wind and rain from the storm had been lashing the entire coast for several days, almost like a boxer softening up his opponent with jabs before landing a haymaker. In the late afternoon of September 14, with hurricane-force winds (over 75 miles per hour) buffeting the town and tides surging to nearly ten feet above normal, the haymaker was swung at Cape May.

Sometime before five o'clock that afternoon, a wave described as a "40 foot [high] tidal wave" crashed into the town. The towering wall of water demolished Cape May's boardwalk, destroyed Convention Hall (musical instruments from the building were found scattered about the area), and splintered two piers (Hunt and Pennyland). Roads were not only washed out but buried by tons of sand and debris. Three hundred families had to be evacuated.

Thus began a swath of unprecedented devastation along the Jersey Shore. Ocean City suffered a fate similar to that of Cape May: the boardwalk was devastated, the roof blew off the Breakers Hotel, and the mast of the *Sindia*, which had been jutting out of the beach as an Ocean City landmark for more than forty years, was snapped off at the sand line.

As always when weather is at its most violent, the strange and unpredictable happened. In their book *Great Storms of the Jersey Shore*, Larry Savadove and Margaret Thomas Buchholz recounted an amusing incident in Ocean City, in which a family had to flee their home just as they were sitting down to dinner. Later, the table leaf, with dishes of meat, peas, and potatoes lined up neatly, was seen floating down the street.

Atlantic City also bore the storm's fury. The Grand Dowager of the Jersey Shore suffered extensive property damage, including the loss of the entire boardwalk near the Absecon Inlet. The storm cut the world-famous Heinz Pier in half, sending great chunks careening down city streets. On Madison Avenue, eight teenage boys maneuvered a forty-foot section of Boardwalk down the street, like Huck Finn poling a raft down the Mississippi. Countless homes and businesses were flooded by seawater. Structures were tossed around like pieces on a Monopoly board. Convention Hall, the Armory, and the railroad station were packed with dazed evacuees, who were stunned by the storm's sudden fury. That night Coast Guardsmen patrolled the devastated city, making it seem more like a bombed-out city from the ongoing world war than the sun and fun capital of the Jersey Shore.

Because of its precarious position dangling off the coast, Long Beach Island is always a ripe target for storms, and the Hurricane of 1944 was no exception. Besides the normal damage caused by the wind and tides, a mammoth wave—some say it was thirty feet high—inundated the southern part of the island. The inexorable wall of water knocked houses from their moorings and set them floating on what had been solid ground but was now turned into a lake by the storm. The buildings that stayed put lost walls, roofs, and whatever else the hurricane could pry off. Huddled in their homes as the water rose around them, people watched once-solid structures and mountains of debris go floating by on the street as if they were dried leaves caught in an autumn breeze.

Pictures of the southern part of Long Beach Island in the storm's aftermath show such utter devastation that it's hard to believe that the area wasn't the victim of a massive explosion. Buildings were not merely damaged but annihilated; little remained of many except for piles of wood and brick. In Harvey Cedars alone, so many homes were either destroyed or severely damaged that it was deemed impossible to tell where the structures had once stood.

The northern part of the coast was attacked with the same viciousness. Officials in Shore towns in Ocean and Monmouth Counties also reported a giant wave—some said it was fifty feet high—that crashed into the shoreline, destroying whatever was in its path. Piers, boardwalks, homes, and businesses were strewn about like toys thrown by an angry child. The boardwalks that were wrecked read like a road map of shore towns: Bay Head, Point Pleasant, Belmar, Ocean Grove, Asbury Park, and Long Branch.

Of course, the rest of New Jersey didn't escape the hurricane's wrath. The northeastern part of the state suffered the most rainfall, with Rahway and Elizabeth reporting over eleven inches. Rahway was also the single-day rainfall champ, with six inches falling on September 13. Trees, the soil around their roots already softened by the rain preceding the hurricane, were uprooted by the thousands, littering roadways, yards, and train tracks throughout the state. Included among these were orchard trees; seven hundred thousand bushels of apples were blown from trees by the storm, which helped contribute to agriculture losses totaling three and a half million dollars.

Overall property damage was estimated at twenty-five million dollars. Nearly seven hundred buildings were destroyed, and over thirty-six hundred damaged. The storm took eight lives, all in shore communities.

The day after the hurricane the air was as still as death. People ventured out of their homes, looked at the devastation, and just shook their heads. In just a matter of hours their lives had been turned inside out, uprooted like many of the trees lying scattered about. These memories would linger long indeed.

Nor'easters are storms unique to the small portion of the United States that New Jersey inhabits. To someone from Kansas, a nor'easter is an icy wind that comes roaring down from Canada and acts like a super air conditioner, plunging the entire region into the deep freeze. But to a New Jerseyan, the word "nor'easter" means much more than that—as it did during those fateful March days in 1962, when the most memorable of all nor'easters arrived.

March 5, 1962, was just another Monday in New Jersey. At the Algonquin Theatre in Manasquan (Monmouth County), Jerry Lewis's latest film, *The Errand Boy,* was playing. Whitewall tires were selling for $35.54 a pair, and twenty-seven pieces of furniture cost a mere $329. The New York Yankees were beginning preparations to win—yawn—yet another world championship. For entertainment, people enjoyed watching the life and death struggles of an intense TV doctor named Ben Casey. On the international scene, President John F. Kennedy struggled with escalating Cold War tensions.

The weather forecast for that day was "cloudy, chance of snow, mixed with rain developing," not much of a herald for the arrival of the greatest nor'easter of them all.

Actually, the Great Nor'easter was two storms: one had come steaming over the middle portion of the country, spreading snow and cold in its wake, while the other had formed off the Georgia coast. The two joined forces, then began heading north up the Atlantic seaboard.

The timing couldn't have been worse. The storm arrived during spring tide, which is when the sun and moon are aligned with the earth and tides are higher than normal. To make matters worse, at the same time a strong high-pressure system stalled over Newfoundland, blocking the storm's path. New Jersey was in the bull's-eye of the storm's wrath.

All this was unknown on March 5. The weather was bad—a steady east wind along with driving rain combined to make it a miserable day—but nothing out of the ordinary.

By the next morning, however, it was becoming obvious that this was no ordinary storm. Damage reports were trickling in from some Shore communities: the Loveland Town Bridge had collapsed in Point Pleasant; Ocean Grove's boardwalk was damaged; there was flooding in Sea Bright, Atlantic Highlands, Bradley Beach, Long Beach Island, Ocean City, Sea Isle City, and numerous other towns; and, perhaps most surprisingly, the storm hadn't abated. If anything, it was increasing in intensity.

Tuesday, March 6, was D–Day—"Destruction Day"—for many Shore towns. That morning, police on Long Beach Island discovered that the ocean had broken through the protective barrier of sand dunes at Holgate; seawater was racing across the street and joining Barnegat Bay on the other side of the island. Alarmed authorities began evacuating Holgate. But the pain had just begun for Long Beach Island.

Up and down the Shore, things got bad quickly on that fateful Tuesday. Bulkheads, such as the one that protected Sea Isle City, held under the fearful onslaught of the pounding waves. Unfortunately, the waves were so high that the water simply flowed over the bulkheads as if they weren't there. The water swept into the streets of Sea Isle City, quickly submerging streets and rushing into basements. The Fean Hotel, the Madeline Theater, the Excursion House, the Amusement Center, and other businesses in Sea Isle City were washed away by the waves. Virtually all of the town's twelve hundred residents had to be evacuated.

Everybody waited for the wind to swing around that day, to come from the west, and not the east, so that it would stop pushing great mountains of ocean water in front of it. What no one knew was that the storm, locked firmly in place by the blocking high, had created a thousand-mile fetch (an area where ocean waves are generated by wind) far out in the ocean. As the wind roared down this incredibly long fetch, it piled up more and more water in front of it, until by the time the waves arrived at the shoreline they were as big as three-story buildings.

Shakespeare called it "the hungry ocean," and this storm was proving how voracious the sea's appetite could be. Wildwood, Absecon Island, and Ocean City became actual islands as seawater cut their mainland links. Brigantine lost practically all of its "protective" sand dunes. Forty-foot-high sand dunes on Island Beach were either moved or destroyed, changing in a geological blink the island's topography.

The hungry sea ate more than sand. In Asbury Park, sections of the boardwalk were buried under tons of wind-whipped sand. Boardwalks just vanished in Bay Head, Seaside Heights, Long Branch, Sea Girt, Sea Isle City, Atlantic City, Cape May, and numerous other Shore communities. Structures were flattened as if they'd been made of cardboard.

People kept waiting and waiting for the wind to weaken, for the waves to diminish, for the terrible storm to finally leave. For two and one-half days, and five consecutive high tides, the relentless nor'easter battered the shore. Low tide ceased to exist; it was high tide, higher tide, highest tide.

While much of the Shore got rain or sleet from the storm—and even the rainfall totals weren't much, averaging just about two inches at Atlantic City—the interior sections of the state got snow. This was bad news for a Boston cabdriver, who had decided that he had had enough of winter that year. Without bothering to inform his superiors, he turned his hack south for Florida and was happily motoring through New Jersey when the storm forced him to a halt in New Brunswick. There he was intercepted by the state police, who interrupted his trip long enough to escort him to the Middlesex County Jail.

Although the entire state, and particularly the Shore, was hard hit by the storm, the hands-down winner of the "most devastated" award was Long Beach Island. The eighteen-mile barrier island was breached by the ocean and bay in five places. The worst was at Seventy-ninth Street in Harvey Cedars, where a channel more than sixty feet wide and fifteen feet deep was established where once there had been roads, sand, and homes. Nearly 50 percent of the town's ratables were lost.

The rest of the island fared little better. By the time Wednesday, March 7, dawned, the storm had destroyed the sand dunes, beaches, and whatever else the island had been counting on for protection. This left buildings at the ocean's mercy, and the raging surf delivered the knockout blow. Houses were ripped from their moorings and sent careening into the swirling waters. The island six miles at sea was nearly put out to sea permanently: overall it lost 270 homes, with 180 more suffering severe damage.

Finally, on Thursday, the storm began to weaken. Gradually during the day the wind and rain slacked off, and the tides did not surge in with the violence of past days. Friday dawned clear and breezy; nature had simply worn itself out.

Slowly, the state began shaking out the cobwebs and climbing to its feet. Along the Shore, however, it was a different story. A week after the storm, a newspaper story about Harvey Cedars said: "Nobody lives in Harvey Cedars anymore. There are no roads. There is no drinking water. Wreckage is everywhere and where there is no wreckage there is just sand. . . . The houses are everywhere, in no order, sometimes piled two or three together. Around them crushed and mangled cars and trucks lie half buried."

The week after the Great Nor'easter began just like the previous week. The Algonquin was showing *Second Time Around*; an "automatic" dryer was selling for ninety-nine dollars, and Ben Casey was again battling death. It seemed like just another week—but for thousands of Jersey Shore residents, it would never be the same again.

Perhaps the only good thing about the 1962 nor'easter was that it was over. The state would not see its like again. It was, those in the know assured weather-weary New Jerseyans, the "storm of the century."

Fifty years later, we were hearing that again. Unfortunately, it seems to many that Hurricane Sandy will never be over. More than a year after it struck, many New Jerseyans were still reeling from the storm's effects.

New Jersey has been hit by bad storms before—nor'easters, blizzards, hurricanes. Some of those storms are described in this chapter. Usually, however, a storm hits, it's messy and inconvenient for a bit, there's some road flooding and other infrastructure problems, and after a little while things go back to normal. Not so with Sandy. Once that storm roared ashore on the night of October 29, 2012, New Jersey—and the lives of thousands of people—would never be the same again. And for many the effects of Sandy are still going on.

Initially, when Sandy formed as a late season hurricane, it was supposed to stay far out in the Atlantic and not even be a threat to land. But the more it churned her way north from the Caribbean, the more that weather forecasters warned that Sandy was going to make a weird left turn out in the ocean and, like a bad driver, plow straight into New Jersey. That happened on October 29.

Meteorologically, there are numerous reasons why Sandy deviated from the normal path that hurricanes take for New Jersey and became such a disastrous storm. A blocking high-pressure system over Greenland. An upper-level low-pressure system forcing the jet stream to take a path up the East Coast. A stalled cold front that pulled the storm toward it. There was this, and there was that.

None of that matters. What does matter is that Sandy slammed into New Jersey like a runaway freight train hitting a wall of wet tissue paper. When it did, it destroyed buildings, devastated lives, and changed the state—probably forever.

Although it smashed the entire state, because it came roaring in off the ocean Sandy was particularly brutal to the Jersey Shore. One place that the storm was extremely vicious with was Seaside Heights, a small town on Barnegat Beach Island in central Jersey where thousands annually flocked in warm weather to enjoy its beach and amusement-filled boardwalk. Within a matter of hours, the boardwalk where a million pleasant memories had been made for so many people was ripped up and destroyed, the storm showing little sentimentality. The boardwalk's iconic roller coaster, a thrilling but yet nonthreatening ride where countless parents took their chil-

Damage to the Point Pleasant
boardwalk from Sandy.

The Point Pleasant boardwalk was ripped up as far as the eye could see.

Boardwalk buildings were totally destroyed by Sandy.

dren for a soaring, wind-whipped view of the Atlantic beneath, was tossed into the ocean like so much useless scrap metal—a maker of memories no longer.

The quiet beach community of Mantoloking was almost completely destroyed. Natural gas fires in South Mantoloking burned throughout the night, the eerie blue glow emanating from the soggy ground making it look like Hell on Earth. Besides the Shore, parts of many other towns were underwater—Hoboken, Jersey City, Sayreville among them. More than 2.7 million people statewide were without power—fallen tree limbs were twisted around down power lines, making restoration of power all the more difficult. Without electricity, gas stations couldn't pump gas, grocery stores couldn't keep food refrigerated, cell phones and computers were useless— people were cold, hungry, and desperate. There was no communication and no comfort. All that was missing were the zombies.

Homes were flooded, ripped off foundations, torn apart. Everywhere in the piles of debris of plasterboard and paneling that lined streets and sat forlornly in parking lots and traffic islands were sad, waterlogged memories of lives now devastated—a child's doll, pages from a photo album, clothing, a tattered and faded sports flag with the words "Giants Rule" on it.

And the lives. The lives taken, the lives ruined, and the lives changed forever. Sandy claimed thirty-nine New Jersey residents, ranging in age from four to ninety-four. They died of hypothermia, of falls, of drowning, and in other ways from this cruel storm. Thousands more had their lives ripped from beneath them—elderly couples planning to live out their retirement in a little house at the Shore, the people whose Shore home had been passed down in the family for decades, and the young couples just starting out who had sunk all of their money into their dream house at the coast. All of them now glassy-eyed and silent, staring aimlessly into space.

In the years to come, as the jagged scar of this time fades, and history takes over and does what history always does, which is reduce a tragedy down to statistics, the numbers will jump off the page: second-costliest hurricane in U.S. history; twenty-four affected states; six million people without power; seven thousand people forced into emergency shelters; twenty thousand flights cancelled; largest Atlantic hurricane on record; and on it goes.

However, for those of us in New Jersey who lived through it, Sandy can never be reduced to numbers. It will, and will always remain, the storm that changed our lives and our state.

Of course, many other storms have wrecked havoc in New Jersey.

One of the worst was the Hurricane of 1821, which is the first hurricane whose eye passed over the state. This storm came boiling up out of the Atlantic in early September, and struck the state hard on the afternoon of the third. As the *Sussex Register* reported: "A very severe gale of wind from the S.E. accompanied with heavy rain, visited this place last Monday afternoon . . . prostrating the fences to the ground, uprooting and twisting from their trunks the largest trees, and leveling the corn and buckwheat with the earth." Another casualty of this storm was a unique area of Long Beach Island called Great Swamp. Located where the northern portion of Surf City is today, Great Swamp was a freshwater oasis of animals and tall cedar trees nestled within the sand and salt of Long Beach Island. The hurricane's winds knocked down the trees, and the waves poured saltwater into the immediate area, turning Great Swamp into a marshland. Today Surf City is built on the bones of Great Swamp.

Although New Jersey gets hammered with hurricanes and nor'easters, there's other weather activity the state misses out on. Tornadoes, as a rule, don't hit the state very often; when they do, they usually last just a few minutes, rather than the much longer time that the devastating midwestern twisters spend on the ground. The state has had its share of tornadoes, though: on June 19, 1835, one struck New Brunswick, killing five people on its seventeen-mile rampage. Fifty years later, a twister ricocheted back and forth across the Delaware River from Camden to Philadelphia, killing six people and causing five hundred thousand dollars in damages. Possibly the worst tornado in recent memory was the one that struck at Seabrook, Cumberland County, in 1975, causing ten million dollars worth of damage.

Ironically, the Great Blizzard of 1888 did not produce the most snow ever in the state. That distinction goes to the February blizzard of 1899, which dumped almost inconceivable amounts of snow throughout New Jersey. Accumulations of two feet were considered puny; Warren County, with thirty inches of the white stuff, Mercer with thirty-four, and Gloucester with thirty-six were far more the norm. The winner of the rather dubious honor for most snow went to Ocean and Burlington Counties, each of which had forty inches of snow.

Ice storms tend to be more local events, hitting a particular area or county rather than an entire state. In late February 1902, however, the most severe ice storm on record blanketed much of the state with sleet and ice. Telegraph, electric, and telephone lines from north to south were knocked down by the sheer weight of the ice, which also disrupted railroad traffic. As might be expected, trees took the heaviest hit. A weather observer in Somerville mourned "so many of our beautiful shade trees with their top branches broken off by the heavy sleet." An observer in Rancocas wrote that the storm "broke trees down with the weight of the ice—such devastation has never been seen here before. The town looked as though a tornado had struck it. Pine forests suffered great damage."

Although lightning strikes can occasionally be deadly to people, lightning mostly strikes trees and causes damage to buildings. On Saturday, July 10, 1926, a single lightning bolt caused more than seventy million dollars worth of damage in New Jersey. A bolt from a summer thunderstorm struck a building containing explosives at the United States Naval Ammunition Depot at Lake Denmark in Rockaway Township (Morris County). The strike caused the building to explode, which led to a series of chain-reaction explosions at other magazines on the compound. Each explosion brought a new wave of debris hurtling into the air, flames leaping skyward, and shells and other explosives whistling to earth where they, too, exploded. The next day, the *New York Times* described the area as "charred and smoking. Not a blade of grass nor a green shrub remains. Trees are stripped of branches. The ground is pitted with craters."

DID YOU KNOW?

- New Jersey's coldest morning—and record low temperature—occurred on January 5, 1904, when the temperature at the New Jersey Weather Service's River Vale location (Bergen County) dropped to a bone-chilling minus 34 degrees Fahrenheit. Not to be outdone, Layton in Sussex County checked in with minus 31 degrees F. The temperature dipped below zero throughout the entire state with the exception of Cape May City, where it was a balmy 0 degrees F.
- The hottest days in New Jersey were July 9 and 10, 1936, when the temperature was at least 100 degrees Fahrenheit everywhere in the state except at Atlantic City, where "cooling" sea breezes kept the mercury at 94 degrees. The hottest reading ever recorded in the state was on July 10, 1936, at Runyon in Middlesex County: an egg-frying 110 degrees Fahrenheit.

- New Jersey's weather played a critical role in United States independence. A storm on Christmas night in 1776 helped keep the Hessians who were occupying Trenton indoors and largely unaware of what was happening outside. That enabled George Washington and his small force to approach the town and capture it after a brief fight. This victory revived the flagging morale of the Continental troops and helped keep Washington's largely volunteer army together.

Subsequently, Washington's army suffered through the brutal winter of 1779–80 at Morristown. This was the famous "Hard Winter," when the Delaware River was frozen for an incredible seventy-five days (December 21, 1779–March 4, 1780), and Philadelphia recorded just one day in January when the temperature went above freezing. A thermometer in New York City during January reportedly registered a reading of minus 16 degrees Fahrenheit; by mid-month every principal port from Maine to North Carolina had frozen over. Washington's troops endured the bitter weather at Morristown while living in makeshift log cabins. In February, a Continental soldier at Morristown wrote that the "ink freezes in my pen, while I am sitting close to the fire."

Ghosts, Tall Tales, and Legends

Deep in the Pinelands, in a room lit only by the flickering glow of a candle, a pregnant woman struggled to give birth.

Outside, a fearsome thunderstorm had suddenly boiled up. The night sky, so peaceful just minutes ago, was now the scene of a heavenly sound-and-light show of massive proportions; thunder exploded in the darkness, while lightning ripped jagged holes across the black curtain of night.

In the small home, a group of elderly women who were assisting their pregnant neighbor looked at one another uneasily. Several pulled their shawls tighter around their bony shoulders; something was not right. They could *feel* it.

In unison, they turned to the small bed, where the woman was tossing and turning in agony as the birthing time approached. There were rumors that she was involved with sorcery and witchcraft; some even whispered that she had been in league with the Prince of Darkness himself. In the warmth and security of their own homes, the women had dismissed these stories as nonsense. Now, with the storm raging outside, and the candlelight casting eerie shadows on the walls, the women felt the cold hand of fear touch their hearts. What if they hadn't been just stories after all?

All at once, the moment to bring life into this world arrived. Forgetting their fears, the women quickly and efficiently attended to their neighbor. Shortly, a healthy baby boy was delivered. The women wrapped him in a homemade blanket and handed him to the anxious mother, who smiled wanly. The women smiled too; all that talk about witchcraft had been just that—talk. Everything was fine.

That's when the baby began to change.

First its human features melted away, as if they were made of wax that had suddenly become white-hot. Then the fat, chubby body stretched out like a rubber band, until it looked more serpentine than human. From its feet sprang horse's hoofs; from its shoulders sprouted bat wings. With a terrible sound of cracking bone, the face stretched and grew until it became a horse's elongated snout.

As the women and the birth mother watched in stunned disbelief, the thing that had once been a human child but was now something else entirely rose up on its two back legs until its horrible head grazed the ceiling. It snarled at the frightened women; smoke came from its nostrils. With a fierce cry, the creature began whipping its heavy, forked tail about the room, beating the women—including the mother—mercilessly. Finally, with a guttural sound, the beast flew up the chimney and out into the darkness, its great wings sounding like thunder in the suddenly still night.

So was born the Jersey Devil, the unlucky thirteenth son of Mother Leeds.

Unquestionably the state's most famous legend, the Jersey Devil is also New Jersey's most popular folk tale. Ever since his—or, more properly, its—birth in 1735, the devil has been embraced by each succeeding generation, which adds its own special twist to the tale so that the story changes just as rapidly as its audience. Each new version of the story adds another chapter to the life of this strange and fascinating creature.

Some say he was born as described above, a normal baby doomed to become a monster by his mother's interest in the black arts. Others say that Mother Leeds, already burdened with twelve children, was driven to despair when she found herself pregnant for the thirteenth time. "I hope this time it's a devil," she shouted angrily, forgetting the old axiom to be careful what you wish for, because it might come true.

Whatever the circumstances of his birth, the devil flew off that night to begin a life tormenting the residents of the Pinelands. Everything from crop failures to droughts and fish kills has been blamed on this infamous beast.

Although everyone in the Pinelands knew about the Jersey Devil (Walter Edge, two-time New Jersey governor and United States senator, said that when he was a boy in Atlantic County, he and his friends were "threatened with the Jersey Devil, morning, noon, and night"), the creature was just a regional phenomenon until one amazing week in 1909. Then, clearly making a bid for larger fame, the devil swept out of the Pinelands during the week of January 16–23 and instituted a reign of terror unparalleled throughout western New Jersey. From Camden to Trenton, the devil rode on wagons, attacked animals, killed chickens, tried to break into homes, and terrorized citizens in numerous cities. Not only did hundreds of people see the creature, but the incidents were reported in newspapers throughout the state. Suddenly everyone knew the Jersey Devil.

After that spree, however, the devil became shy once again and retreated deep into the forest, where it has largely remained to this day. It still makes occasional forays, however, like the one in 1966 during which a poultry farm near the Mullica River was attacked by something that went on a savage rampage, killing over two dozen ducks, geese, cats, and dogs—including a ninety-pound German shepherd.

In recent years, civilization has nibbled at the corners of the Pinelands, and it's the opinion of some that the Jersey Devil is dead, killed by the encroachment of concrete and asphalt. This, however, seems like a premature obituary. The wily creature has been considered dead before (most notably in 1925, when its "carcass" was put on display by a Gloucester County man who supposedly shot the beast), but it has always turned up again. It seems as though it would take a lot more than urbanization to kill so cunning a creature.

Today, every time the wind blows hard in the Pinelands, or there's a crash in the underbrush, it's blamed on the Jersey Devil. Oh yes, we say with a grin and a wink, that's him, that old devil. Then we hurry on our way, particularly if night is coming on, and the shadows are getting longer, and mysterious sounds are creeping closer to us with each dying flicker of the sun.

For who knows what really lurks deep in the strange, uncharted region of pine forests and cedar water of the Pinelands? Here, where the wind moans through the trees, where distant lights flicker and vanish without warning, and where the wet, swampy ground sometimes seems to reach out and grab at your feet, there are clearly things best left unknown—and unseen. One of these could well be the Jersey Devil.

DID YOU KNOW?

It's awfully hard to kill the Jersey Devil. The creature has been reported dead, only to turn up again, more times than Elvis. Vivid proof of this came in the early nineteenth century. Naval hero Stephen Decatur paid a visit to the Hanover Iron Works to make sure that the cannonballs being made were the right size and shape for fighting the Barbary pirates. While lining up a shot on the firing range, Decatur saw the Devil flying right across the target area. With cool precision, Decatur sent a shot right through the beast. The Devil, however, ignored the wound and continued on its way.

What does the Jersey Devil look like? Although descriptions and portraits often vary, a few elements have remained consistent in the legend. See if you can guess which body part most commonly describes the Jersey Devil:

1. Body of a (kangaroo, horse, chicken)
2. Head of a (rat, zebra, dog)
3. Face of a (bat, snake, horse)
4. Wings of a (dove, duck, bat)
5. Feet of a (donkey, wildebeest, pig)

Answers: 1, kangaroo; 2, dog; 3, horse; 4, bat; 5, pig.

Of course, the Jersey Devil isn't the only legend to emerge from the Pinelands. This vast, mysterious wilderness has many more tales to tell, tales like that of "Fiddlin'" Sammy Giberson.

Sammy was born in Burlington County in September 1808, and if he wasn't playing a fiddle at the moment of his birth he almost certainly picked one up the instant his doctor smacked his bare bottom. By the time he was a man, no one in the Pinelands could make the catgut sing like Sammy.

One night, after partaking of the local refreshment at a New Gretna inn, Sammy began proclaiming his fiddling excellence. "I could even beat the devil in a showdown," he boasted.

A gasp went up from the audience. It wasn't wise to challenge Old Scratch like that.

Later that night, Sammy headed home. Suddenly the moon scurried behind some clouds and the air turned sharply colder. Sammy looked up and saw a stranger barring his way.

"I hear you think you can beat me dancing and fiddling," said the stranger ominously. When Sammy asked who he was speaking to, the stranger drew himself up to his full height.

"The devil," he snarled. "Now start playing."

Sammy knew that he would have to play as he'd never played before. Pulling out his fiddle, he began playing for all he was worth, and the devil began dancing. For hours the contest continued; first Sammy played, then the devil. Each was the equal of the other.

Finally, with dawn approaching, the devil admitted that Sammy was indeed a superb fiddler. Suitably impressed, Satan promised to teach Sammy some tunes that no mortal had ever played before.

The devil must have kept his word, for from this point on Sammy Giberson became the most amazing fiddle player the world had ever seen. He could play just as well lying on the ground as he could standing up, and the music he played was like nothing ever heard by human ears. When people asked where he had learned these times, Sammy just smiled.

Soon it was whispered that Sammy disappeared into the deep woods with his fiddle on certain nights. Before long the sound of two instruments would come floating through the pine trees with strange, haunting music. The residents called the tunes devil duets.

Finally, death claimed Sammy Giberson. His fiddle was locked in its black box and placed on a shelf. That, however, did not silence it. People swore that they could hear music coming from the box—the same mysterious music that Sammy used to play. Eventually the fiddle vanished.

There are those who claim that the fiddle didn't just disappear; they say that Sammy reached out from the grave and took it himself. The proof, they confide, can be heard late at night: if you listen closely, you can still hear the sound of Sammy's music, floating through the trees from the deepest, darkest part of the forest.

The white stag of Shamong is another classic Pinelands tale. It seems that one stormy night many years ago, a stage coach was lurching along on the rutted roads, trying desperately to reach the warmth and security of the Quaker Bridge Hotel. Frantically the driver whipped his team of horses, as the thunder crashed above him, and the rain came down in stinging bolts from the angry heavens. Desperate to reach shelter, he was overjoyed when he suddenly saw a light in the distance, which he knew came from the hotel. With a triumphant cry he urged his team on.

All at once, from out of nowhere, a great white stag suddenly appeared in the road directly in front of the stage. With a shouted oath the coachman reined in his horses. As he got down to investigate this strange phenomenon, the creature vanished as dramatically as it had appeared. His curiosity piqued, the driver walked down the soggy roadway a bit, to see if he could find any evidence of the stag.

Suddenly the coachman's eyes grew wide. Up ahead, camouflaged by the driving rain until he was right on top of it, was a bridge across a raging river—or what was left of a bridge. The storm and the rushing water had torn it apart, and if the coachman had continued to push his horses forward the entire stage would have plunged into the river. Since then, white stags have been considered a good luck symbol in the Pinelands.

Legends. Tall tales. Are they wholly imagined or is there some shred of truth at their center? Are they merely fabrications, or are they the stuff of cold, hard fact? Before you answer, consider the strange case of Peggy Clevenger of the Pinelands.

Put simply, Peggy Clevenger was a witch. Not a black-clad, broom-flying Halloween witch, but a real witch, the type who knew how to make natural forces do her bidding.

Everyone in the Pinelands knew what Peggy was. Usually they gave her a wide berth, but sometimes that wasn't possible. This was the case when a man thought that Peggy had bewitched him. Declaring that he was going to kill her, he drew Peggy's picture, then cut up some silver coins and loaded them into his shotgun. Unfortunately, his aim was off: when he fired he hit Peggy's hand in the picture. The next day, Peggy was seen with a badly mangled hand. She said her dog had done it, but everyone knew better.

"The old devil," grumbled the shooter. "If I'd only got her heart instead of her hand, I'd fixed her."

Peggy had the ability to turn herself into a rabbit. Once a few boys were out with their hunting dog when a rabbit was spotted. The boys and dog all gave chase and seemed to have the rabbit cornered, until it jumped into the window of Peggy's house. In the twinkling of an eye Peggy was at the same window, glaring out at them. Boys and dog turned tail and ran.

Supposedly, Peggy kept a hotel called the Half-Way Place, which was so named because it was halfway to the Jersey Shore from the Pinelands. Considering the whispers about Peggy, and what went on in that hotel, it's a fairly safe bet that few people ever signed the guest register of the Half-Way Place.

Among the many other stories told about Peggy was that she kept a large cache of gold hidden in her house. This supposed fortune proved to be her undoing.

One night, a fire roared through Peggy Clevenger's house. With the first light of dawn, rescuers poking through the still-smoldering ashes found Peggy's body—with her head cut off. Plainly, no fire had done that. It was murder, pure and simple, and suspicion immediately fell on Peggy's daughter and son-in-law, who had been seen at her home the night of the fire.

Despite a lack of evidence, this was the accepted version of Peggy's death for several years. Then a Pinelands man got terribly sick, and it seemed obvious that he was going to die, but he didn't, despite getting sicker and sicker. People began saying that he couldn't die, because he was harboring a terrible secret that needed to be told before he could be released.

Finally, after months of suffering, the man gave in to the inevitable: He admitted that he had killed Peggy for her gold—which he never found—and set the fire to cover his tracks. No sooner had he confessed than he closed his eyes for the final time.

Whatever happened to Peggy Clevenger's gold? Did someone else find it, or is it still out in the forest, lying under a bed of pine needles, waiting to be discovered? Is it possible, as the locals say, that Peggy's headless body is still searching for it, wandering through the Pinelands on its eternal quest? Is anyone brave enough to find out?

Ghosts are among the most terrifying of all supernatural phenomena. The idea that some restless souls continue to walk the earth after their death sends a chill down the spine of even the bravest mortal. New Jersey has its share of these strolling spirits.

On May 6, 1937, the dirigible *Hindenburg* exploded while trying to land at Lakehurst in Ocean County. The disaster, which was reported around the world, spelled the end of lighter-than-air transport. Since ghosts are often associated with tragedy, perhaps it's only logical that the ghost of an airman has been reported in Lakehurst. The ghost haunts Hangar Number One at the Naval Air Station; several officers have reported seeing the spectral figure, which vanishes when approached. Is this spirit someone involved in the *Hindenburg* disaster, or is it the ghost of a former soldier who was once stationed at Lakehurst and was killed in a war? No one knows—and the ghost isn't telling.

Ghosts sometimes turn up in the strangest places. In Union County, the ghost of Hannah Caldwell, a woman killed by a stray bullet during the Revolutionary War, reportedly haunts the Union County Courthouse in Elizabeth. Railroad tracks throughout the state are where you'll find the Hooker Man (also called the Long Valley Ghost). According to legend, this one-armed apparition was struck by a train while walking on the tracks in life and is still taking his strolls—although in a different reality. In Branch Brook Park, on the border of Newark and Belleville, a spectral figure in white has been seen floating near a tree where a fatal car crash killed a honeymooning couple.

Then there's the phantom of Parkway Exit 82.

As if it's not difficult enough to drive the Garden State Parkway, with its ubiquitous toll booths, there have been reports of ghostly activity near Exit 82 in the Toms River area. Supposedly, on nights when the fog is thick, a very tall person suddenly runs out onto the roadway and frantically waves motorists down, as if he desperately needs help. When the drivers slow down, the figure disappears. Supposedly, this stretch of the Parkway has been the scene of an unusual number of accidents. Could some of these be the result of the Phantom of Exit 82? No one knows, but think twice when driving along that stretch, especially on foggy nights.

Another eerie ghost story concerns a place called the Water's Edge Cafe in Jefferson Township (Morris County). Originally built by Alfred T. Ringling of circus fame, the structure became a restaurant in the 1940s. The first ghostly sightings were reported in the 1960s. The British owner of the building repeatedly saw a shadowy figure on the stairs and in one of the rooms. The ghost was described as having dark hair and hateful eyes. When questioned, the spirit identified itself as Armon Hirsuit, but a search of local history books turned up no record of that name.

Soon the restaurant began showing signs commonly associated with a haunting, including sudden cold spots in rooms and objects moving with no apparent cause. Other ghosts popped up: One was a woman in a powder-blue Victorian dress, who told a psychic that she was the eatery's caretaker; another was a male ghost with dark hair, who was wearing a suit with a wide collar.

Who were these ghosts in life? What was their connection to the building that still attracts them today, long after their death? This type of information can hold the key to understanding hauntings, but the answers are often difficult to obtain. It's rare to not only know who a ghost is, but why he or she remains in a certain place. That's precisely what occurred in Basking Ridge, however.

Bill Baily's dream had always been to build a large house that could be used as an artist's colony, but he died unexpectedly in 1931, before the house was finished. His wife, Sarah, kept the dream alive, and in 1936 the large, rambling structure was finally completed. Given Bill's love for the house, it probably shouldn't be too surprising that his ghost began appearing throughout it. His wife remained in the house until 1941, when it was turned into a boy's school. Bill wasn't heard from much until the mid-1970s, when another couple bought the home. Before you could say "Boo," windows starting opening and closing, the television began channel surfing on its own, and strange noises came from all over the house. The topper came in 1986, when during a test for paranormal existence Bill himself suddenly appeared at the front door.

Ironically, that episode seemed to help both sides. The couple learned to get along with Bill, and he apparently decided to leave them alone. Bill remained very protective of the house he loved, though, even to the point of closing the windows when it rained. (Now that's the kind of ghost we should all have!)

Another New Jersey house that seems to have not-just-mortal occupants is an old Victorian structure in Midland Park. Although more than one ghost has been reported there, the spirit that everyone seems to see is that of a small yellow and white cat. This feline phantasm stays mainly in a third-floor bedroom, where even those who don't see it often find a warm spot on the bed and a small, round indentation on a comforter or blanket.

From early in the twentieth century comes a ghostly New Jersey tale identified only as occurring somewhere across from the South Branch Raritan River. There, in a place known as the haunted meadow, was often seen "a man riding on a rig without horses or shafts to it, just as if he sat perched about four feet above the bare axle, on which the two wheels turned almost like lightning."(Quarrie 271) From the wheels of this ghostly wagon came blue light, which sparked out continuously as the vehicle careened around the dark meadow at high speeds. Some said it was the ghost of a man called Joseph Pittenger; others claim that the meadow was simply haunted. As proof, they cited the fact that cows placed there at night to graze would go wild, stampeding in all directions as if the demons of hell were after them.

In 1964 the legendary folklorist Father Henry Charlton Beck related a story of the haunted of St. Boniface Church in Jersey City. According to Beck, who was quoting a nineteenth-century magazine article, the house of worship was infected by a cacophony of hideous sounds: "At one instant the house would seem still as a tomb, and then suddenly a burst of wild voices would seem to issue simultaneously from all parts of the building, reverberating along the aisles in fierce laughter, and dying away only to give place to a second succession of shrieks more ghastly and unusual than the first."

The ghost apparently caused quite a stir in Jersey City. Crowds of people searched for the spirit, who was spotted on the church steeple by a young girl. She described the ghost as "gigantic in appearance, with eyes hollow and fiery, like marsh lights, and wearing a long flowing robe which resembled a cloud, so vapory and mistlike was its texture."

A poltergeist was supposedly the cause of some mysterious events at a New Egypt (Ocean County) farm. After a slow start in which it amused itself by moving kitchen utensils and hairbrushes around, the mischievous spirit began hurtling deadly objects, including a hail of spice jars, through the air,. Terrified, the family called in psychic investigators from a nearby college. They managed to get rid of the cranky ghost—but not before one of the investigators was nearly killed when a forty-five-pound tinker's anvil inexplicably launched itself at his head, just barely missing him.

Although many people dismiss ghosts as figments of overactive imaginations, new stories of inexplicable phenomena are constantly coming to light. In 1994, for example, it was revealed that Courtroom 1 in Toms River (Ocean County) was being plagued by a number of strange occurrences: doorknobs jiggling by themselves, motion detectors tripped inside empty rooms, lights turning on and off, and sightings of spectral figures like a neatly dressed middle-aged man and a tear-shaped figure that looked like white smoke. Another possible haunting has been reported at Hudson County Community College in West New York, which is housed in a former convent. Employees at the college report hearing strange sounds and voices, and one caught a glimpse of a female ghost in a black dress carrying books.

Another thing to consider is this: If indeed there are no such thing as ghosts, then why are there nearly one hundred cases of homes in New Jersey where no other explanation except supernatural activity has been found for mysterious occurrences?

Perhaps we're laughing off the reality of ghosts too quickly.

Those who lived around Lake Hopatcong in Morris County certainly weren't laughing two hundred years ago. That's when a strange beast that reportedly lived in the lake was scaring local inhabitants half to death.

According to the story, the creature was so large that next to it an ox seemed like a fawn. The beast had a horse's head, an elephant's body, and sported a huge set of antlers. Sometimes its great head would suddenly burst from the water with a violent splash, rising up like the periscope of some horrible submarine.

What happened to this gigantic creature? No one knows for sure. The Lenape Indians told the early settlers of Boone Town (Boonton) that the beast had drowned while crossing the lake on thin ice. Its carcass, they said, was at the bottom of the lake. When the settlers rowed out to the spot the Indians had described, they could see, on the bottom, a huge skull with antlers extending ten feet in length.

Legends are very much a part of the cultural heritage of the Ramapo Mountain People, who live in and around the towns of Mahwah and Ringwood. One of the best-known is the tale of Jack o' Lantern.

According to the story, the Jack o' Lantern is a mysterious light that suddenly appears in the woods at night. If you go toward the light it vanishes, only to reappear somewhere else. The more you follow the light the more it darts from place to place. Soon you are hopelessly lost.

Another Ramapo legend concerns a magic barrel full of gold that rolls down a mountain every night at midnight. If a person can stop the barrel before it disappears into an old well, he or she is entitled to all the gold it contains. But there's always a catch in the world of the damned: if someone stops the magic barrel, monsters and snakes will suddenly appear, forcing the person to flee for dear life. Supposedly the magic barrel is still at it, merrily rolling down the mountain every midnight and waiting for someone to figure out how to claim it.

The Screech Woman is a particularly eerie Ramapo tale. Her name comes from the hair-raising scream that she emits at night—screams that race through the mountains like the clarion call of death, chilling everyone who hears it.

Like the Pinelands, the Ramapo Mountains are a strange and mysterious place. Who knows what inhabits these hills, especially late at night, when the mortal world is asleep and things unseen emerge to spend a few hours on earth?

What gives us pause, in these increasingly uncertain times, is the fact that the more science and technology teaches us about our world, the less we seem to know. For example, what has caused the plague of misery to descend on many of the people who worked on the Route 55 extension in Deptford (Gloucester County)? Reports say that the New Jersey Department of Transportation was warned not to build this road because it went over a sacred Indian burial ground. The warning was ignored, the road was built, and now many of the workers have had their lives tragically altered by heart attacks, car accidents, miscarriages, and misfortunes that have befallen family and friends.

The devil, you say? Don't say that too loud in New Jersey. You never know who—or what—is going to respond.

Historical Happenings

As one of the original thirteen states, New Jersey has seen a lot of history come its way. Indeed, even when it was a colony New Jersey was making history, such as when it established the first Indian reservation in 1758.

In a state with so much history to its credit, it's difficult to only a point to a few examples as the definitive moments in its past. The events in this chapter, therefore, have been chosen not only because of their historical significance but also because of their unusual nature. It's safe to say that the people you're about to meet—among them an egotistical radio performer, a sullen general, and a brave young woman—and the events they've participated in or caused to happen are all unique, interesting, and have had consequences that went far beyond the boundaries of this state.

The news coming from the radio on the night of October 30, 1938, was anything but good for the United States.

At home, the Great Depression still had its grip firmly around the nation's throat, despite the best attempts of President Franklin D. Roosevelt to break it. Abroad, a shrill-voiced dictator named Adolf Hitler was making increasingly belligerent speeches that seemed to many like a prelude to war. It was an uneasy time.

But as people settled around their radio on that Sunday evening, one day before Halloween, they had no inkling of the drama that was about to unfold—a drama that would soon make them, as well as a part of New Jersey called Grovers Mill, part of American folklore.

That night, most people tuned into Edgar Bergen's popular *Chase and Sanborn Hour*. The ventriloquist and his wisecracking wooden sidekick, Charlie McCarthy, commanded 35 percent of the radio audience. A mere 3.6 percent of the listeners tuned to a competing program on the CBS radio network called *The Mercury Theatre on the Air*.

The Mercury Theatre was the brainchild of Orson Welles, the twenty-three-year-old "boy genius" of Broadway. But his reputation had not helped his ratings, and the prospects didn't look good for the show about to be broadcast: a reworked version of H. G. Wells's 1897 story titled *War of the Worlds,* a tale of Martians invading the earth.

There were problems with *War of the Worlds* from the beginning. The novel took place in turn-of-the-century England, and its leisurely style reflected that era. Orson Welles knew that if the story was to be successful on American radio, it would have to be juiced up, modernized, and moved to the United States. Thus, except for the central idea, the entire novel was scrapped and an entirely new script was written—in a typewriter-torching time of six days.

The authorship of this script has been a source of controversy for years. Many people credit Howard Koch, a young playwright who had just begun writing for the Mercury Theatre. In his 1970 book about the show, *The Panic Broadcast,* Koch does nothing to discredit this notion. However, until the day he died Welles adamantly claimed that he and other Mercury members did "as much of the writing . . . as the writers themselves." He was particularly incensed at Princeton University psychologist Hadley Cantril, who wrote a psychological profile of the broadcast in 1940 called *Invasion from Mars.* After going round and round with Cantril about authorship, Welles fired off this blistering telegram: "Howard Koch did not write *The War of the Worlds.* Any statement to this effect is untrue and immeasurably detrimental to me."

The script that caused all the controversy replaced H. G. Wells's prose with a series of terse news bulletins, in which the alien invasion was presented to listeners as if it were actually happening at that moment. Not only did the bulletins make the story immediate and believable—this was when radio broadcasts were routinely interrupted by special bulletins bringing the latest bad news from Europe—but they also confused the listeners' sense of time. Having frantic bulletin after frantic bulletin piling up made it plausible that events that should have taken hours were happening within minutes.

How was Grovers Mill selected to become so famous? According to Koch, it was pure coincidence. While driving in New Jersey on Route 9 the day before beginning work on the script, he realized that he needed a starting point for his invasion, so he stopped at a gas station and asked for a map. He could have been given a map of any state in the union, but since he was in New Jersey, the attendant displayed his state pride by handing him a map of the Garden State.

"Back in New York starting to work," Koch wrote, "I spread out the map, closed my eyes and put down the pencil point. It happened to fall on Grovers Mill."

For the next six days, the script was written, rewritten, rehearsed, and polished—tasks that normally took weeks, not days. Koch called those six days a "nightmare."

So, when the Mercury Theatre took to the air on that fateful October 30, the chance that it would be a historic broadcast was most unlikely. Consider: Welles tinkered with the script right up until air time; members of the Mercury troupe thought the show "dull"; and, just a fraction of the radio audience was tuned in.

As usual that Sunday night, millions of people initially opted to hear Edgar Bergen banter with Charlie McCarthy. Twelve minutes into the show, Nelson Eddy came on to sing "Neapolitan Love Song." As was common then, many listeners began flipping through the dial—what today's television generation calls channel surfing—until Bergen and McCarthy returned. About four million of these station wanderers stopped at the CBS radio network.

What they heard was a progressive series of frantic "news bulletins" and "eyewitness reports" about some very frightening happenings at the "Wilmuth Farm" in Grovers Mill. Having missed the show's beginning, when it was plainly stated that the program was an adaptation of *War of the Worlds*, the newcomers were plunged into a maelstrom of horrifying news about the arrival of creatures from Mars. To a jittery populace thoroughly conditioned to having ominous news bulletins break into their radio programs, and who trusted radio as a reliable source of information, there was no doubt that what they were hearing was real.

The panic starred to build. People began calling their friends, family, or neighbors, to warn them that the earth was being invaded by tentacled creatures with saliva dripping from "rimless lips." The news spread like wildfire; the American Telephone Company reported that telephone volume increased 39 percent during the broadcast, and 25 percent the next hour.

Meanwhile, back in the studio, Welles and his crew blithely continued with their program, unaware of the panic they were causing. When they finally got word, an announcement was made that it was only a radio show. It was forty-two minutes after the broadcast began. It was also much too late.

By then pandemonium reigned. The growing number of listeners, to their horror, had heard familiar New Jersey landmarks and place names fall to the

Martian machines: Princeton, Trenton, the Pulaski Skyway, Bayonne, and Newark—all destroyed or captured by the evil aliens. The fight at Grovers Mill between the Martians and the "State Militia" was described as "one of the most startling defeats ever suffered by an army in modern times." Out of 7,000 soldiers, just 120 were reported to have survived; the rest were "strewn over the battle area from Grovers Mill to Plainsboro, crushed and trampled to death under the metal feet of the monster, or burned to cinders by its heat-ray."

The broadcast ended with Welles, playing a Princeton astronomer, discovering that the Martians had been killed by germs that they had no biological defense against. In his playful epilogue, Welles said that the broadcast was the Mercury Theatre's Halloween version of "dressing up in a sheet and jumping out of a bush and saying Boo!" However, it's doubtful that many people heard those final words; they were too busy fleeing from the Martian invasion in one of the greatest instances of mass hysteria ever recorded.

Martian landing monument at Grovers Mill.

As might he expected, the broadcast caused extreme consternation in the Trenton-Princeton area, scene of most of the "fighting." "Alarm Centers on Princeton" reported the *Newark Evening News* of October 31, 1938. "Terror and hysteria persisted well past midnight in Princeton in the wake of 'War of the Worlds' broadcast last night," began the story. Hysterical telephone callers overwhelmed Princeton police headquarters, which had just one man on duty. A dozen undergraduates at Princeton University were called home by frantic parents. A man rushed into a Kingston church screaming that the world was coming to an end, while in Dutch Neck people prayed in the streets. State police headquarters in Trenton was flooded with phone calls, and traffic was reported as "unusually heavy" at Penn's Neck and on the Brunswick Turnpike (Route 1).

Other parts of the state fared no better. East Orange police headquarters received more than two hundred calls from frightened people who wanted to know how to escape the Martian's poison gas. Two families from Manhattan burst into the Maplewood police station, frantically wondering how they could get home now that the Pulaski Skyway had been destroyed.

In a single block in Newark, more than twenty families rushed out of their houses with wet handkerchiefs and towels over their faces to thwart the poison gas. Panic-stricken, they began dragging furniture and other belongings out of their homes and loading them into their cars so that they could flee before the Martians arrived. It took an ambulance, three police cars, and an eight-man police emergency squad to calm them and unsnarl the traffic jam they had created.

In Orange, a movie theater was emptied by a man screaming that the world was ending, and frantic children were reported running through the streets in their pajamas. In West Orange, patrons fled in terror from a restaurant, leaving half-eaten meals—and unpaid bills.

Adding to the excitement in North Jersey was the fact that electric lights throughout Bergen County flickered from 6:15 to 6:30 P.M. This helped convince people that the invasion was real.

The Jersey Shore didn't escape the "Martian Menace" either. A man from Bradley Beach raced out of the house in his pajamas and ran down to a nearby bar where he knew his son to be. Wild-eyed, he burst into the bar and ordered his son home. A Red Bank resident was so convinced he smelled poison gas and smoke that he called the police and asked what he should do.

When all was said and done, it was left for a man who lived on the "Wilmuth" (actually Wilson) farm to have the final word on the entire affair. The Andersons were one of three tenant families living on the Wilson farm. On the night of the broadcast, Mrs. Anderson, who had been listening to the show, burst in on her husband James, who had gone to bed, and told him that Martians were reportedly all around them, dealing out death and destruction. Mr. Anderson got up and went out to the front porch, where he was greeted by bullfrogs croaking, crickets chirping, and the stars beaming down at him from a crystal-clear night sky.

"Darn fools," he snorted, and went back to bed.

Initial reaction to the broadcast was swift. The next day, newspapers ran front-page stories vilifying Welles. Soon, however, more thoughtful journalists like the *New York Tribune*'s Dorothy Thompson praised Welles for showing just how easy it was in the new age of mass communication to stampede a cattle-like public.

The show, she wrote, demonstrated "the incredible stupidity, lack of nerve and ignorance of thousands . . . [and] proved how easy it is to start a mass delusion."

"Mr. Welles . . . made . . . the perfect demonstration that the danger is not from Mars but from the theatrical demagogue," she added.

As for Welles himself, it has always been assumed that he never intended to cause a nationwide panic and that his apologies for doing so were sincere. However, years later, Welles admitted during a television interview that he felt at the time that radio's reputation as a voice of authority had become too great and that he thought people should question it instead of just blindly obeying.

"[I felt] it was time for someone to take the starch . . . out of some of that authority: hence my broadcast," he said. There are also indications that Welles timed the broadcast to have the news bulletins become more urgent at precisely the moment when he knew listeners were spinning their dials away from Bergen and McCarthy.

Today, we smugly assume that we're too sophisticated to fall for anything so obviously contrived as an invasion from Mars, despite the fact that a baseless on-line rumor can go viral in minutes and have millions convinced that it's true. If such a hoax is successful again, we won't react like the folks who, after listening to and finding out that the War of the Worlds broadcast was imaginary, stormed a Peruvian radio station and burned it to the ground.

In grade school, children are taught that Boston's famous Tea Party was a prelude to the American Revolution. The events of December 16, 1773, when a party of patriots dressed as Indians dumped a load of British tea into Boston Harbor to protest Britain's taxation policies, stands as a legendary moment in our national heritage.

What's not generally taught, however, is that New Jersey had its own Tea Party, one that was just as bold and daring as the one in Massachusetts.

Today the picturesque town of Greenwich in Cumberland County lies peacefully alongside the Cohansey River. Its main street, called Greate Street, is lined with historic homes dating back a century or more. It's the type of town where you can practically hear the birds taking a breath between songs as you walk underneath the large, leafy trees that dot the thoroughfares.

But on the evening of December 22, 1774, peace was the last thing to be found at Greenwich. That night the town was a bubbling, foaming cauldron of anger, all of it directed at the British ship *Greyhound,* and a cargo of tea it had brought into Greenwich. Before the night was over, Greenwich would have its own Tea Party.

The series of events leading up to Greenwich's crowning moment in New Jersey history began on December 12, 1774, when the *Greyhound,* with J. Allen in command, appeared in Cohansey Creek. Since the ship was too small to have transported the tea across the Atlantic Ocean from its initial loading point at Rotterdam, Holland, it's likely that the *Greyhound* met a larger British ship somewhere (possibly in Delaware Bay) and took the tea on board at that point.

Taking the tea on board was one thing; finding someplace to unload it was quite another. As Allen made his way up the Delaware River, someone probably told him that tea was not exactly a popular item to be bringing into the colonies right then. In October, the citizens of Annapolis, Maryland, had forced the owner of the ship *Peggy Stewart* to burn his vessel because it contained imported goods from England, including several chests of tea. Philadelphia had turned back the *Polly* with its load of tea by refusing permission for the captain to dock. The Boston Tea Party had made tea the lightning rod for all the injustices that the colonies felt Great Britain was perpetrating against them, and Allen was sailing into the gathering storm with an incendiary cargo on board.

Then he thought of Greenwich—and a man named Daniel Bowen.

Bowen was a known British loyalist living at a house-warehouse in Greenwich owned by John Sheppard. Allen decided to sail into Greenwich, which was then a thriving port, transfer the tea to Bowen's house, and then return for it after all the furor had died down. After all, this was Greenwich, and not a hotbed of insurrection like Philadelphia or Boston.

Thus the *Greyhound* landed at Greenwich on December 12, and the tea was unloaded and stored in the cellar of Bowen's residence without incident. (According to the *Bridgeton Chronicle* of November 13, 1874, this building was located directly across from the town's open market square.) Allen must have mentally patted himself on the hack; with a little forethought, he had defused a potentially dangerous situation.

He couldn't have been more wrong.

Allen's crew was spotted unloading the tea, and by the next day word of what was being stored at Bowen's was spreading throughout Cumberland County. The first General Congress of the colonies, which had met in Philadelphia in September 1774, had recommended that the colonies not import any British goods or merchandise, especially tea. Yet here was the foul stuff, sitting in a Greenwich basement. This did not sit well with the county's patriots; a meeting was called for December 23 in Cohansey Bridge (now Bridgeton) to decide what to do about it.

(The exact sequence of events is somewhat ambiguous. Most accounts have Allen landing on the twelfth, and unloading the tea the same night. However, *Dunlap's Pennsylvania Packet* of January 9, 1775 states that the tea was unloaded on December 22. In view of the fact that the tea incident occurred on the twenty-second, it's likely that the correct landing date was the twelfth, which would have given the participants ample time to arrange their "party.")

Events would make the meeting superfluous, however. In the fading light of December 22, men from Cohansey Bridge, Greenwich, Fairfield, and other towns gathered at the home of Richard Howell, four miles outside Greenwich. From there the group, numbering about two dozen, went to the Fithian residence, where they donned "war paint" and feathers. When they emerged, there was no doubt about their final destination: Greenwich.

It was dark by the time the group arrived in Greenwich. Within minutes the night sky was lit up by the flames of an enormous fire burning in the market square—a fire fueled by the chests of tea that the men had carried out from the warehouse across the street. The Greenwich Tea Party had begun.

Monument to the Greenwich tea burners.

Word quickly spread among the citizens, who rolled out of their beds and headed down to the site of the blaze. There they found the "Indians" dancing in glee around the fire, as the despised symbol of English authoritarianism went up in smoke.

Not everyone, however, could bear to part with their tea so easily. One of the raiders was a man named Henry Stacks, who also dearly loved British tea. While the fire burned, Stacks quietly collected all the precious leaves that he could and stuffed them into his pockets, coat, shoes, and wherever else they would fit. Unfortunately, he was spotted; someone stuck the name "Tea Stacks" on him, and there it remained for the rest of his life.

No sooner had the fire died out than the "Indians" vanished. The next day, Fithian wrote in his diary: "Last night the Tea was by a number of persons in disguise taken out of the House & consumed with fire. Violent & different are the words about this uncommon Manoeuvre among the Inhabitants.

Some rave, some curse & condemn, some try to reason; many are glad the Tea is destroyed, but almost all disapprove the Manner of the destruction."

Almost immediately, legal machinery began to grind. The Cumberland County Committee of Safety, passed resolutions condemning the act, and several attempts were made by the British judiciary to prosecute as many of the "Indians" as possible. These efforts came to naught; many people secretly approved of the action (including the sheriff, Jonathan Elmer, whose brother had been of one of the participants), and finding a jury that would convict was impossible.

As the years slipped by, New Jersey's patriotic Tea Party faded into history. Greenwich lost its status as an important port. The advent of the centennial anniversary of the Tea Party reawakened the spirit of 1774. A huge celebration was held in Greenwich to mark the occasion. In November 1874, the *Bridgeton Chronicle* said: "[These] patriotic sons of Cumberland County were among the first to strike the blow which gave us a name and prominence among the nations of the globe." It was, said the paper, a bold and daring act "of which the inhabitants of this county have a just reason to be proud."

Thirty-four years later, a monument to the tea burners was dedicated on Greate Street, where it remains to this day.

The events in Greenwich and elsewhere throughout the colonies were all leading up to one thing: the Revolutionary War. Almost four years after the Greenwich Tea Party, New Jersey was again the site for a critical event that helped propel the fledgling nation toward its freedom—and, in the process, produced a beloved American tale.

It was June, 1778. After a cool start, the month had turned blistering hot—bad news indeed for the British troops, whose wool uniforms and heavy packs, weighing up to eighty pounds, proved too much for some men as they struggled across the heat-seared New Jersey landscape. (On June 26, the English lost two hundred men to the heat.) General Henry Clinton, commander of the British force of eighteen thousand soldiers, had abandoned his occupation of Philadelphia on June 17 and 18 to consolidate his army with other English troops in New York City. He planned to march across New Jersey to Sandy Hook; from there his army would sail to New York. Smack in the middle of Clinton's path lay the little village (population one hundred) of Monmouth Courthouse, or Freehold, as it is known today.

Reoccupying Philadelphia was a great psychological boost for the American forces. George Washington wasn't content with a moral victory, however. He wanted a battlefield triumph to show the mettle of his army. When he learned that the British were leaving Philadelphia, he put his own army into motion from Valley Forge. On June 24, Washington camped at Hopewell, while Clinton stopped at Allentown, twenty miles to the southeast.

Washington held a council of war to determine his army's next step. Some of his officers urged a pitched battle now, before the British got safely to New York. Others agreed with the more cautious views of General Charles Lee.

Lee was a vain, egotistical, stubborn man whose motto in modern terms would be "My way or the highway." Outspoken to a fault, Lee had fought on the side of several European powers, including England, before settling in Virginia just before the revolution began, and he became the second-ranking officer in Washington's army.

Possibly because he had served with various spit-and-polish European armies, Lee didn't have much regard for the ragtag colonial forces. He therefore favored a guerrilla war, fearing that colonial troops couldn't stand up to the British in a face-to-face battle. Finally, Washington decided to attack the British, but with just a small segment of his army.

A detachment of four thousand men under General (the Marquis de) Lafayette was sent against the British. By the time the troops reached Englishtown on June 27 their number had swelled to five thousand. Lee was now in command, after initially turning down the assignment, then changing his mind. The plan seemed simple: attack the rear of the British Army, but don't bring on a full-scale battle.

Soon after daybreak on Sunday, June 28, Lee moved his troops forward, seeking to cut off and capture several columns of British cavalry and light infantry (about six hundred men) in the army's rear. Lee was so sure of victory that he turned to Lafayette and said, "My dear Marquis, I think those people are ours." He sent the same optimistic message to Washington, indicating that a quick, bloodless victory was in the offing.

By midday, however, as temperatures soared into the nineties, Lee's fortunes fell. Clinton, upon learning that the colonials were preparing to attack, decided to meet the assault in strength. He turned around the entire First Division, a force of about nine thousand men, and sent them hurrying to the rear. To his dismay, Lee found that instead of fighting several hundred

British troops, he was about to battle thousands. Faced with a rapidly deteriorating situation, Lee retreated.

All this was occurring unbeknownst to Washington. After a leisurely breakfast at the Englishtown home of Dr. James English, Washington headed for the front, expecting to hear of or even witness a colonial success. Much to his surprise, however, he began encountering troops who told him that Lee was retreating, not attacking, and that the colonials seemed headed for another defeat.

Washington, at the very least astonished and more than likely furious, rode on and encountered Lee on the battlefield. What followed was one of the most controversial exchanges in United States military history.

Galloping up to Lee, Washington reined in his horse and snapped: "I desire to know, sir, what is the reason, whence arises this disorder and confusion?"

Lee was stunned. Expecting to be cordially greeted, and maybe even complimented on the way he had maneuvered his forces ("Flattering my-

View of Monmouth Battlefield State Park.

self," Lee said later, that his conduct would draw "Washington's congratulations and applause"), Lee was startled by the vehemence in his commander's tone, and could stammer only "Sir—Sir!" in response.

Later reports would have Washington chewing out Lee, calling him a "damned poltroon" and swearing "till the leaves shook on the trees."

After a few more remarks, Washington rode forward to take command, leaving Lee behind to lick his wounds. For Charles Lee, the war, and his career, were over.

(A few months later, a court-martial found General Charles Lee guilty of not following Washington's orders to attack and of a "disorderly retreat." Lee left the army in disgrace.)

Quickly Washington rallied his troops, and, despite his earlier admonishment about not fighting a general engagement, was soon doing exactly that. All during that blazing hot day, the colonials stood their ground against the crack British troops. That night, Clinton slipped away to Sandy Hook, leaving the Americans in control of the battlefield.

DID YOU KNOW?

Facts About the Battle of Monmouth

- The Battle of Monmouth was the longest sustained battle in history until Gettysburg, lasting from dawn until nightfall.
- Although it is commonly considered a draw (even though the British army left the field during the cover of darkness), the battle was actually a great victory for the colonial army, which, despite General Charles Lee's trepidation, proved that it could stand toe-to-toe with the legendary English forces.
- Having proved that the Continental Army could stand up to the British Army, the battle sent confidence levels soaring among patriots, the Continental Congress, the army, and even Washington. As such, the battle can be considered a turning point of the Revolutionary War.
- It was the last major fight in the North between British and American forces during the war.
- It was the only battle of the war in an open field in which the main forces of both armies, and most of their commanders, participated.
- Lee died on October 2, 1782. Although his court-martial might have been politically orchestrated, there is no doubt that Lee was not very pleasant, as he proved in his will: [I do not wish to be buried] "in any church or church yard or within a mile of any Presbyterian or Anabaptist meeting house; for, since I have resided in this country, I have kept so much bad company when living, that I do not choose to continue it when dead."

It was during the battle that the second extraordinary event of the day occurred: the story of Molly Pitcher.

We have all seen images of Molly Pitcher, petticoats billowing in the breeze, determinedly loading a cannon while battle smoke wafts about her. But did this really happen, or is it just a Revolutionary tall tale?

While it seems that we can (fairly) safely say that the event did actually take place, the woman who was known as "Molly Pitcher" remains a shadowy figure.

As near as can be determined, this is what happened: Molly was bringing water to the men of General Stirling's colonial artillery brigade, which included her husband, who were waging a fierce duel with their British counterparts. This was hard, sweaty work, and some men were overcome by the blistering heat and passed out at their posts. When her husband went down from the heat (not, as popularly believed, from being shot), Molly jumped in and took his place.

As stirring as this story is, however, it didn't immediately become part of American folklore. In fact, it wasn't until the American centennial in 1876—nearly a century later—that "Molly Pitcher" sprang to life. As the United States prepared to celebrate its hundredth birthday, a teacher in Williamsport, Pennsylvania, named Wesley Miles remembered how an old woman named Molly McCauly had taken care of him as a young boy in Carlisle, Pennsylvania, when his mother was ill, and how she had related stories about loading the cannon at Monmouth. Miles thought it would be proper to honor this patriotic woman, who was by then lying in an unmarked grave in Carlisle.

To get the ball rolling, he wrote a letter to the *Carlisle Herald* extolling Molly's deeds at Monmouth. This initiated a fund-raising campaign, which culminated in the dedication of a monument to Molly in Carlisle on July 4, 1876. The inscription read, in part: "Mollie McCauly, Renowned in History as Mollie Pitcher, The Heroine of Monmouth."

The effects of Miles's letter were destined to reverberate throughout American history. The publicity surrounding the monument unleashed Molly Pitcher fever across the United States. Suddenly everyone wanted to know more about this previously forgotten woman, who had risked life and limb for the cause of liberty. Thus began the glorification of what had been a simple story: Molly's husband wasn't overcome by heat, he was wounded (in some versions, even killed); Molly wasn't an ordinary-looking soldier's wife,

The plaque honoring Molly Pitcher
at Monmouth Battlefield State Park.

but a doe-eyed goddess; Molly didn't merely load the cannon, she recited patriotic platitudes as she let each cannon ball fly; and so on.

Today, the story has assumed such mythical proportions that it's hard to find the truth behind all the patriotic ardor. Thanks to the diary of Joseph Plumb Martin, a colonial who fought at Monmouth, and a few other eyewitness accounts, it's reasonably certain that a woman did bring water to Stirling's parched soldiers, and did actually help fire a cannon. Martin, in fact, related an interesting story about Molly:

> While in the act of reaching for a cartridge and having one of her feet as far before the other as she could step, a cannon shot from the enemy passed directly between her legs without doing any other damage than carrying away all the lower part of her petticoat. Looking at it with apparent unconcern, she observed that it was lucky it did not pass a little higher, for in that case it might have carried away something else, and continued her occupation.

Who was this brave, cool-headed woman? Most historians and writers have identified her as Mary Hays, wife of John Casper Hays of Carlisle. Others believe that Molly was the wife of William Hays, a Carlisle barber, who records show did indeed enlist in the colonial army on May 10, 1777, as a gunner in Colonel Thomas Proctor's Pennsylvania artillery regiment. Thanks to legal documents, we know that he had a wife named Mary. (Unfortunately, there is no reliable evidence that her maiden name was Ludwig, as is so often stated.)

As was common then, Mary, who was about twenty-four at the Battle of Monmouth, followed her husband into the army rather than remain home alone. Those acquainted with her said that she smoked, chewed tobacco, and swore with the best of them—certainly a far cry from the sweet, innocent beauty so often pictured!

After the war, Mary and William returned to Carlisle (even more reason to doubt that Molly's husband was killed at Monmouth!), where William died in 1787. In 1793, Mary married John McCauly, who died in 1813. Molly Pitcher/Mary McCauly passed her remaining years alone, working odd jobs in Carlisle and telling people about her battlefield heroics. One person described her as of average height, muscular, strong, heavyset, kind, and "a very busy talker." The heroine of Monmouth died in 1833, at age seventy-nine.

DID YOU KNOW?

Was "Molly Pitcher" really two women?

This is the interesting hypothesis offered by Henry Charlton Beck in his book *Fare to Midlands*. Beck, the father of New Jersey folklore, told the story of a man who was convinced that history had confused two women: the "real" Molly Pitcher, Mary Hays, and another woman named Margaret Cochran. According to Beck, Cochran also followed her husband, who was an artillery gunner, into the army. When her husband was seriously wounded at the Battle of Fort Washington in November 1776, she took over his cannon and continued firing it until she too was hit by enemy fire. Her husband died of his wounds, and Margaret was taken prisoner by the British. Eventually she was paroled, but her wounds never healed, and she became completely disabled. Because of her role in the battle, she became known as Captain Molly, but her later years were filled with pain and loneliness, and she eventually turned to prostitution. She died of gangrene around 1800.

The existence of Margaret Cochran and her heroics at Fort Washington are confirmed by a 1779 United States Congressional resolution, which voted Margaret Cochran Corbin (her married name) a pension because she "was wounded and disabled in the attack on Fort Washington, whilst she heroically filled the post of her husband who was killed by her side serving a piece of artillery."

Has history confused and merged Margaret Cochran and Mary Hays into one "Molly Pitcher"?

Will we ever know the truth? The search for Molly Pitcher continues.

If it hadn't actually happened this way, the strange events surrounding the cruise ship *Morro Castle* in September 1934 would seem to certainly be straight out of a disaster movie. Captain murdered? Ship ablaze? Crew abandoning ship while ignoring passengers? Mysterious vials of sulfuric acid? Certain crew members acting oddly? Call Hollywood and cue the director; all that's needed are the giant robots.

Surprisingly, all of those things are part of the real yet surreal saga of the *Morro Castle*. The strange occurrences surrounding the ship's demise have spawned a cottage industry second only to the *Titanic* as far as "what happened?" And because a lot of it happened off the New Jersey coast, what happened to the *Morro Castle* is one of the more unusual happenings in New Jersey history.

On the morning of September 7, 1934, as the ship was returning to New York City from Havana, veteran captain Robert Willmott told Chief Engineer George White Rogers to locate and throw away two vials of sulfuric acid that he had learned had been smuggled aboard the ship. The captain feared sabotage, public riot—even personal injury from the acid. Rogers went looking, found two vials of what he said were not acid but a fluid that could be used as a stinkbomb, and tossed them overboard. Later Willmott told First Officer William Warms that "something is going to happen tonight. I can feel it." Willmott seemed nervous and jumpy, suspecting someone was trying to kill him.

To make matters worse, the weather was terrible—foggy and rainy—and the passengers were forced indoors. As dinner approached, the captain complained of not feeling well, and just ate melon for dinner. Indeed, Willmott was a no-show at the Captain's Farewell Dinner that night. Around 7:30 that night Willmott was found slumped over his bathtub, his knees on the floor, dead. He had apparently been giving himself an enema when the attack came that killed him. The ship's doctor said that he had died of a heart attack brought on by acute indigestion.

Willmott's death caused every officer aboard ship to advance one grade in rank. While this may seem perfectly fair, it also meant that men were in positions that they did not understand and were not familiar with. As the ship made its way up the Jersey coast the weather rapidly deteriorated; the rain came down in sheets, the winds tore across the boat, and towering waves battered the vessel. The crew members had to use all their skills to battle the storm.

Then, around 2:45 in the morning on September 8, a fire was discovered in a small storage closet. The crew wasted precious minutes running around trying to determine what to do and who was in charge instead of attacking the fire immediately. By the time they did so it was too late. In fifteen minutes the fire went from one room to six rooms on several different decks.

Here is where the inexperience of the crew came into play. The *Morro Castle* had fire doors, but nobody closed them. The fire hose system was such that only six hoses could be operated at one time, but the crew had nearly two dozen hoses in operation, meaning that barely enough water to cause a puddle trickled out of the hoses.

With lifeboats burning and people panicking, new captain Warms sent the ship at top speed through the gale, desperate to reach port. Unfortunately, all the wind did was feed the fire. Passengers poured out of their staterooms, but having not been drilled in emergency situations, just gathered at the rear of the ship and watched the flames approach.

About five miles off Manasquan, the engines were stopped; even though the anchor was dropped, the ship began drifting north, carried along by the raging sea. With the heat and smoke unbearable and the metal deck becoming so hot it blistered feet inside shoes, passengers began jumping overboard, trying desperately to save themselves. Many of the crew abandoned the ship, taking space in the lifeboats without helping the passengers into them before ordering them lowered. One lifeboat that could hold 60 had only 30, and 27 were crew. Ultimately, only 6 of the ship's lifeboats made it into the water, and only 85 total seats were filled out of a capacity of 408. The final death total was 86 passengers and 49 crewmen.

Rescue ships both professional and private rushed to the scene to fish people out of the water. Even the governor of New Jersey, Arthur Harry Moore, rode over the water in a plane, pinpointing survivor locations for ships to find. Unfortunately, many people drowned or died of shock.

Aflame, the stricken ship drifted up the coast, attracting hundreds of people onto the central Jersey beaches to watch the surreal scene of a large ship burning out of control casually float by. The *Morro Castle* finally came

The burning hulk of the *Morro Castle* came to rest in this approximate area of the ocean. (Convention Hall is to the right).

Monument outside Convention Hall in Asbury Park commemorating the *Morro Castle* incident.

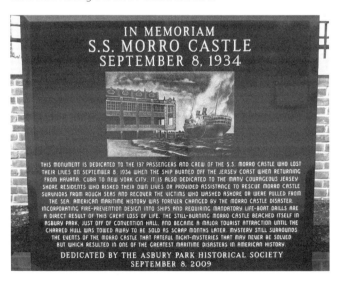

IN MEMORIAM
S.S. MORRO CASTLE
SEPTEMBER 8, 1934

THIS MONUMENT IS DEDICATED TO THE 137 PASSENGERS AND CREW OF THE S.S. MORRO CASTLE WHO LOST
THEIR LIVES ON SEPTEMBER 8, 1934 WHEN THE SHIP BURNED OFF THE JERSEY COAST WHEN RETURNING
FROM HAVANA, CUBA TO NEW YORK CITY. IT IS ALSO DEDICATED TO THE MANY COURAGEOUS JERSEY
SHORE RESIDENTS WHO RISKED THEIR OWN LIVES OR PROVIDED ASSISTANCE TO RESCUE MORRO CASTLE
SURVIVORS FROM ROUGH SEAS AND RECOVER THE VICTIMS WHO WASHED ASHORE OR WERE PULLED FROM
THE SEA. AMERICAN MARITIME HISTORY WAS FOREVER CHANGED BY THE MORRO CASTLE DISASTER.
INCORPORATING FIRE-PREVENTION DESIGN INTO SHIPS AND REQUIRING MANDATORY LIFE-BOAT DRILLS ARE
A DIRECT RESULT OF THIS GREAT LOSS OF LIFE. THE STILL-BURNING MORRO CASTLE BEACHED ITSELF IN
ASBURY PARK, JUST OFF OF CONVENTION HALL, AND BECAME A MAJOR TOURIST ATTRACTION UNTIL THE
CHARRED HULL WAS TOWED AWAY TO BE SOLD AS SCRAP MONTHS LATER. MYSTERY STILL SURROUNDS
THE EVENTS OF THE MORRO CASTLE THAT FATEFUL NIGHT-MYSTERIES THAT MAY NEVER BE SOLVED
BUT WHICH RESULTED IN ONE OF THE GREATEST MARITIME DISASTERS IN AMERICAN HISTORY.

DEDICATED BY THE ASBURY PARK HISTORICAL SOCIETY
SEPTEMBER 8, 2009

to rest in the ocean just off Convention Hall in Asbury Park. The burned-out ship was a tourist sensation. More than one hundred thousand people poured into town to view the spectacle, drawn by the nonstop media reports. The town's boardwalk, getting ready for its off-season slumber, revved back up, and it presented an eerie sight: the sound of amusements and rides and people having fun just yards away from a tragic scene that had cost so many their lives.

The ship was eventually towed away, but in its wake it has left a cottage industry of "what really happened"? Was the captain murdered? How did the fire start? Was sabotage involved? Was the ship secretly running guns to Cuba? What about the suspicious activities of some of the crew?

Only one thing is certain: the *Morro Castle* incident ranks as one of the most bizarre happenings in New Jersey history.

It was two A.M. on July 30, 1916. All around the huge munitions storage site called Black Tom Island in Jersey City, just across from the Statue of Liberty, everything was quiet.

It would not remain that way for long.

"At 2:08 [A.M.]" said the *New York Times* of July 31, 1916,

a million people, maybe five millions, were awakened by an explosion that shook the houses along the marshy Jersey shores, rattled the skyscrapers on the rock foundations of Manhattan, threw people from their beds miles away and sent terror broadcast, swept into nothingness $5,000,000 worth of ammunition, and started fires and bred another explosion that did damage estimated at $20,000,000 more.

The *Times* likened this tremendous roar, which was heard as far south as Maryland, to "the discharge of a giant cannon." It was far more than that, however: it was a dagger thrown at the heart of America by foreign agents—a dagger thrown with unerring accuracy that struck one of New Jersey's most populous cities.

Before 1870, Black Tom was nothing but a barren, windswept rock jutting out of New York Harbor. Then the Central Railroad of New Jersey purchased the site as a storage area and enlarged it, turning it from an island into a twenty-five-acre promontory. It still retained its curious shape, described as looking like "a monster's head and neck."

By 1916, as World War I raged in Europe, Black Tom was a bustling warehouse site owned by the National Dock and Storage Company. The island had become the principal storage and overseas shipping location for tons of munitions and explosive powders made in the Northeast and Midwest. Seventy-five percent of all munitions and armaments sent from the United States to Europe left from the greater New York–New Jersey area, and most of this came from Black Tom.

Despite the official neutrality policy of the United States in this stage of the war, most of the munitions that left Black Tom went to the Allied powers of Great Britain, Russia, and France. The nation's sympathies were clearly with the Allies and against Imperial Germany. Indeed, to many of the immigrants who had only recently escaped to America from Europe and now worked at Black Tom, the island was a symbol: each crate of munitions loaded was another blow against the kaiser.

The kaiser was aware of this, thanks to Germany's well-organized intelligence network. A blow at this facility would both hurt Germany's enemies and show the United States that its phony neutrality had its price. Black Tom was marked for destruction.

Many of those who emigrated to the United States were processed at Ellis Island, just a mile away from Black Tom, and settled in Jersey City, Hoboken, Bayonne, Hackensack, and other nearby New Jersey waterfront towns. For them, Sunday, July 30, was a day off, a brief break in the grueling six-day workweek. Many people probably went to sleep that night thinking about what they would do with their free day: go to church, walk in the park, or just sit at home and relax.

Those dreams were rudely interrupted at 2:08 in the morning, when the first titanic blast from Black Tom rocked the entire metropolitan area.

Thousands of skyscraper windows were shattered by the force of the shock wave, sending daggers of glass hurtling down to streets below. Just across the water, both the Statue of Liberty and buildings on Ellis Island were hit by chunks of flying shrapnel. The entire harbor lit up, as if a massive Independence Day celebration was taking place.

"A great pillar of flame . . . lit up the sky with a red glare," reported the *Times*.

After the initial explosion came a series of smaller ones. "Car after car and barge after barge of high explosives ignited," the *Times* said. "Some burned rapidly and some burned slowly, but all burned furiously."

Thousands of people rushed out of their homes and poked their heads out of (probably broken) windows to see what had happened. It was utter pandemonium.

"Men, women, and children left their homes in their nightclothing," said the *Times*. "Many declared they had been thrown out of bed by the force of the concussion." (This caused a death: Arthur Tosson, a ten-week-old boy who lived on Central Avenue in Jersey City, was thrown from his crib by the force of the explosion and killed.)

The force of the explosion was so great that members of the Reagan family of Deal, forty miles away from the blast, were nearly thrown from their beds by its power. Ten miles farther south, guests of the New Monmouth Hotel in Spring Lake were awakened by the concussions.

Incredibly, firemen who had been on Black Tom at the time of the explosion, and who were battling a fire initially thought to have caused the blast, were not killed. "Firemen, blackened by smoke and their clothing torn to tatters, came staggering out of the smoke, but they were too dazed to tell what had happened," said the *Times*.

As explosions continued to bombard the harbor, frantic evacuation efforts began for those on nearby Ellis and Bedloe's (now Liberty) Islands. Dodging shrapnel (and occasionally being struck by it), boats removed twenty-five family members of Statue of Liberty staffers to Governor's Island.

On Ellis Island, the scene was much worse. Immigrants who thought they had finally escaped the horrors of the Great War now suddenly found themselves apparently right back in it. Under a shower of shrapnel, and illuminated by the fiery red glow from Black Tom, 353 frightened people from the Great Hall were loaded onto the ferry Ellis Island and conveyed to the Battery in New York City. There, four policemen were stationed to make sure no one tried to disembark.

The immigrants were not the only ones frightened. The six A.M. mass at the Mission of Our Lady of the Rosary church in Jersey City was packed to the rafters. "I can assure you," Father A. J. Grogan told a questioner, "there were many praying on their knees who had not been inside a place of worship for a long time."

Finally the explosions on Black Tom stopped, and investigators were able to ascertain the damage. The next day, July 31, the *New York Times* told the chilling story:

Thirteen warehouses of the National Storage Company were destroyed. There remained no vestige of those nearest the base of the explosion. Not a brick to mark where they had stood—only black holes in the ground and blackened ends of broken piers pointing like death fingers through the debris-littered surface of the harbor. Where on Saturday stood huge brick warehouses there remain only giant mounds of blazing and smoking ruin, while all about them are the wreckages of barges and railway rolling stock and other debris.

Ellis Island looked as if it had been attacked by enemy planes. Every window in the Great Hall and the hospital were shattered, the hospital's roof had caved in, holes pockmarked building walls, and the lawn and walkways were covered with glass, wood cinders, and other debris.

Jersey City was also hit hard. Damage to City Hall alone came to $25,000; virtually every window and glass door in the building was broken, and the ceilings in the courtroom and the Assembly Chamber were destroyed. The beautiful stained-glass windows of St. Patrick's Church were ruined, as were windows in scores of churches, businesses, and homes.

Glass, in fact, was the biggest casualty in the Black Tom explosion. Plate-glass damage in Jersey City was estimated at $50,000, and $35,000 in Hoboken; similar losses in Manhattan and Brooklyn totaled $300,000. The entire damage total was $20 million, which didn't count the estimated $5 million in lost munitions.

Before the flames died down investigations were launched to find the cause of the explosion. Initial speculation was that sparks from freight cars had caused a fire on a barge, which had spread to the munitions warehouses. Incredibly, with a war raging in Europe and Black Tom's critical importance to the Allies, no one seemed to suspect sabotage.

"On one point the various investigating bodies agree," reported the *New York Times* of July 31, 1916, "and that is that the fire and subsequent explosions cannot be charged to the account of alien plotters against the neutrality of the United States."

It would take more than two decades to find otherwise. Finally, after years of investigations, charges, countercharges, dead-end leads, and false hopes, Germany in 1939 was found by an international commission to be responsible for the Black Tom explosion. As near as could be determined, three German agents snuck onto Black Tom around midnight and set small fires in some of the boxcars containing dynamite. They also placed explosives with time fuses there. These were the cause of the initial explosion at 2:08 A.M.; the highly incendiary cargo of munitions on the piers and in the warehouses did the rest once the fire reached them.

The Black Tom explosion was part of an aggressive campaign of sabotage waged by Imperial Germany against the United States in the three years (1914–1917) leading up to America's entry into the war. The campaign was successful because people mistakenly believed the United States could hide behind its oceans and watch the affairs of the world from a distance. Thus, security at Black Tom, as well as other sensitive sites, was shockingly lax. The explosion, however, brought the war to the nation's doorstep and changed the way Americans felt about their safety. In that sense, the Black Tom affair was the beginning of our sense of vulnerability to the world's problems.

Today Liberty State Park, with its lush greenery and flags snapping in the breeze, stands on the site of Black Tom. Few visitors to the park suspect that they are standing on the site where a massive explosion occurred.

DID YOU KNOW?

- In January 1929, while American investigators were closing in on Germany's role in the Black Tom explosion, the German government produced a report that blamed—in all seriousness—the entire thing on New Jersey's infamous mosquitoes! The report claimed that a night watchman had started a fire on Black Tom that night to "drive away the mosquitos. . . . It [Black Tom] was about the worst place in Jersey, on account of the swamps there." Even though the report was quickly discounted, New York newspapers had a field day laying more blame at the feet—or on the wings—of New Jersey's mosquitoes.

- Black Tom was not the only New Jersey munitions site struck by Germany. On January 11, 1917, the Canadian Car and Foundry Company plant in Kingsland, which was making artillery shells, was burned to the ground in an explosion and fire reminiscent of Black Tom. For hours artillery shells rained down on Kingsland and nearby Rutherford; losses were estimated at $17 million. Again, however, no one initially considered sabotage as a motive.

A Town Treasury

Towns are like people; each has its own personality, shaped and molded by experiences. Most people keep their personality bottled up inside them, so that when you pass someone on the street you don't know whether they're happy or sad, quiet or loud, outgoing or shy. On the other hand, a town's personality is always on display. A deserted street lined with abandoned factories and shuttered buildings reveals the sadness of prosperity gone bust, while streets full of shops, businesses, and people hustling to and fro mean vibrance and vitality.

Each town in this chapter has its own individual personality, shaped by events and marked by the actions of its citizens. As you read these stories, you might he surprised to discover that they are very similar to where you live.

It remains today, as it has since its founding back in 1869, an oasis of quiet and solitude along the Jersey Shore amid the often frenetic atmosphere of other coastal towns. This is entirely within character, for it's a town that prides itself on retaining the relaxed, unhurried atmosphere of the nineteenth century even as the twenty-first century races along in a blur of information overload. In a world of information superhighways, this town is like a letter from an old friend: warm, cozy, and personal, something to be cherished and experienced again and again. It's "God's Square Mile" along the Jersey Shore—the town of Ocean Grove.

The story of Ocean Grove begins with the curious fact that if not for the dreaded New Jersey mosquito, there wouldn't be a town of Ocean Grove. (At least, not where it's presently located.)

In July 1867, the Reverend William B. Osborn, a Methodist minister, attended the first national camp meeting for the promotion of holiness in Vineland, New Jersey. During that time, Osborn and the Reverend J. R. Andrews of Vineland spoke about the need for a permanent camp-meeting town. Both agreed that it should be by the sea, so that rest and salvation could go hand in hand.

Osborn and Andrews enthusiastically explored the New Jersey coast, which then consisted of little but scrub pines, sand dunes, and bramble bushes, with a few towns (Cape May, Long Branch, and Squan, now Manasquan) tucked in between.

Finally, a site called Seven Mile Beach (now Avalon and Stone Harbor) was selected, and Osborn and Andrews went to Philadelphia to purchase the land from the owners. Before the deal was finalized, however, Andrews suddenly remembered something; turning to Osborn, he said, "There is one thing we have forgotten."

"What is that?" the minister replied.

"The mosquitoes," said Andrews. "We don't want to buy the mosquitoes."

Osborn looked at his friend. "That's so," he said, and just like that, the deal was canceled.

Thus the search began again, but this time with the proviso that no (or at least as few as possible) mosquitoes come with the property. As might be expected, this was a hard condition to fulfill in New Jersey, and the search lagged.

In February 1868, Osborn came upon an extremely foreboding spot: towering above the beach were sand dunes that gradually sloped to the west until they reached the turnpike, which was nothing more than a narrow, rutted, one-lane dirt path running from Long Branch to Squan. Growing out of the dunes were thick clusters of briers, stumpy pine trees, and a veritable forest of bushes, within which lived rabbits, birds, and an assortment of other creatures. The area was surrounded by thick woods and several small lakes.

Most people would have taken one look at this inhospitable wilderness and walked away. Osborn, however, saw something else here, something that he thought could be the answer to his long search. Struggling through the brush, he made his way down to the site of present-day Founders Park; there, despite a thick covering of snow on the ground, Osborn knelt and prayed.

Even with God's help it took several more visits before Osborn was convinced that the sand-choked, tree-filled stretch of coastline should be the site of a permanent camp-meeting town. Finally, after coming back to the spot one final time in the summer, Osborn decided that his search had ended. Indeed, without icy winds, bitter cold, and snow to contend with, there was much to like about the area: the ground was high, the lakes seemed pleasant, and the tall trees afforded abundant shade. Surprisingly enough, there were also no mosquitoes. (A map prepared a few years later by Dr. John B. Smith, the state entomologist, shows the entire coastline filled with mosquitoes except Ocean Grove.) Deciding to call the new town Ocean Grove (where the first part comes from is obvious, while "grove" referred to the vast number of trees), Osborn hurried back home to begin the preparations that would make his dream a reality.

So it was that in the summer of 1869, a hardy band of nineteen people (seven ministers, plus four faithful followers and their families) arrived at the chosen site. One wonders what thoughts must have been going through their heads as they gazed upon the desolation that greeted them. In her book, *In the Beginning, God,* Mrs. W. B. Osborn described the pioneers' arrival: "When we first entered, where now our gates are, the driver stood in front of his carriage and lifted the limbs, so as to crowd our conveyance through the brush and drooping branches of the trees. The heavens were black, the grass wet, and the sands half-knee deep."

Any gloom was quickly dispelled by Reverend Osborn. Alighting from his carriage, he led the small band on a tour, extolling the virtues and beauty of the area. Before long the group had pitched its tents and begun the arduous job of carving a town out of the wilderness. The first camp meeting was held by candlelight in one of these tents on the evening of July 31, 1869.

In March 1870, the New Jersey legislature granted Ocean Grove a charter. The Ocean Grove Camp Meeting Association began selling lots in its new seaside community. According to Mrs. Osborn, the first buyer was James A. Bradley, who subsequently went on to found Asbury Park.

Despite occasional doubts about what the Camp Meeting Association was trying to do, Osborn never lost his burning faith in its mission, nor his unshakable belief that the Jersey Shore was the place in which to do it. At one point, Osborn tried to get the Reverend Joel Croft to buy a lot in Ocean Grove.

"What have you there?" asked Croft.

"Sand and the ocean," Osborn replied, "but in twenty years there will be a continuous city from Long Branch to Cape May." He could not have been more right.

In all, 373 lots were sold. By then, the first permanent building in the town, housing a book store, post office, and business office of the association, had been erected.

Much hard work was expended to transform the inhospitable terrain into a region in which people would want to live. The first annual report of the Camp Meeting Association lists these labors, most of which were supervised by the apparently indefatigable Osborn: forty thousand trees trimmed, thousands of trees cut down, thousands of loads of sand removed, the entire area brushed and cleared of debris, and roads cut, graded, and graveled.

In fact, James A. Bradley was so impressed with Osborn's ability that he asked him to become the superintendent of Asbury Park and offered to supply the capital and share the profits with him. Osborn refused. "I founded Ocean Grove for the glory of God," he told his friend, "but I am not in the money-making business."

By 1876, the little community that had begun with nineteen people in tents was on its way to becoming one of most popular spots on the Jersey Shore. The railroad was bringing an estimated fifty thousand people to the town, which netted the train company forty-seven thousand dollars in receipts for its first year of operation. The flood of visitors, however, was a mixed blessing, as the president of the Camp Meeting Association noted diplomatically in the seventh annual report: "Our quiet has been somewhat disturbed by the influx of excursionists, who never stay long enough to be impressed by their surroundings, and being unsettled themselves, unsettle everybody about them."

The main visitors to Ocean Grove were business and professional men and their families, who were attracted by the combination of religion and recreation in this new community by the sea. One of the activities that visitors and residents alike enjoyed was congregational singing. In 1889 a reporter for the *New York Tribune* wrote that the sound of ten thousand worshippers raising their voices in song was audible a mile away, creating "such a volume of sound that the roar of the surf sounds like the bass notes of a distant organ."

Of all the buildings in Ocean Grove, none is more famous than the Great Auditorium. This magnificent structure dominates the entire town, attracting visitors from all over.

The auditorium was built in 1894 to commemorate Ocean Grove's twenty-fifth anniversary. The number of worshippers attending services in the town was straining the existing building to capacity, and all agreed that a new auditorium seating ten thousand people would be a wonderful way for Ocean Grove to celebrate its silver anniversary.

The cost of such a structure was estimated to be $50,000, a sizable sum. However, the citizens of Ocean Grove swiftly rose to the challenge; virtually

The Great Auditorium in Ocean Grove.

the entire amount ($42,900) was pledged in just a single day of Sunday services.

Ground was broken for the new auditorium on December 2, 1893. Incredibly, it took just three months to build this massive structure. (Today it would take three months just to approve the plans!) The final cost was $69,112.16. The building opened on July 1, 1894, and was dedicated during August of that same year.

It is the focal point of Ocean Grove, and a long and illustrious list of people have appeared at the Great Auditorium throughout the years, including Enrico Caruso, John Philip Sousa, Billy Sunday, Billy Graham, Duke Ellington, Will Rogers, Pearl Bailey, Booker T. Washington, Helen Keller, and Dr. Norman Vincent Peale.

Numerous United States presidents have chosen the Great Auditorium as a forum for unveiling important policy pronouncements. William

McKinley used it to announce his imperialistic policy toward the Philippines in 1899. In 1911, as the clouds of war thickened over Europe, President William Howard Taft mounted the great stage and urged that arbitration, rather than violence, be used to settle international disputes.

But of all the many dignitaries who have come to Ocean Grove, the most poignant visit was that of Ulysses S. Grant in the summer of 1884. The former president had been severely criticized in the press for the recent failure of his Wall Street brokerage firm. Many people had lost a lot of money and blamed Grant, even though it would later be revealed that the trusting Grant had been unaware of his partner's shady dealings. By the time he returned to Ocean Grove that summer, for a reunion of army chaplains, he was no longer the hero who had saved the Union during the Civil War, but an old man sick in both body and spirit, who needed crutches to walk and had to be helped into his seat.

A preacher and former Union soldier named A. J. Palmer had been chosen to introduce Grant to the huge audience waiting to hear him speak. Palmer, far from being cool toward Grant, launched into a stirring discourse about the general's many virtues, sweeping the audience along on the power of his words. At the conclusion, Palmer looked down at the much-maligned hero and cried out: "And no combination of Wall Street sharpers shall tarnish the luster of my old commander's fame for me!"

With a roar of approval the normally restrained Ocean Grove crowd leaped to its feet. For several minutes they cheered Grant wildly, with men throwing their hats in the air and women waving handkerchiefs.

Grant finally struggled to his feet and began to speak. After a few halting words, he suddenly stopped and burst into tears. "This young man has overcome me," he cried out, and proceeded to sob uncontrollably for several minutes before an audience in which many eyes were undoubtedly wet as well. Eventually the old general took his seat, remarking that never before had he been unable to control his feelings.

It was Grant's last public appearance. One year later, he was dead.

Demonstrating its affection for a former hero on whom others had turned their back was right in tune with Ocean Grove's character, for the town inevitably went its own way. This was especially true in the rules that governed community life. Fueled by the Camp Meeting Association's desire for a Christian town, there were many edicts that might seem overly restrictive today. The sale of liquor was banned, and hotels and merchants were forbidden to stock either tobacco or novels (it was felt that such frivolous reading distracted from more serious reflection). On Sundays, no business could be conducted, no amusements were allowed, and no newspapers were delivered. The gates leading out from the community to the surrounding area were closed at midnight Saturday and not reopened until midnight Sunday, blocking all traffic except emergency vehicles.

Not everyone found this type of life appealing. In 1893, a writer for an early travel guide was amazed that so many people would willingly spend their summer vacations in "a religious autocracy, which is severe in both its positive and negative regulations."

But this view was the exception rather than the rule. Somehow, as the nation swept into a twentieth century filled with world wars, flappers, Prohibition, gangsters, suburbia, hot rods, beatniks, hippies, and riots, Ocean

The first freshwater well in Ocean Grove was called Beersheba. The fountain in the middle of this ornate structure stands on the original spot of the first well.

Thornley Chapel is typical of the Victorian-style architecture throughout much of Ocean Grove.

Grove seemed unaffected. With its gingerbread-trimmed buildings, quiet boardwalk, and tree-lined walkways, the town seemed to have found a way to keep time at bay. Even the much-ridiculed Sunday traffic ban brought back memories of a quieter, simpler time, when a person could walk down the street without getting run over by a car or choking on exhaust fumes.

But nothing stays the same forever, not even Ocean Grove. In 1979 the New Jersey Supreme Court declared the town's form of government unconstitutional. Out with the government went many of the prohibitions, including the Sunday driving ban. Now the town is part of Neptune Township.

Yet the modern world has only intruded up to a point. Ocean Grove today still remains remarkably true to its roots: a peaceful, picturesque place, where quiet reflection, common courtesy, and good feeling are present in abundance.

Great Auditorium Statistics

Cost: $69,112
Square footage: 36,225
Highest point: 55 Feet
Seating capacity: 10,000 at first, now 6,500

The Great Auditorium Pipe Organ was built at a cost of $27,000 by Robert Hope-Jones in 1907, one of the true geniuses in organ construction. The instrument, which contains 8,000 pipes ranging from 32 feet high to smaller than a lead pencil, is considered one of the most unique and powerful organs in the United States.

James A. Bradley's involvement in Ocean Grove, and subsequent founding of Asbury Park, helped bring civilization to that untamed region. In an article for the *Asbury Park Journal,* Bradley related how he, quite innocently, became an integral part of the history of the Jersey Shore:

> One afternoon in May, 1870, I was walking along Broadway, New York, and suddenly ran against our friend, David H. Brown, Esq., Treasurer of the Ocean Grove Association.
>   "How is Ocean getting on?" [Bradley asked.]
>   "Very fairly," said he, "why don't you buy a lot? Those who have their names put down now have first choice."
>   "Well, put me down for two."

Later, when Bradley went to Ocean Grove, he liked what he saw, despite the opinion of his manservant, who called the place "a wilderness." During an exploratory trip in the surrounding area with Osborn, Bradley came upon the desolate spot that would someday become Asbury Park. Anxious that Ocean Grove have a friend as its immediate neighbor to the north, Bradley bought the land and began planning his own community.

Millville is primarily known today as the home of the New Jersey glass industry, and with good reason. During the industry's heyday around 1900, only Pittsburgh produced more glassware than this Cumberland County town.

The area that would someday be Millville was first visited by Europeans sometime around 1754. What they found was a wilderness of sandy soil, trees, and wild huckleberry and blackberry bushes nestled beside the Maurice River. Early European settlers never saw a river they didn't try to tame, and the Maurice was no exception. A log bridge was built across the water, and the area was christened "The Bridge." Later a sturdier bridge replaced the first one, and the name changed to "New Bridge" or "Maurice River Bridge." A few houses popped up here and there, but in no real sense was it a town.

This changed in 1795, when Joseph Buck came to New Bridge. Buck was a veteran of the Revolutionary War who had seen action in many important engagements, including the siege of Yorktown. According to some reports, he was also present when Major Andre, the British spy caught in the Benedict Arnold plot, was hanged.

After returning to civilian life, Buck married Ruth Seeley and settled in Bridgeton, New Jersey. For three years (1787–1790) he served as the Cumberland County sheriff.

At some point Buck discovered New Bridge and apparently liked what he saw, for he acquired a house on the west side of the Maurice River. By this time the region was more developed, spurred by Henry Dunker and Joseph Smith, who had arrived in the area in 1790, formed the Union Company, and built several lumber mills on a lake.

Buck agreed with the plans of Dunker and Smith for the region. In fact, when the former Continental soldier let his imagination wander, he foresaw a vast colony of mills located along the Maurice River, with elegant manor houses uptown for the owners. In 1795 Buck decided to develop the area. Either because of Buck's plan or because of the mills already on the lake, the town gained a new name: Millville.

Enthusiastically, Buck embarked upon his vision by buying up land in Millville and building a large house there, but time was against him. He died eight years later, in 1803, his dream unfulfilled. Fewer than two dozen buildings marked the spot where Buck had imagined an industrial center.

Buck died before witnessing the defining moment in Millville's history, although it wasn't apparent as such when it first happened. In 1806 an Irish immigrant named James Lee opened the first glass factory in Millville along the east bank of the Maurice River. Lee was a restless man who had previously operated a factory in Port Elizabeth called the Eagle Glass Works, and he didn't remain in Millville long either. Within a few years he sold his factory there and moved to Kensington, Pennsylvania, where he embarked on yet another glass-making venture. But although Lee's stay in Millville was short, his legacy was long.

Glassmaking and Millville were a natural combination. To make glass, sand is subjected to very high temperatures and then allowed to cool; the better the quality of sand, the better the quality of glass produced. Millville was blessed with not only a huge supply of fine-grained sand with few impurities but also a vast supply of wood in nearby forests for the glassmaking furnaces.

Lee's window-glass factory, along with an iron foundry established several years later, brought the first real progress to Millville. People came to the area to work in the factories, and this pool of workers attracted other industries. Soon Buck's vision began to be realized. Millville's population soared from a few hundred people in the early 1820s to nearly five thousand in 1870.

If Lee's glass factor was the first defining moment in Millville's history, the second was surely the arrival in town of Dr. Theodore Corson Wheaton in 1883. Born in the South Jersey community of Tuckahoe in 1852, Wheaton had degrees in both pharmacy and medicine when he brought his family to Millville to live. The entrepreneurial Wheaton practiced medicine and also ran a pharmacy and a general store.

In 1888, Wheaton's inquisitive mind turned to the type of glass used by physicians and pharmacists, and he decided to expand his business ventures even further by entering into the glass business. Buying into the small Shull-Goodwin Glass Company, Wheaton soon found that he was fascinated by glassmaking. Believing that the industry had a strong future, he bought out the remaining partners, and by 1889 the entire one-building operation was his. From these humble beginnings rose the mighty T. C. Wheaton Company (today Wheaton Industries), one of the leading glass manufacturers in the world.

Sparked by Wheaton, the glass industry roared forward in Millville, as well as the rest of South Jersey, and by the dawn of the twentieth century the town was famous as a glassmaking center. In 1908, the Philadelphia newspaper *The North American* "celebrated" Millville's fame in a jingle:

Jersey is a funny place, mosquitoes, frogs & sand,
And half pint flasks to fit the pocket are in great demand.
So the make flasks by thousands in the pint and half pint size,
And when they get a stock on hand they change & make glass eyes.
Now Millville is the city that this jingle is about,
They have no demon ruin saloons—they voted them all out.
Most every workman owns his home and buys his children shoes,
That's something that is hard to do if you "hit up" the booze!

A few years earlier, an ode of a much different sort was written to the city by a young poet named Carl Sandburg, who lived in Galesburg, Illinois.

Millville Sign with its Holly City logo.

In a combination of prose and poetry simply called "Millville," Sandburg expressed his feelings about the New Jersey town: "Down in southern New Jersey, they make glass. By day and by night, the fires burn on in Millville and bid the sand let in the light."

In a subsequent paragraph, Sandburg described the town: "Millville by night would have delighted Whistler, who loved gloom and mist and wild shadows. Great rafts of wood and big, brick hulks, dotted with a myriad of lights, glowing and twinkling every shade of red. Big, black flumes, shooting out smoke and sparks, bottles, bottles, bottles, of every tint and hue, from a brilliant crimson to the dull green that marks the death of sand and birth of glass."

At the height of its glory, the Millville glass industry consisted of over a dozen companies, all making glass "by day and by night." The names of many of these companies have long since slipped into history: International Glass Company, Caloris Company, Commercial Flint Glass Company, Glove Graduate Company, Nelson Creamer, Howard Davis, Kimpron Haupt, Eastern Glass, L. G. Nester, Frederick and Dimmock, Morris, Stuhl Laboratory, and Wheaton.

Glass does not tell the whole story of Millville though. The town is also known for another product, something that has nothing to do with factories and furnaces and everything to do with sunlight and rain: holly trees.

Millville's "holly-days" began in 1926 when Clarence Wolf, president of the Silica Sand Company, sent out packages of holly culled from local trees to the company's forty-six customers as Christmas gifts. The response was so enthusiastic that he continued doing it year after year. By the late 1930s, Wolf didn't want to rely on wild trees for the holly, so he planted an orchard of nearly three thousand trees. By the 1950s, thanks to the care of Wolf and horticulturist Dan Fenton, the orchard contained forty-four hundred trees of thirty different varieties.

Because Millville holly had become so well known throughout the United States, the city commissioners proclaimed the town the Holly City of America in the 1950s, a distinction that it still retains.

DID YOU KNOW?

A former New Jersey governor and a key aide to President Franklin D. Roosevelt are two of Millville's most prominent citizens.

Although born in Medford, Edward Casper Stokes grew up in Millville after moving there with his family in 1871, when he was eleven years old. After graduating from Brown University in 1883, Stokes returned to Millville and got a job in a bank. He then began a slow but steady rise up the political ladder, serving in the state assembly and senate before being elected governor on the Republican ticket in 1904, defeating Charles C. Black by fifty-one thousand votes.

Leon Henderson, on the other hand, found success not in Trenton but in Washington, D.C. Born in Millville on May 26, 1895, Henderson's childhood was spent in deep poverty. To help support his family, he quit high school and took a job in a glass factory, but a teacher talked him back into school. He put himself through college by working odd jobs and playing semipro sports.

By 1941 Henderson was a key figure of Franklin D. Roosevelt's administration. That year he was made director of the Office of Price Administration, and charged with controlling inflation during the war years. The fact that he did so, through a series of price controls and a rationing system, was considered a minor miracle by many Washington observers. This was a highly public post, and the cigar-smoking, plain-talking Henderson made the front covers of both *Life* and *Time*. In later years, he gained fame again for bringing the nation's first federal senior citizens housing project to Millville.

In July 1778, during the Revolutionary War, four Continental army soldiers stopped for a picnic at the Passaic Falls, near a tiny village of ten houses called Acquackanonk. Later, one of the picnickers wrote about that lazy afternoon in northern New Jersey: "We composed some excellent grog, then chatted away a very cheerful half hour—then took our leave of the friendly oak—its refreshing spring—and the meek falls of the Passaic."

The men were George Washington, Alexander Hamilton, the Marquis de Lafayette, and his aide-de-camp, James McHenry (who recorded the brief respite in his diary). Although their stop at the "meek falls" that day was short, the impression it made on Hamilton was long indeed. Thirteen years later, as the first Secretary of the Treasury of the United States of America, Hamilton chose that peaceful spot as the showcase for what he hoped the young country would someday become—and in so doing founded the city of Paterson.

Born out of the clash of philosophies between two of this country's Founding Fathers, nurtured on the hum of the cotton spindle, and hardened by repeated failures that left it barely alive, few cities in the United States can claim as colorful a past as Paterson. Throughout its often-turbulent history, Paterson has attracted both speculators and innovators; it has made some people rich and dashed the dreams of others on the rocks of failure. It has lent its name to the title of an epic poem, been the scene of an ugly labor strike, and built products that have changed the course of American history.

The beginning of Paterson dates to the beginning of the United States, and a duel of ideologies between Hamilton and Thomas Jefferson. To Jefferson, the future of the United States was in its farmers and the agrarian society they would create. "Cultivators of the earth are the most valuable citizens, the most independent, the most virtuous," Jefferson wrote, "and they are tied to their country, and wedded to its liberty and interests, by the most lasting bonds." Hamilton, however, dismissed an agrarian society as weak and ineffective. The only way for the United States to become strong enough to deal with the powerful nations of the world, he felt, was for it to develop a centralized government based on a robust industrial economy. He favored aligning the federal government with industry: "There is no purpose to which public money can be more beneficially applied than to the acquisition of a new and useful branch of industry," he said.

As the government's financial head, Hamilton could put the nation's money where his philosophy was. In 1791, he proposed that the federal government spend one million dollars (which was then 2 percent of the national debt) to build a "national manufactory" that would, in effect, be an industrial urban complex, run by a group called the Society for Establishing Useful Manufactures (SUM).

Because of the water power that would be needed to run the factories, Hamilton chose Acquackanonk as the site for this bold experiment. A surveyor had already estimated that Great Fails would be able to drive 247 wa-terwheels. The presence of nearby quarries, a large supply of timber (both for burning and building), and nearby deposits of bog iron ore were additional factors that helped steer Hamilton to choose the quiet village for his plan.

Congress, already suspicious of many of Hamilton's ideas, was in no mood to agree to a scheme that would have made the federal government the country's biggest manufacturer. Undaunted, Hamilton turned to the private sector; he wrote an SUM prospectus and turned it over to New Jersey's governor, William Paterson, to guide through the state legislature. When he did so (both the governor and some New Jersey legislators be-came stockholders in the new corporation, although the phrase "conflict of interest" never seems to have occurred to anyone), Hamilton named the new manufacturing community after the governor.

The governor's political skills enabled the SUM to get the sweetheart deal of the century (the eighteenth or any other, for that matter). Among the benefits that the charter granted were: exemption of SUM employees from poll taxes, general assessments, and routine military duty; a ten-year tax exemption for SUM property and buildings; the right to hold a lottery to regain projected financial losses; exclusive domain over the Passaic River; and, most significantly, the right to govern its own lands.

In May 1792, the SUM got things off and running by purchasing seven hun-dred acres in the vicinity of the Passaic Falls. Thanks to the salesmanship abili-ties of Hamilton's friend William Duer, the governor of the SUM, six hundred thousand dollars worth of stock in the fledgling industrial empire was quickly sold. Hamilton was gratified to find foreign investors also very interested in what was happening in New Jersey. It seemed as if his vision was correct.

Then, just as quickly, disaster struck. A stock speculation scheme that Duer was masterminding unraveled, sending him to jail, causing a national financial crisis, and giving the SUM a severe black eye. Many SUM stock-holders were hit hard by the economic downturn and lost interest in putting any more of their money into this great industrial experiment. Hamilton, who had initially seen himself as strictly an advisor to the SUM, leaped in with both feet to save his tottering manufacturing city. But nothing seemed to go right: French architect Pierre L'Enfant—who designed Washington, D.C.—was hired to plan the new industrial complex, but his ideas were too elaborate and expensive and he was dismissed; it was difficult to recruit local workers to staff the factories; and not enough skilled artisans were available to manage and supervise the mills.

Bleeding red ink, suffering from indifferent management, and severely undercapitalized, the SUM threw in the towel in 1796. Only two factories—a four-story stone cotton mill and a smaller building that was used for bleaching and printing—had been completed. The SUM sold off most of its machinery and whatever goods had been produced, and halted operations. Without the prospect of jobs, people deserted the area, and the population plummeted. Paterson's first great era had ended in failure.

Although down, Paterson was not out. Its first revival began when Roswell Colt, a member of the family whose name would someday be on the gun that "won the West," and whose relationship to Samuel Colt would bring the ultimately famous gunmaker to Paterson, became governor of the SUM in 1809. Although not directly involved in manufacturing anymore, the society still owned significant land and water rights in the town, and thus stood to benefit when, slowly but surely, industries were attracted by the Passaic River waterpower that the SUM had harnessed through a series of canals, called "raceways". Factories began popping up in Paterson, although too late for Hamilton, who had been killed in the famous duel with Aaron Burr in 1804, to see his dream finally realized. When the War of 1812 cut off European goods to this country, there was almost no manufacturing capacity in the United States to replace them—except in Paterson.

Paterson boomed during the war years. At the start of 1815, a manufacturing census reported eleven cotton mills, a card and wire mill, a rolling mill, and a sawmill in operation, and a population of fifteen hundred.

When the war ended in 1815, however, so did Paterson's boom years, as European products came flooding back into the marketplace. The British deliberately undersold U.S. manufacturers to regain their foothold with American consumers. This caused the cotton industry to collapse, which spun the country into several years of economic stagnation.

Once again Paterson hit the skids. The downfall was colorfully chronicled in an article in an 1859 edition of *Scientific American*: "The streets were again deserted; mills were locked up and stood in gloomy solitude; the spindle rusted in the socket; the wheel rotted in its pit; and the spider wove his cobwebs upon looms whose clatter drowned the workmen's song."

Reports of Paterson's death were greatly exaggerated once again. The United States was changing, becoming just as acclimated to the sound of the worker's wheel and the clatter of the loom as it was to the gentle clip-clop of the plow horse; manufacturing was becoming the driving force in the U.S. economy. By 1821, the *True American* reported that Paterson contained nine mills with a total of more than over 650 employees. Between 1821 and 1827 the number of spindles in Paterson cotton mills jumped from 12,600 to 23,938, while the total amount of cloth produced grew by a million yards. Paterson had risen again from the ashes, and this time the comeback lasted longer.

Now firmly established as a manufacturing center, Paterson grew steadily throughout much of the nineteenth century. When the depression of 1837 destroyed the cotton industry, Paterson switched to machine making and steamed forward. In the 1840s another milestone was reached when silk manufacturing began in the town. In time the silk industry would make the town internationally famous (Paterson became internationally known as "Silk City"); it would also make a very few men very rich, and breed a resentment that led to a cataclysmic labor strike in 1913 that nearly destroyed Paterson.

Hamilton had hoped that Paterson would become a crucible of ideas and manufacturing vitality, and in this he was correct. The town attracted people of vision and resourcefulness, and their achievements stamped the city as the epitome of American can-do ingenuity.

From Paterson came inventions that would change the world, such as Samuel Colt's revolutionary repeating revolver and John Holland's first practical submarine. The locomotive, which transformed America, was born in Paterson in the 1830s when an English train engine arrived in town in pieces and a local carpenter named Thomas Rogers decided that he could build one just as easily. He could, and did, and by 1880 Paterson was producing 80 percent of the locomotives made in the United States. Even into the twentieth century, Paterson was still the source of epoch-making events; when Charles Lindbergh crossed the Atlantic Ocean alone in 1927, his plane, *The Spirit of St. Louis*, was propelled by an engine made at the Wright Aeronautical Company in Paterson.

By the 1960s, however, Paterson was ailing. Having been born and nurtured on manufacturing, Paterson suffered the pangs of withdrawal as industry throughout the Northeast heeded the siren call of cheap labor and headed first to the South and then overseas. The city seemed old and tired, unable to summon up its old clan; even the once-mighty Great Falls of the Passaic became a shadow of its former self, thanks to an SUM decision that diverted 75 million gallons of water a day out of its normal flow. This turned the majestic waterfall into little more than a dripping faucet, and the Passaic River into a polluted disgrace that William Carlos Williams called "the vilest swillhole in christendom." (Williams's widow claimed that the stench of the river was so powerful that it actually peeled paint off houses.)

Today, with the Passaic Falls clean once again and its many historic districts displaying a variety of architectural gems, Paterson may not be Silk City anymore, but it remains a fascinating town.

One of the greatest American writers of the twentieth century, New Jersey–born William Carlos Williams, selected Paterson as the title and general subject of his greatest work: the five-volume poem *Paterson.*

Born in Rutherford (Bergen County) on September 17, 1883, Williams earned a medical degree from the University of Pennsylvania in 1906. He returned to Rutherford, where he practiced medicine and wrote for the rest of his life. The basic concept of *Paterson*—linking the city with modern man and to a broader extent, American life—took Williams more than fifteen years to work out. The poem's prose and poetry mixture, and the complex images and structure of the piece, proved difficult for him. "That God damned and I mean God damned poem *Paterson* has me down," he wrote in December 1943. "I am burned up to do it but don't quite know how. I write and destroy, write and destroy . . . I flounder and flunk."

Williams persevered, however; the first *Paterson* volume was published in 1946 to critical acclaim. Subsequent volumes appeared in 1948, 1949, 1951, and 1958. The poem, said one critic, is "Whitman's America, grown pathetic and tragic, brutalized by inequality, disorganized by industrial chaos, and faced with annihilation." At the time of his death, on March 4, 1963, Williams was working on a sixth volume.

Although Paterson was the country's most strike-ridden city between 1850 and 1914, no one was prepared for the consequences of the Silk Strike of 1913, which not only became one of the most devastating labor disputes in American history but also destroyed virtually all the participants.

The silk industry began in Paterson in 1841. By 1880 the town was preeminent in the nation's manufacture of silk and was dubbed "Silk City." However, although silk's success made the business owners rich—Catholina Lambert, one of the manufacturers, ostentatiously flaunted his wealth by building a medieval-style castle on a mountain top for his home and amassing a huge art collection within its stone walls—for most it meant nothing more than hard labor, long hours, and meager wages. Finally, on February 25, 1913, weavers walked off the job in the Docherty Mill to protest the decree that workers work four looms instead of two. Not only would this have doubled the workload, it would eventually reduce mill jobs by half. Other mills quickly joined the walkout; before long 24,000 silk workers were out on the street.

The strike quickly escalated into a war between the silk owners and the Industrial Workers of the World (IWW) labor union. The workers who had begun the strike with legitimate grievances were caught in the middle; what had begun as a job action for workers' rights evolved into a grim struggle for survival between two iron-willed opponents. For month after desperate month the strike dragged on as both sides grew weaker; workers had to send their children out of town because there was no food, while mill owners were hemorrhaging money.

Finally, after five months, unable to bear their families' hardship anymore, the ribbon workers broke with the IWW and came to an agreement with the owners. This leak in union solidarity soon became a flood, as other workers rushed to settle as well.

The strike produced no winners. Workers gained almost no concessions; the IWW lost both power and prestige; and the silk owners were greatly weakened financially. However, the biggest loser of all was Paterson. The strike saddled the town with a reputation as a seething cauldron of worker fervor, an image that frightened away other industries and helped drive the city into decline. Meanwhile, the silk industry, which had been slumping anyway, was pushed over the brink. By 1938, just six thousand workers were left in an industry that had once employed four times that many. Paterson was "Silk City" no more.

"We are now going to settle a Town at the Falls, at a place reported . . . to be without compare to any other yet known: None equal for pleasant healthful air; Lovely Situation; second to none for Fertility."

And so it was that, in 1679, a group of recent immigrants from Great Britain to the New World, including the writer of the above words, William Emley, set off to start a town. The community that they began would be known by various names throughout its history, but we know it today as one of the most prominent towns in New Jersey history: Trenton.

When the group arrived at the "Falls," they found other English settlers already there, including Mahlon Stacy, the principal landowner in the area. Stacy had long been singing the praises of the region, writing about peaches (an unknown fruit to the English) that "hang almost like our onion" and delicious wild fruits that grew in abundance, like strawberries and cranberries.

The area that would soon be called Trenton was ideal, not only for farming, but for carving out a life. Rain was plentiful in the summer, the winters were not too harsh, and the soil was easily tilled. The surrounding forests contained a variety of hardwood trees needed for building homes and heating them. In addition, there was the broad Delaware River, which would not only provide drinking water, but could also be used to power mills. (What the early settlers would discover through trial and error, however, was that the shallow Assunpink Creek was far better for this purpose than the unreliable Delaware, where the water level always seemed to be going up or down, never reliably enough, however, to power a waterwheel.) In 1680 Stacy foreshadowed the region's future as an industrial power by building a gristmill of logs.

Initially the region had been known as the Falls or the Falls of the Delaware. When more settlers came, the name changed to the Yorkshire Tenth, because the settlers were Quakers from Yorkshire in England who had been assigned ten shares of land each. In 1714 came another, and more permanent, name change, with the arrival of William Trent. Trent was a wealthy merchant from Philadelphia who planned to develop the area. He bought Stacy's eight hundred acres, built a brick house near the Delaware (which still stands today), and rebuilt Stacy's wooden mill out of stone. Not surprisingly, as the dominant force in the community, Trent's name began to be associated with it, and soon the Yorkshire Tenth had become "Trent's Town," which was later shortened to Trenton.

Helped by its location along the river, which brought many travelers and settlers to the area, Trenton grew slowly but steadily throughout the first half of the eighteenth century. Although still good for agriculture, the area began to take on a more industrial flavor. Trent had expanded Stacy's single mill into a complex, and added an ironworks. In 1731 a steelworks was built by Isaac Harrow, and several tanning works were also established in Trenton.

By 1775, when war came to the colonies, Trenton, a community of about one hundred buildings, laid out along seven or eight picturesque streets with the river in the background, was often described as a "pretty town." As the citizens of Trenton listened to the fiery speeches of the patriots and heard the Declaration of Independence read from their courthouse steps, they little realized that this "pretty village" would shortly become the turning point in the Revolutionary War.

Few stories in United States history are more stirring than the tale of George Washington taking his ragtag hand of weary and dispirited soldiers across the Delaware River on a cold Christmas night in 1776 and surprising the Hessian mercenaries who were occupying Trenton. The story has been told many times and does not need to be repeated here; suffice it to say that without the victory at Trenton, the American bid for independence might well have been snuffed out before spring arrived.

After the war was won it was time to think about the peace, and a major decision for the congressional delegates of the new country was where to locate the national capital. Several Founding Fathers, among them James Madison, pushed for the government to be centered at Trenton, which was then the geographic center of the United States. (Madison, in fact, wrote confidently that Trenton "is to become the future seat of the Federal Government.") Southern congressional delegates, however, did not agree, and so a compromise was reached: the government would be alternated between Annapolis, Maryland, and Trenton, until a permanent site could be decided upon.

This "government by pendulum," as Bordentown's Francis Hopkinson tartly called it, reached Trenton in November 1784. Unfortunately, excitement over Congress' arrival ran so high that members of the state legislature also flooded into town at the same time, anxious to see the national leaders in action. This created a severe shortage of rooms for the Congress. However, before beating a hasty retreat out of town (and whatever oversized chairs and bathtubs they had wedged themselves into for sleeping), the congressional delegation did vote one hundred thousand dollars to be spent to erect federal government buildings "on the banks of either side of the Delaware." It was easy to see that they meant Trenton.

This appeared to lock it up for Trenton, but even as the citizens were celebrating, forces were moving to undermine their hopes. Southerners still disliked placing the capital there, feeling that the city was too far north (in this dispute can be seen the earliest shadows of the Civil War, nearly eighty years in the future). Then, unexpectedly, George Washington weighed in against Trenton, saying that if the federal buildings were placed on the Delaware, they would be "improperly placed for the seat of the empire."

Washington's pronouncement punctured Trenton's euphoria. The final blow came in September 1785, when Congress refused to appropriate the hundred thousand dollars approved the previous year. Sentiment in Congress for a capital along the Delaware collapsed and could not be revived. Trenton had to content itself with becoming the permanent capital of New Jersey in 1790.

Trentonians shook off the disappointment and buckled down to the business of improving their town. By the mid-nineteenth century, sparked by the completion of the Delaware and Raritan Canal and its feeder canal, which enabled raw materials to be brought in and finished goods out easily, Trenton was thriving as an industrial center. Led by Peter Cooper's Iron Company (established in 1845) and the wire rope factories of John A. Roebling Sons (1848), the city became one of the predominant manufacturing regions on the East Coast. The rubber industry, ironworks, and textile industry all helped fuel a population explosion of 300 percent from 1840 to 1860. In one decade alone, from 1850 to 1860, the population grew at an amazing 166 percent, from 6,461 to 17,228, as people came to Trenton in droves to claim the explosion of jobs caused by the industrial activity.

Trenton roared into the twentieth century in fine fettle, proud of its past and full of confidence in its future. The famous slogan "Trenton Makes—the World Takes" summed up the city's pride in its industrial sector, which seemed as if it would be vibrant forever.

It didn't work out that way, for reasons not totally within Trenton's control. The post–World War II suburban stampede from the cities (Trenton's suburbs grew by 40 percent between 1940 and 1950) coincided with the decline of manufacturing all across the northeastern United States. As the city's industrial lifeblood ebbed, Trenton was caught in a downward spiral typical of many big American cities, faced with the triple-whammy of an aging physical plant, shuttered factories, and a shrinking revenue base.

Today Trenton is fighting hard to bounce back. Don't bet against this capital city.

For seventy years, from the mid-1880s to the mid-1950s, the name "Bordentown" did not just mean a small town at the tip of northern Burlington County. It also meant the Manual Training and Industrial School for Colored Youth—the only state-supported co-ed all-black boarding school north of the Mason-Dixon Line.

By the 1880s in America, the promise of equality for African Americans that the Civil War and Reconstruction had held out had been replaced by the reality of Jim Crow and segregation. Blacks were especially fleeing the South, where lynching and the Ku Klux Klan were common, for the less-restrictive North. It was in this atmosphere that the Reverend Raymond Rice opened the school in 1886 in the living room of his New Brunswick home. The idea behind the school was to teach African Americans skills so they could become self-sufficient in an increasingly hostile world.

Rice quickly moved the school to Bordentown, a small community about twenty-five miles south in Burlington County. Founded in the first part of the eighteenth century and named for Joseph Borden, the town had seen its fair share of notable residents, including Francis Hopkinson (who signed the Declaration of Independence), patriot writer Thomas Paine, and Patience Lovell Wright, America's first female sculptor. Another notable resident had been Admiral Charles Stewart, commander of the *U.S.S. Constitution* (popularly known as "Old Ironsides") in the War of 1812. It was to Stewart's four-hundred-acre former estate that the school moved in 1896.

Statue of Thomas Paine in Bordentown, celebrating the time he lived in the town.

(This led to the school sometimes being called "Old Ironsides" or the "Iron-sides Normal School.")

In 1894 New Jersey designated the Bordentown school as the state's in-structional institution for vocational education. Nine years later the New Jersey Board of Education formally took control of the school.

Although it was supposed to train blacks to be self-sufficient, the school initially stuck fairly close to a "classic" education, emphasizing history, En-glish, classic languages, and other academic fields. In 1913 Booker T. Wash-ington suggested that the school also offer courses in vocational skills, such as in the new field of auto repair. Under the stewardship of William Valentine, who became the school's third principal in 1915, the school did exactly that, with such success that it soon became known as the "Tuskegee of the North."

It was to tiny Bordentown, with its one main street, that notables, includ-ing Eleanor Roosevelt, Albert Einstein, and Paul Robeson, came to see and lecture at this highly regarded institution for black education. The school was run year-round and offered not just formal education but also practical lessons to prepare its students for the outside world. The institution had its own farms, orchards, and cattle, offered sports such as tennis, and in gen-eral provided African American youths with a nurturing environment that they probably wouldn't have found in public education and allowed them to develop to their full potential.

But the handwriting was on the wall for segregated facilities, and the landmark *Brown vs. Board of Education* decision in 1954 drove one stake into the school's heart. The other was thrust there by Governor Robert Meyner, who wanted the land and buildings for a mental health facility and became a fierce critic of the school. The school couldn't combat both of these things, and closed in 1955.

Today a few buildings of this historic institution remain, slowly deterio-rating. Despite its historic significance, no one has come forward with any ideas to save what's left for posterity. A documentary called *A Place Out of Time* was produced about the Bordentown school. The site is today used by the state's juvenile justice system. Ironically, a place that once helped Afri-can American youths escape the prison of Jim Crow segregation has now become an actual prison.

When New Jersey Was Hollywood

"Cameras were everywhere, grinding out dramas. Burglaries and dynamite and fat men rolling down hills, and nobody even turned to look at them. Kindly old ladies didn't blink an eyelid when three galloping Mexicans were shot and killed at their very door."

Of course, this quote must be about Hollywood. Like Pavlov's dog, we are conditioned to make certain assumptions in life, and one of these is that movies are made in Hollywood. After all, where else would the sight of robberies, murders, and explosions be so commonplace that passersby stifled yawns at the sight of such mayhem?

The answer is: Fort Lee, New Jersey.

Today, Fort Lee is assumed to be merely the last exit in New Jersey before the George Washington Bridge. But like most other assumptions made in haste and ignorance, those about Fort Lee are wrong. There is a story to be told here, in this Hudson County community of thirty thousand people, a fascinating story of heroes and villains, combining all the elements of classic cinema. It is a tale of the time when not just Fort Lee, but all of New Jersey, was the undisputed movie-making capital of the United States, and Hollywood was just an unknown town in California.

There is no question that Thomas Alva Edison belongs on the roster of New Jersey's greatest citizens. The Wizard of Menlo Park was one of those rare people who moved humanity forward through the force of his own genius. His many inventions helped make the late nineteenth and early twentieth centuries an exciting and optimistic time, when wondrous new devices like the phonograph and the electric light seemed to spew forth from Edison's lab almost daily.

Edison's claim to the invention of motion pictures, however, is cloudier. Despite the popular perception that the concept of moving pictures sprang full-blown into his mind from nothingness, others had been pursuing this idea for years before Edison and his employee, William K. L. Dickson, began serious work on it at Menlo Park in the early 1890s. Although both were brilliant men, the two don't seem to have conceived of anything incredibly new in the development of motion pictures. Their real genius was in taking preexisting elements, such as nitrocellulose film, clock gears, and other mechanical parts, and arranging them into the proper components that would enable pictures to move.

That they did this, and more, is beyond dispute. In March 1893 Edison patented a machine called a Kinetoscope, which was a coin-operated device that could be used by just one person to view moving pictures. Realizing the commercial potential of movies, Edison built the famous "Black Maria" at West Orange, the world's first motion picture studio. Within three years came the Vitascope, a machine that could project movies (which Edison bought from two men in Washington, D.C.) for viewing by an audience. Edison used these as the building blocks to swiftly forge a major role in the fledgling motion picture industry. Although it had competitors, particularly overseas, the Edison company was the dominant United States film manufacturing company in the early years of film.

Because it was Edison's home, New Jersey contributed many of the subjects and locations for early films. In the beginning people were astonished by the mere fact that pictures moved, so most early films involved nothing more elaborate than the surf breaking on the beach or people dancing. Audiences soon tired of the novelty, however, and began demanding more sophisticated films. Among the first films to employ a story line were Edison's *A Morning Alarm, Starting for the Fire,* and *Fighting a Fire* (1896). These three short films were actually one long movie of the Newark Fire Department doing the things described in the titles. Because of their narrative structure, the films could be shown independently or in sequence. New Jersey also supplied the location for Edison's famous *Great Train Robbery* (1903), which was shot on location in the Essex County Park reservation and on the Erie and Lackawanna Railroad near the Passaic River.

Still, audiences were not satisfied. Early movies were primarily made by businessmen who often didn't vary scenery, story elements, or camera angles from one film to another. In fact, movies became such a turnoff that theater owners showed them only at the end of vaudeville programs, knowing that the appearance of a film would make the audience leave. Obviously, more variety in a movie's characters, plot, and scenery was needed. The day that filmmakers realized this was the day that New Jersey's Golden Age of Movies truly began.

Although the first films were shot indoors, moviemakers quickly realized the advantages of outdoor locations. The use of natural light and the ability to utilize various backgrounds, plus the availability of ready-made props, made outside filming superior to inside shooting. Freed from the confines of the studio, movie plots became more diverse, mixing drama, comedy, and romance all within a single film. Stories were no longer written by businessmen, camera operators, and directors, but by professional writers, who knew how to create coherent narratives.

New York City, which provided most of the actors and movie-making capital, was initially the most popular source for outdoor locations. The city's gritty streets became the source of reels of urban dramas.

The problem was that those same gritty streets were not very helpful when making westerns, Civil War films, sea stories, or numerous other types of pictures. Although early audiences were unsophisticated, it's doubtful they could be convinced they were watching two cowboys shoot it out on the open range while a streetcar was rumbling past in the background. Filmmakers began searching for scenic vistas, open fields, and sparsely populated towns; they found it all in New Jersey.

New Jersey had everything the movies needed: beaches, mountains, farms, woods, and fields. In particular, the northern part of the state presented filmmakers with a smorgasbord of locations: it offered not only sprawling urban centers like Jersey City and Newark but also miles of unspoiled countryside, and plenty of sparsely inhabited towns, all within a relatively short distance of each other. (In 1910, the population of Jersey City was 267,779; just a few miles to the north and east, Fort Lee had just 4,472 people, while Leonia contained barely 1,500.) Movie crews began packing up their cameras and casts and heading across the Hudson.

Before long, it seemed as though you couldn't turn around in New Jersey without bumping into a movie crew. In those simpler times, shooting a film didn't require a small army of equipment and people. Often the director, cameraman, and crew would cruise around in cars until they found a location that suited their storyline. Everyone would pile out, the director would position the single camera, the cast would get a few perfunctory instructions, and movie magic would begin.

Long before the star system ruled Hollywood, the first real "stars" of the silver screen were New Jersey towns and locales. Asbury Park, High Bridge,

Bayonne, Edgewater, Sea Bright, North Bergen, New Brunswick, Linden, and scores of other towns were used in everything from slapstick comedies to tear-jerking melodramas. Actors and actresses soon became intimately familiar with the New Jersey countryside. Actress Linda Arvidson, later to become the first wife of pioneer director D. W. Griffith, said that she was "made love to on every rock and boulder for twenty miles up and down the Hudson." In fact, the Palisades region was used so often in films that in 1910, a writer in the *Dramatic Mirror* complained about the repeated use of "Jersey scenery" in the movies.

Of all the New Jersey locations used, no place topped Fort Lee. For an all-too-brief time, the tiny town along the Palisades was the cinematic capital of the world.

It's fitting that both Fort Lee and the movies were attracted to each other, for each was just taking its first tentative steps at the beginning of the twentieth century. The town, originally named Fort Constitution but changed to honor Revolutionary War general Charles Lee, was incorporated on March 29, 1904, just as the movies were coming into their own as public entertainment.

Fort Lee had several advantages for film companies. It was just across the Hudson from New York City, and it was built up enough to provide facilities such as restaurants and hotels that the movie companies needed, but still largely rural and thus ideal for filming many different types of pictures. Most important, it had Coytesville.

Located in the northern part of Fort Lee, the Coytesville section looked exactly like a prairie town in the Old West. It had dirt roads, wooden frame buildings, and neither telephone nor telegraph wires. Best of all, it had Rambo's Roadhouse, which looked so much like a western saloon that one expected to see Wyatt Earp or Wild Bill Hickock come ambling out the front door any moment. Scores of cowboys were destined to come out of Rambo's, step onto the wooden front porch, hitch their fingers in their gunbelts, and walk out to the dirt street for a shoot-out.

Although Coytesville might not appear in Fort Lee's civic brochure, it delighted filmmakers. They were scouting near and far for authentic-looking western locations, and here was one practically in their backyard. And not only horse operas could be filmed in Fort Lee; the easy accessibility of forests, meadows, and the towering Palisades cliffs meant that the town could be virtually anything the director wanted it to be.

A trip to Fort Lee from New York City was relatively simple. Film people took either the train or subway to 125th Street, where they caught the ferry for the trip across the Hudson. Once in New Jersey, either a trolley or horse-drawn buggy would take them to that day's location.

Fort Lee had gotten a small taste of movie life in 1909, when Edwin S. Porter shot *Rescued from the Eagle's Nest* on the sheer cliffs of the nearby Palisades. The star of that adventure film was a young man named David Wark (D. W.) Griffith, who would soon make his mark on the young industry not as an actor, but as a director.

A short time later, when Griffith became the principal director at the American Mutoscope and Biograph Company, he remembered Fort Lee. Soon he was routinely bringing his cast and crew over from the city to make *The Man and the Woman, The Fatal Hour, Balked at the Altar, The Curtain Pole, A Tragic Love, Lucky Jim,* and dozens of other films.

Always a pioneer, by 1912 Griffith had moved on to California. However, he had blazed a trail to Fort Lee that others were quick to follow. Champion Studio, which specialized in westerns, had already settled in Coytesville in 1910. Now others came to town: Eclair (a French film company), Peerless, Willat, Universal, Paragon, Solax, and Lincoln all built studio facilities in Fort Lee.

Suddenly, sleepy little Fort Lee found itself in the spotlight. It took to its new role of film capital with gusto.

Virtually everything in the town was available for rent to the film companies, from a sturdy oak on someone's property that would make a good hanging tree for western ne'er-do-wells to an entire home. (Everything means *everything*—as evidenced by the youngster who would greet film people with the question, "Hey, you wanna rent me mudder?") The town boomed as hotels, restaurants, garages, blacksmiths, stables, and just about every other business benefited from the needs of the movie companies.

Most importantly, the emergence of this new industry in Fort Lee meant jobs, and plenty of them. It's estimated that one-third of the town's population was employed by the studios in building sets, carrying scenery, painting props, and doing other odd jobs, while another third were extras. Wages were excellent; even the lowest-paid studio employee averaged between $100 and $150 per week—a veritable fortune during those times of low taxation and an even lower cost of living.

The studios' needs were endless. Most averaged fifty-two pictures a year, and it wasn't uncommon to have several different film companies working within plain sight of each other. In one instance, crews from the Biograph and Reliance studios were shooting on opposite sides of the same fence. The activities of the studios might be as simple as renting a farmer's pasture for a day or as complicated as constructing an entire German town and then destroying it. (This was done, on the site of present day Fort Lee High School, for the film *The Kaiser: The Beast of Berlin*.)

The most in-demand spot of all was Rambo's. The bottom floor appeared as a saloon, hotel, sheriff's office, and just about any other type of building that heard the jingle of a cowpoke's spurs in the Old West. Actors and actresses often dressed and put on makeup in the second-floor rooms. Behind the building was a cistern with a pump that performers used to clean off their makeup at day's end. Fort Lee residents looking for work as extras would congregate at Rambo's and wait for the film companies to arrive, hoping to be noticed.

Rambo's also became a gathering place for everyone connected with the movies. The hotel had a hundred-foot grape arbor on one side, and under this it placed a long plank table, with benches on both sides, to feed the hungry filmmakers. Although Rambo's menu never varied—ham and eggs, bread and butter, coffee, and homemade apple pie—everyone ate with the huge appetite that trekking around the New Jersey countryside all day provided. After dinner, everyone would sit around the long table trading stories and gossiping until it was time to either go back to work or go home.

With so many films in production simultaneously, Fort Lee became like some bizarre Disneyland, where a walk on the street could bring you face to face with an Indian, a cowboy, a sailor, a knight, a soldier, a southern belle, and dozens of other characters. In the evening, when darkness brought filming to a halt, many actors went in full makeup to parties and dinners at the homes of local residents.

Unfortunately, time has erased the names of most of those who made movies in Fort Lee. How many except diehard film buffs recognize the names Mable Normand, Florence Lawrence, Irene Castle, Alice Brady, and Stuart Holmes? All were stars during the early days of movies—all are largely forgotten today.

A few names have survived throughout the years. Mary Pickford, "America's Sweetheart," made over a dozen films in New Jersey, while Douglas Fairbanks shot four films there. Lionel and Ethel Barrymore also made a handful of films in the Garden State, as did Lillian Gish. On the other side of the camera, famous directors who plied their trade in New Jersey included D. W. Griffith (over eighty films, made mainly in the Fort Lee area), Raoul Walsh, and Mack Sennett.

New Jersey also gave rise to some modern film empires. William Fox (20th Century Fox) and Lewis Selznick (father of David O. Selznick, who made *Gone With the Wind*) both got their start in Fort Lee. Fort Lee was also home to the remarkable Alice Guy Blache, who, through her Solax Studio, was the first female film director and studio executive.

Of all the interesting people who made movies in Fort Lee, none is more fascinating than Alice Guy Blache. In an era when women were expected to be seen and not heard, Blache was the guiding creative and business force behind Fort Lee's Solax Studios.

Alice Guy began her filmmaking career in France in the 1890s, where she acted in and directed numerous pictures for the Gaumont Company. She married Herbert Blache in 1907 and came to the United States, where she became involved in the fledgling film industry. In 1910 Alice Blache, her husband, and a partner founded the Solax Company in Flushing, New York. Two years later the Blaches built a production facility in Fort Lee at a cost of $100,000 (an enormous sum for that time).

Although both husband and wife were equal partners in Solax, Herbert Blache was still involved with Gaumont, so many of the business and artistic decisions fell to his wife. Widely recognized as the first female director in the history of film as well as the first person actually to call herself a "director," she helmed many of the Solax productions, which largely consisted of one- and two-reel comedies and adventure films. Even those pictures that she did not direct were under her artistic control, making her the dominant figure at Solax and the first female studio executive in history. Alice Blache was involved in practically every aspect of the Solax films, from writing the story to selecting the props. Because of her astute business instincts and artistic ability, she commanded great respect among the hardheaded businessmen who ran the film companies.

But while she campaigned vigorously to break the domestic shackles that bound most women back then, ultimately Alice Guy Blache could not escape those confinements herself. The breakup of her marriage deprived her of the masculine presence needed to gain admittance into the boy's club of American movie making, and she found herself isolated from the film community. Eventually she retired to France.

Of all those who achieved stardom in Fort Lee, however, none was more colorful (or more unusual) than Theda Bara. She burst to prominence in 1914 in William Fox's *A Fool There Was*, playing a "vamp" (short for vampire, and meaning a woman who sucked the life out of men). Scenes of her gloating over the fallen body of her male victim caused a sensation; the word "vamp" entered the popular lexicon, and Bara became an overnight success.

Sensing an opportunity, Fox threw his formidable publicity machine behind Bara. The press was swamped with accounts about how pleasant little Theodosia Goodman (Bara's real name) from Cincinnati was the most vile temptress in history, how no man could resist her, and how her lips burned like fire when kissed. Yarns were woven about her mysterious past as an exotic Arabian princess. Over a five-year period, Bara starred in more than three dozen pictures, many of them reprising her vamp characterization. By 1919 the public, growing either tired or bored, had turned its back on Bara, but she had been one of the first of a breed quite common today: the publicity-produced celebrity.

Another silent film star from the Fort Lee era, Pearl White, left us an even more enduring phrase than "vamp." In 1914, White made the Pathé Studio serial *The Perils of Pauline*, which featured the title character getting into all manner of precarious situations. Indoor scenes were filmed at Pathé's studio on Congress Street in Jersey City, and outdoor sequences were shot throughout the area (including on a hill behind Christ Hospital in Elizabeth).

The scene that grabbed the public's attention was shot on the Palisades cliffs near Fort Lee. It showed the lovely Pauline once again in danger, this time dangling from the cliffs, holding onto nothing more than a spindly tree jutting out from the rocks, while the Hudson rushed by below. The public was so enamored with that scene that people began calling such situations "cliff-hangers," and the term has remained in use to the present day.

Celebrities often went to Fort Lee to see what all the fuss was about, and sometimes to make a film of their own. Harry Houdini arrived in town to make *The Man from Beyond,* a film about, remarkably enough, an escape artist. Baseball slugger Babe Ruth also came to Fort Lee to star in a picture called *Babe Comes Home*, which had—surprise—a baseball plot.

So the years passed in Fort Lee, and the rest of New Jersey: women hanging off cliffs, shootouts in the street, heroes and villains fighting to the death, and tearful embraces between long-lost lovers. It was a time when the distinction between fact and fiction blurred, and sometimes even merged, such as when the citizens of one New Jersey town thought that the bank holdup being filmed was real and began firing actual bullets at the "robbers."

Exciting, unpredictable times indeed. Yet by 1919, they were just about over. Many of the Fort Lee studios had either closed or were in the process of shutting down and heading west. By 1925, the once-burgeoning film industry in Fort Lee—and the rest of New Jersey—was virtually extinct. A number of different factors had combined to kill the golden movie goose.

The first occurred in 1913, when Cecil B. DeMille made *The Squaw Man* in a tiny California town called Hollywood. To his fellow producers back east, DeMille sent enthusiastic reports of long, warm days full of sunshine. Griffith was also firmly ensconced in California, and he probably added to the praises that the Golden State's temperate climate was receiving. In New Jersey, filmmakers who were struggling with frigid winters (Linda Arvidson would remember: "[In winter] our makeup would be frozen, and the dreary, cold damp rooms in the country hotels made us shivery and miserable") and humid summers must have read these reports with envy, and interest.

Not just makeup and shooting schedules affected by the weather. Forced to shoot in the studio during the winter, directors had to turn up the intensity of indoor lights. The heat generated, combined with the extraordinarily flammable silver nitrate film stock, made fire a constant danger. (This was one of the causes of a fire in 1914 that virtually destroyed the Eclair studio.)

Transportation was also influenced by nature's unpredictability. Many filmmakers depended on the Edgewater ferry to get back and forth across the Hudson, but a storm or harsh weather meant that the boat ran on an irregular schedule—if it ran at all. More than once film companies got stuck on either side of the river because the water was too churned up to allow the ferry to operate.

"It was the rotten New Jersey weather that killed the movie business in Fort Lee," declared former movie stuntman Gustav Nelson in 1961.

On top of the weather, filmmakers in New Jersey also had to deal with another problem: the Edison company and its business allies.

Virtually from the beginning of motion pictures, the Edison company had sought to control the domestic film industry through its patents. For ten years Edison fought bitter court battles with its U.S. competitors (mainly the American Mutoscope and Biograph Company) over patent infringement. After losing several court decisions, the Edison company changed tactics. In 1908 it was the guiding force behind the formation of an association with the other major filmmaking companies called the Motion Picture Patents Company (MPPC). Through various schemes, such as charging exhibitors a weekly two-dollar licensing fee in order to show films and setting a strict production schedule, the Motion Picture Patents Company sought to control the entire motion picture industry.

Today we would call the MPPC a monopoly. Back then the word was "trust," but it meant the same thing. Some filmmakers went along with the trust; others, calling themselves "independents," resisted, and continued to make movies in defiance of the MPPC. In response, the trust sent out detectives to enforce its edicts—and their roughhouse methods didn't include politely asking the independents to stop.

The result was much like a Mack Sennett comedy. An independent company would be filming somewhere, when word would come that trust detectives were prowling around the area. The cameraman would pick up the camera and dash away, leaving cast and crew innocently milling about in full costume and makeup, as if that was the sort of thing they did every day just for the fun of it. After a period of time, the company would reunite with the cameraman and filming would begin again, until the next time that the trust detectives approached, when the whole process would be repeated.

In the 1967 book *One Reel a Week,* pioneering cameramen Fred J. Balshofer described the difficulties of working with one eye always on the lookout for trouble:

> The towns of Fort Lee and Coytesville were so small it was a cinch for McCoy [the main trust detective] and his added assistants to hound us. McCoy and his cohorts appeared every place we went to photograph around Coytesville. Some in our company would spot one of the spies approaching and give me the signal. I folded the legs of the tripod, put the camera over my shoulder, and took off down the road or into the woods. . . . The continued nuisance had the effect of making it impossible to work since all of us had become too jittery to concentrate.

It would be difficult to make a cake, much less a movie, under these circumstances. As filmmakers searched for ways to escape the trust's odious enforcers, California gestured once again. Not only was it three thousand miles away from the trust, it was larger, and full of unknown towns. A film company could vanish in the state's wide-open spaces and work unimpeded. As Balshofer said: "Los Angeles with its mild climate and sunshine beckoned as an escape both from the winter months of the East as well as the ever-present Patents Company detectives."

Already reeling from the twin evils of poor weather and the trust company methods, the New Jersey film industry was dealt a death blow by World War I. Government rationing deprived the studios of coal, which they desperately needed to heat their large, drafty buildings.

Finally, it all became too much; the exodus from New Jersey (and in particular Fort Lee) to California began.

Of course, no one in New Jersey could know that trickling away to California was an industry whose glamour and economic power would one day captivate the world. There were no government commissions or politicians ready to bestow tax breaks on industries to keep them from leaving. Indeed, movie people were frowned upon back then as low-class entertainers, and perhaps many people in Fort Lee and throughout New Jersey were glad to see the last of the performers and their industry, gaudy makeup, extravagant costumes, silly play acting, and all,

By 1925 the film industry had virtually vanished from New Jersey. Fort Lee caught its breath and settled down to become a thriving middle-class town. Changes came, of course; Coytesville could no more remain like a town in the Old West than Dodge City could remain a cowboy town waiting for the return of Wyatt Earp. Soon the streets were paved, telephone and electrical wires were strung from newly erected poles, and newer, more modern buildings were constructed in the once-popular cowboy haven. Even Rambo's changed, although much later than the rest of the area. Progress spread its concrete and steel fingers throughout Fort Lee, irrevocably altering the town and wiping away the movie memories. The open fields where Indians, cowboys, knights, soldiers, and lovers had cavorted before the camera became the approach to the George Washington Bridge.

"Thus passeth the glory of the world," proclaimed the *New York Herald Tribune* of Sunday, October 26, 1947, underneath a picture of an abandoned, dilapidated Fort Lee film studio. The newspaper might well have added: "And never to return this way again."

It's the Natural Thing to Do

So far, every chapter of this book has exploded the myth that New Jersey is nothing more than macadamized highways and superfund sites. However, there are always a few holdouts who cling to their repudiated beliefs until the bitter end.

For them, this chapter is the bitter end. This is the story of the "natural" New Jersey—places like the Forsythe Refuge near Atlantic City and Great Swamp near Morristown, where nature has not been paved or cemented over and has instead been allowed to flourish in all its glory. This chapter is the story of trees, flowers, animals, insects, and a host of other things having nothing to do with roadways and rest stops. (And this doesn't even include the Pinelands, which is unique and deserves its own chapter.) From the seashore to the mountains, and everywhere else in between, the "natural" New Jersey shines like one of nature's brightest jewels—and all anyone has to do to find it is pull off the highway.

From numerous points in the Edwin S. Forsythe National Wildlife Refuge in Oceanville, you can look up and see the tall buildings and casino hotels of Atlantic City looming on the horizon. This is New Jersey's version of the Odd Couple: a major wildlife refuge that shuns development coexisting next to an urbanized metropolis that entertains millions of visitors each year.

The preserve was originally established in 1939 as the Brigantine National Wildlife Refuge. A second section, Barnegat, was founded in 1967. The two were combined under the Forsythe name in 1984, in honor of the late Congressman Edwin B. Forsythe, a staunch friend of the refuge.

More than two hundred thousand people per year, many of them dedicated bird watchers, journey to Forsythe's Brigantine Division, which is one

Sea gull at Forsythe wildlife refuge, showing
how close it is to Atlantic City.

of the most heavily visited wildlife refuges in the United States. (Everyone
visits Brigantine because that's where the public-use facilities are located.)

Almost 90 percent of the Forsythe Refuge (Brigantine Division from
here on, unless otherwise noted) is tidal salt meadow and marsh, inter-
spersed with shallow coves and bays, which serve as resting and feeding
habitat for water birds. Fish and shellfish use the calm tidal waters as nurs-
eries, and also for spawning and feeding.

The refuge is located directly on one of the Atlantic Flyway's most active
flight paths. More than 275 species of birds frequent the 24,000-acre natural area during the migration season. Among these are a variety of ducks,
geese, sandpipers, egrets, and bitterns.

Of all birds, herons are particularly well represented at Forsythe; nearly
a dozen species nest at the refuge. Snow geese and the majestic glossy ibis

Birds at Forsythe.

are other birds that are frequently found there. Forsythe also has, at times, approximately 90 percent of the Atlantic population of brant, a small, dark goose whose extremely fussy eating habits limit it to a diet of just a few plants. (Brant are so picky that when a blight in the 1930s decimated its favorite food, eel grass, the population nearly died out due to starvation.)

During the migratory seasons, Forsythe practically overflows with birds. Tens of thousands of ducks, geese, wading birds, and shorebirds concentrate at Forsythe during these periods, stopping to feed and rest before resuming their journey. It's not uncommon during migratory periods to see massive squadrons of shorebirds flying in formation and practically blotting out the sun. When these groups of birds land en masse in one of the tidal pools, the roar they make upon hitting the water is like that of a colossal cannon being fired.

Once they arrive at Forsythe, some birds find that they like it so much that they don't want to leave. Black ducks remain there throughout the summer to nest and raise their young. If the weather permits, Atlantic brant and black ducks also overwinter at Forsythe.

The refuge plays an important part in providing undisturbed nesting habitats for several endangered and threatened species. Special nesting platforms have been erected for peregrine falcons and ospreys. Bald eagles are also seen at the refuge each year.

Although there are a few footpaths through the woods, the best opportunities for viewing birds and wildlife at Forsythe occur along the eight-mile Wildlife Drive. This one-way road loops around the refuge and is wide enough to allow ample space for pulling over to the side of the road whenever desired. (This becomes particularly handy during gosling and duckling seasons, when the parents and their young think nothing of marching right across the road, often stopping traffic—and providing priceless photo opportunities.)

More than six thousand acres of the refuge are designated as a wilderness area, including two of the few remaining undeveloped barrier beaches in

More birds at Forsythe.

New Jersey. This region provides essential nesting and feeding habitat for the rare piping plover, black skimmer, and least tern. The natural habitats of these species have been decimated by human development and increased recreational use of the beaches. The Forsythe Refuge is one of the last places where the birds are guaranteed unimpeded use of beaches.

Even though Forsythe is largely wetlands, there are approximately three thousand acres of woodlands there as well. These contain songbirds, deer, turtles, raccoons, rabbits, muskrats, skunks, and other animals. Even the rare Pine Barrens tree frog sometimes hops over for a visit.

Like people, the Forsythe Refuge responds to the seasons. The natural ebb and flow of light and temperature throughout the year dictate the amount of wildlife activity at the refuge. During the depths of winter, when cold and snow lie heavy on the earth, the refuge is at its most quiet. With the coming of spring and the rebirth of the natural world, Forsythe explodes into life; waterfowl in particular are plentiful during this time, as thousands of birds stop there temporarily on their way to nesting sites farther north. Summer finds life at the refuge again slowing down, although these are usually the months of peak duckling activity. (It's also the time of peak insect activity.) August is when the shorebirds reverse their springtime migration, responding not to clock or calendar but to ancient instincts that tell them that summer's warmth will soon be gone. The autumn brings another spectacular array of birds to Forsythe on their long journey south; more than one hundred thousand ducks and geese have been known to gather in the pools at Forsythe at one time, frolicking in the water like swimmers out for one final fling on Labor Day.

Yet, even as the Forsythe Refuge once again falls under the dreamy spell of winter, it's comforting to know that within a few short months, the skies will once again be filled with birds, signaling yet another spring and another season of renewal at the Forsythe Refuge for all nature's creatures—including us humans.

Despite the popularity of the Forsythe Refuge among the wing-and-feather set, it isn't the only spot in New Jersey that migratory shorebirds frequent on their long journey northward. Each spring, from early May through the first week of June, more than one million shorebirds stop for rest and relaxation along New Jersey's "other coast"—the Delaware Bay.

The migration of shorebirds every spring from Brazil, Argentina, and other South American countries to the far north, with a stopover in New Jersey, is one of nature's most reliable barometers. The concentration of birds along the Delaware Bay coast is the second-largest gathering of shorebirds in the country. (Surprisingly, the largest migration occurs in a wetlands section of landlocked Kansas.)

The birds are migrating primarily from South America to their nesting grounds on the Arctic Bay, a trip of about seven thousand miles. The Delaware Bay coastline is a halfway point on their flight, and nearly two dozen species have chosen the beaches there as the perfect place to rest from their arduous journey.

The Delaware Bay beaches that the shorebirds frequent bear little resemblance to those along New Jersey's ocean. To the birds, however, these small, rocky beaches are every bit as inviting as their Atlantic Coast counterparts; without them, the birds would die.

Many birds fly nonstop from their winter homes in the South straight to the Delaware Bay, a distance of about four thousand miles. Although, like long-distance runners, the birds fuel up before they start, by the time they reach New Jersey the exhausted creatures have hit the wall. Many of the birds lose up to 50 percent of their total body weight during the first part of their flight.

What attracts the shorebirds to the Delaware Bay coastline, besides the opportunity for a little R&R, is something near and dear to every traveler's heart: food. For the shorebirds this means horseshoe crab eggs, a particularly tasty dish that makes their beaks water.

The Delaware Bay hosts the largest concentration of spawning horseshoe crabs along the Atlantic Coast of North America. Although the crabs begin spawning in April and don't stop until the summer is nearly over, May is their peak month for egg laying. By a happy coincidence (unless you're a mama horseshoe crab, that is), this is also the time of peak shorebird activity. During these weeks, horseshoe crabs crawl up onto the beach by the thousands to lay their eggs, sometimes packing the sand so tightly that a person could literally walk on their shells and never touch the ground. After laying their eggs in the sand—350 tons worth, according to some estimates—the crabs head back to the bay. It's a good thing the crabs don't linger to see the results of their labors: water and wave action, and activity by other crabs, unearths many of the eggs, leaving them to be eaten by the ravenous birds.

Thanks to the food and the rest, by the time the birds are ready to resume their trip they have undergone a remarkable transformation. The sleek and rested creatures that depart from the Delaware Bay bear little resemblance to the worn-out, half-starved scarecrows that initially arrived.

After leaving New Jersey, most of the birds go straight to their nesting grounds in the Canadian and Arctic tundra, where they remain for about one month. In that short time they have to establish territories, find mates (obviously, long courtships are out), and start nesting. There's neither time nor the resources to feed—another reason why their stopover at the Delaware Bay is so important to the birds.

The shorebirds stay at the nesting ground just long enough to mate. A few days after their eggs hatch, the adults begin the return trip south, leaving their offspring to fend for themselves. (Since they take a different route south, however, the birds don't stop at the Delaware Bay on the way back.) Over the next few weeks, the baby birds mature, learn to fly and feed, and then take off after their parents, using nothing more than instinct to guide them seven thousand miles.

Clearly, the Delaware Bay beaches play a critical role in the shorebird's life cycle. While residential development on these lands isn't likely, thanks to severe erosion and general inhospitality, there is always the chance that commercial use could someday deprive the shorebirds of one of the few natural areas left on their flight path.

To forestall this, various state and federal agencies, as well as wildlife and conservation groups, have been acquiring this land and managing it for the use of shorebirds and other animals. Today, hundreds of thousands of acres of public land are administered by five agencies along Delaware Bay. Like an oasis in the desert, the rocky beaches of New Jersey's Delaware Bay will. it's to be hoped, forever offer food and rest to the huge flocks of shorebirds that depend on them for their very lives.

The headline on the front page of the December 3, 1959, *Newark Evening News* said it all: "Jetport in Morris Country." In the days that followed, as stunned local residents read about the massive new facility planned by the Port of New York Authority, they discovered that not only were they about to gain a new airport but they were also going to lose an old friend: the Great Swamp.

Born out of the dying gasps of the Wisconsin glaciation some twenty-five thousand years ago, the Great Swamp was (in 1959) approximately four thousand acres of swamp woodland, hardwood ridges, cattail marsh, and grassland. Populated by beaver, foxes, turtles, snakes, and dozens of varieties of fish and birds, the swamp was, like the Pinelands farther south, a New Jersey anomaly: an area of unspoiled natural beauty harkening back thousands of years, and in this case just twenty-five miles from humanity's ultimate monument to concrete civilization—New York City. Thanks to the circumstances of its birth, the Great Swamp for years had been able to survive the urban sprawl that had spread outward from the New York metropolitan area, engulfing farmland and small villages alike. Whether its luck would hold in the face of the Port Authority proposal, however, was anybody's guess.

Thousands of years ago, the massive Wisconsin Glacier moved across northern New Jersey like an invincible army of ice, crushing whatever soil and vegetation it encountered. Then, approximately five thousand years ago, the mighty glacier began to melt and retreat northward. The water flowed into a natural basin surrounded by the Watchung Mountains to form what geologists call Lake Passaic. This ancient lake was estimated to be from 160 to 240 feet deep and 30 miles long by 10 miles wide. After another few thousand years had passed, Lake Passaic began to empty slowly into the Passaic River. Eventually the entire lake drained away, except for some low-lying areas, one of which was the Great Swamp.

When the Europeans arrived in North America and began to explore the region that would someday be called New Jersey, they found the Lenni-Lenape or Delaware Indians living in and around the Great Swamp. Besides animals for food and clothing, the Great Swamp provided the Native Americans with many items that they used in everyday life, such as berries, the juice of which was used to make colored dyes; grasses for covering, roofing, and sweeping; and bird feathers for ornamental and ceremonial jewelry.

On August 13, 1708, British investors purchased thirty thousand acres (about eighteen square miles) from the Delaware Indians. The area included the Great Swamp and cost the British thirty pounds sterling in cash, as well as ten blankets, fifteen kettles, twenty axes, twenty hoes, four pistols, one hundred barrels of lead, twenty shirts, one hundred knives, and other assorted goods.

The Delawares had been content to take what the Great Swamp had been willing to give them. The Europeans, as well as the American settlers who followed them to the area, tried to bend the Great Swamp to their will, with predictable results: most attempts at farming failed because of the mushy ground, while attempts to exploit the forests resulted in excessive chopping down of trees, which exacerbated the problem of excess water. As people abandoned their efforts to make the Great Swamp into something that it could never be, the land reverted to its former appearance: The woods returned to the uplands, while the low areas became even more swampy. As the years rolled by, and bustling communities like Morristown, Summit, and Madison sprang up all around it, the Great Swamp remained a marshy, tree-filled expanse more suited for animals than people.

All this changed, however, with the Port Authority's jetport proposal. To be fair, it wasn't as if the authority suddenly dreamed up the idea to destroy Great Swamp on a whim. Armed with statistical projections that showed almost twice as many passengers and more than twice the cargo tonnage passing through the region's four airports (Idlewild [now John F. Kennedy], LaGuardia, Newark, and Teterboro) in 1965 as had passed through in 1958—and even more in the 1970s and 1980s—the agency saw a clear need to head off overwhelming congestion. After evaluating fifteen sites for a possible new airport, the Port Authority concluded that only the Great Swamp met all the requirements: "There is no other practicable site that would meet the criteria of an airport that the people of northern New Jersey and the metropolitan region must have," said the Port Authority in a report outlining its plans.

Historically, the Port Authority had always gotten its way with proposals such as the one they were now suggesting. This time, however, a group of residents took umbrage at the idea of an airport being dropped right into the middle of peaceful and bucolic Morris County, destroying the Great Swamp in the bargain. They quickly united to fight the proposal.

Thus began what has become an old story today but at the time was a very new tale indeed: the saga of the environment versus the economy. Proponents of the jetport argued that it would bring jobs and business opportunities to the area and create a virtual economic gold mine out of land that, in the case of the Great Swamp, was lying around useless. Opponents countered that the land wasn't useless: it was home to scores of animals, fish, birds, and plants. Furthermore, the proposed airport would wipe out seven hundred homes, as well as churches, schools, and small businesses, and completely transform the character of the region from small-town sleepy to big-city bustling.

For several years the two sides fought it out in New Jersey's own version of David and Goliath: the powerful Port Authority, with its vast wealth and political influence, against a citizen's group of environmentalists, with their coffee klatches and neighborhood meetings. As the pendulum swung to and fro—sometimes the Port Authority would seem on the verge of gaining the necessary approvals, and sometimes the citizen's groups would seem to be riding an overwhelming tide of public support—the fate of the Great Swamp hung in the balance. It had survived thousands of years of natural forces, but could it survive humanity?

The answer was yes. The public pressure and attention focused on the Great Swamp's unique environmental characteristics were too much for the Port Authority to overcome. The Great Swamp Committee of the North American Wildlife Foundation raised more than $1 million to buy over 3,000 acres of land, which were then donated to the U.S. Department of the Interior for a Great Swamp Wildlife Refuge. More than 6,000 private citizens and 422 organizations representing 286 towns and 29 states contributed to the fight to save Great Swamp from extinction. On May 29, 1964, at a ceremony attended by U.S. Secretary of the Interior Stewart Udall, the Great Swamp was officially dedicated as a national wildlife preserve. Four years later, on September 30, 1968, President Lyndon Johnson signed a bill that made the Great Swamp the first wilderness area in the National Wildlife Refuge System. People power had won.

Today, thanks to additional land acquisitions, the Great Swamp National Wildlife Refuge totals over 7,000 acres. More than 220 species of birds, dozens of mammals, and a large variety of reptiles, amphibians, and fish call the refuge home. Animals found at Great Swamp run the gamut from common creatures like the white-tailed deer and rabbits to the rare blue-spotted salamander and bog turtle. Wood ducks, which some call our most beautiful waterfowl, thrive at Great Swamp and produce more than 4,000 ducklings every year. The area also contains a fascinating variety of botanical species, such as ferns, mosses, wild lilies, orchids, and primroses.

A visit to Great Swamp is very different from a visit to most other natural areas. The purpose of the federal Wilderness Act is to let "an area of undeveloped federal land, retain its primeval character and influence . . . where the earth and its community of life are untrammeled by man." Here, in these "outdoor laboratories," the action and evolution of natural life can be studied and observed without the heavy-footed intrusion of humanity. Thus at Great Swamp there are no picnic areas, playgrounds, barbecue grills, or any of the other conveniences found at a park or recreation area. Human involvement is meant to be kept at a minimum.

There are, however, eight miles of hiking trails, winding through pictur-esque, serene landscapes that seem to have come just off an artist's brush. Alone on a path, with just the sky overhead, the trees alongside, and the faint song of a distant bird for company, it's easy to understand why Henry David Thoreau once said: "I enter a swamp as a sacred place [here] there is the strength, the marrow of nature." He could easily have been talking about Great Swamp.

As county parks go, it's pretty large—323 acres of green grass and rolling terrain, a lake, open fields for sports, a fitness trail, bicycling, tennis courts, and more. However, what's particularly striking about Ocean County Park in Lakewood is the quantity of trees it contains. The entrance road off Route 88 is tree-shrouded; hundreds of trees of all different types are scattered all over, like the dense medieval forests seen in Robin Hood movies. It's so unlike the surrounding landscape that it only makes sense when you discover that Ocean County Park was once the vacation home of John D. Rockefeller.

At the turn of the twentieth century, Lakewood was an exclusive winter resort for the high and mighty. It was first discovered in the winter of 1879 by New York City banker Charles Kimball, whose health greatly improved while he was there. He attributed it to the area's pine-scented air, which he believed to be good for the lungs. He hatched the idea of Lakewood be-coming a ritzy winter resort, and before you could say "polo pony" the rich and powerful in the United States were flocking to this small New Jersey town. In the winter the town's population climbed from around twenty-five hundred to nearly seven thousand as society folk drove their luxurious carriages through the streets, danced cotillions, rode to hounds, hosted tea parties for each other, and in general acted like every rich person cliché of that white-gloved era.

No one liked Lakewood better than John D. Rockefeller, who said that Lakewood had "delicious" air. He had become addicted to playing golf and saw in Lakewood a place where he could golf nearly year-round. In 1901 he began buying property in Lakewood, paying what was for him chump change—$87,532—for land in several different locations.

On June 6, 1902, Rockefeller paid $12,500 for the Ocean County Hunt and Country Club property. The group had decided to merge with another

The flag marks the location of John D. Rockefeller's
house in Ocean County Park.

club, and as a result it gave up its original clubhouse. For Rockefeller, this
was perfect; the building was surrounded by a golf course, which was itself
surrounded by seventy-five acres of property covered with spruce, fir, pine,
and hemlock trees. It was a golfer's dream come true.

Golf House—as Rockefeller rechristened the clubhouse—was a large,
three-story building with striped awnings and a glass-enclosed front porch.
There were often sheep contentedly munching away on the front lawn. Besides adding acreage to the estate, Rockefeller planted thousands of trees—
many of which are still there today and in full maturity.

Whether it was the "delicious" air, something in Lakewood agreed with
Rockefeller. "I feel better now than I have in years," he said in 1903.

Rockefeller frequented Lakewood, and Golf House, in the spring and fall
right up until his death. He made occasional renovations to the property,

such as in 1925 when he put an iron fence around it. In 1937 Rockefeller died at the age of ninety-seven, and three years later his son turned the property over to Ocean County, which turned the land into a public park. Golf House itself remained standing until 1966, a slowly deteriorating, elegant yet eerie reminder of the property's former glory days that kids used to sneak into through its basement windows. Today only a flagpole and plaque mark the location.

Ocean County Park offers a variety of outdoor activities. It is a jewel in the crown of the county's park system and contains plenty of green lawns just for spreading out a blanket and reading, listening to music, tossing around the old pigskin, or lying back, relaxing . . . and thinking that you never imagined in your lifetime that you'd be hanging around the same place as John D. Rockefeller.

Like lemmings to the sea, most New Jerseyans sooner or later make a pilgrimage to High Point State Park. This, as the name suggests, is the highest point in the state—1,803 feet above sea level. When you add to that a 220-foot-tall obelisk that you can climb to get even higher, you can see that when people say that they're "looking down" on New Jersey from here, they mean it in the most literal sense!

The history of High Point State Park illustrates land-use planning at its finest. Because the land is tucked away in the northwest corner of New Jersey, it remained isolated and untouched for centuries. The only building project of consequence in the area was the construction in 1888 of High Point Inn near the shore of Lake Marcia.

However, the land probably wouldn't have stayed that way forever had it not been for the Kuser family of Bernardsville, who bought much of the property in 1909. Fourteen years later, Colonel Anthony Kuser and his wife donated ten thousand acres to the state so that the land would be preserved for wildlife protection, bird watching, and water conservation.

Thanks to the Kusers' foresight, today we can enjoy High Point State Park in all its natural splendor. The first stop for many visitors is the 220-foot-high obelisk; the Kusers provided the funds to build this monument to New Jersey's soldiers. The top provides a view of three states—New York, New Jersey, and Pennsylvania—as well as the Catskills, the Poconos, and the Delaware Water Gap. From this height can also be seen Lake Marcia, New Jersey's "highest" lake at sixteen hundred feet above sea level.

Naturally, the main magnet of High Point State Park is its many outdoor activities. Chief among these is hiking (a word to the wise, however; the terrain is frequently uphill and rough). Ten trails run through the park, including a section of the Appalachian Trail. Fishers can try their luck at catching trout and large-mouth bass in season, at the lakes and streams in the park; swimming is also permitted in Lake Marcia during the summer.

Other activities include camping, boating, skiing, snowmobiling, and picnicking. The park also contains the state's first natural area, the 200-acre John Dryden Kuser Natural Area. Dedicated in 1965, the area contains a variety of plants and animals, including a stand of Atlantic white cedar, the famous wood of choice of Jersey Shore boatbuilders.

As you will find out shortly in the chapter about the Pinelands, it was once the home of a vast, iron-producing empire. Even though the fires for the huge blast furnaces that once belched smoke and soot throughout the Pinelands have long since been extinguished, you can relive this unique era in New Jersey history at Allaire State Park.

In 1822, businessman James P. Allaire purchased the five-thousand-acre Monmouth Furnace ironworks from William Newbold for nineteen thousand dollars. For Allaire, owning the newly rechristened Howell Iron Works made sense; he owned a marine engine–building facility in New York City and needed a reliable source of iron.

Within a decade the Howell Works (the name wasn't changed until after Allaire's death) were prospering. At one stretch during the mid-1830s, the blast furnace ran continuously for twenty-one months. Several hundred people lived in the little community that sprang up around the ironworks, which was typical of Pinelands bog iron towns. What was not typical was Allaire's munificence as an employer. He established a school, church, and stage service in his town and built sturdy brick rowhouses for the workers to live in. The virtually self-sufficient village (it even issued its own script in place of money) contained a bakery, blacksmith shop, general store, sawmill, and other businesses. It was about as comfortable an existence as any ironworker and his family could expect.

Allaire ran into financial difficulties in 1847, at the same time that the bog iron industry was entering a decline that would lead to its eventual extinction. With the industry's collapse and Allaire's money troubles occurring concurrently, there was no way the little town could survive. By 1854 just ten employees were left at the Howell Works. The era of bog iron was over, and with it the useful life of the tiny town.

Today, you can relive these days of "ore" at Allaire State Park. A walk through the quaint village nestled amid the shady trees is both relaxing and educational. Some of the buildings remain in operation, including the bakery and general store. (Building operation is seasonal, and dependent on volunteers; it's best to call ahead.) The church at Allaire is reputed to be the only one in New Jersey with its steeple at the rear instead of in the front. A visitor's center explains the history of bog iron.

But there's more to Allaire than just old buildings. At the park you can hike, camp, ride the Pine Creek Railroad (in season), picnic, or just lie on a blanket in the sun. There is a picturesque millpond in the center of the village where children are allowed to fish. In the winter the park offers excellent cross-country skiing.

DID YOU KNOW?

New Jersey has more than forty-five state parks and forests, where you can get in touch with the natural world in many pleasant ways.

Abram S. Hewitt Forest, Hewitt (Passaic County)
Allaire Park, Farmingdale (Monmouth County)
Allamuchy Mountain Park, Stephen's Section, Hackettstown (Warren County)
Barnegat Lighthouse Park, Barnegat Light (Ocean County)
Bass River Forest, Tuckerton (Ocean County)
Belleplain Forest, Woodbine (Cape May County)
Brendan T. Byrne Forest (Burlington)
Cape May Point Park, Cape May Point (Cape May County)
Cheesequake Park, Matawan (Monmouth County)
Corson's Inlet Park, South of Ocean City (Cape May County)
Delaware and Raritan Canal Park, Belle Meade (Somerset County)
Double Trouble State Park (Ocean)
Edison State Park (Middlesex)
Farny State Park (Passaic)
Fort Mott Park, Salem (Salem County)
Green Bank Forest (Burlington)
Hacklebarney Park, Off Rt. 24, Long Valley (Morris County)
High Point Park, Sussex (Sussex County)
Hopatcong Park, Landing (Sussex County)
Island Beach Park, Seaside Park (Ocean County)
Jenny Jump Forest, Hope (Warren County)
Kittatinny Valley State Park (Sussex)

Liberty State Park, Jersey City (Hudson County)
Long Pond Ironworks Park (Passaic)
Monmouth Battlefield Park, Freehold (Monmouth County)
Norvin Green Forest, Sloatsburg Ringwood (Passaic County)
Penn Forest, New Gretna (Burlington County)
Pigeon Swamp Park (Middlesex)
Princeton Battlefield Park, Princeton (Mercer County)
Ramapo Mt. Forest, Oakland (Bergen County)
Ringwood Park, Ringwood (Passaic County)
Stephens State Park (Warren)
Stokes Forest, Branchville (Sussex County)
Swartswood Park, Swartswood (Sussex County)
Voorhees Park, Glen Gardner (Hunterdon County)
Washington Crossing Park, Titusville (Mercer County)
Washington Rock Park, Plainfield (Union County)
Wawayanda Park, Highland Lakes (Sussex County)
Wharton Forest, Hammonton (Atlantic County)
Worthington Forest, Columbia (Warren County)

Roads, Bridges, and Tunnels

Criticism of New Jersey frequently centers on its roadways and, through guilt by association, its other transportation aids such as bridges and tunnels. It's as if the Garden State somehow has more of these than any other state in the country and thus is a fair target for ridicule and abuse.

Such mockery, however, is shortsighted. Because of its dense population and corresponding need to move all of the vehicles that pour out onto the roads at something other than the proverbial snail's pace, New Jersey has frequently been the site of many transportation innovations. The Turnpike, for example, which has been on the receiving end of more corny jokes than the audience at a Las Vegas lounge act, was widely hailed when it first opened as a pioneering achievement in highway development, a road that sped vehicles on their way and propelled the science of highway engineering to the next level. The Pulaski Skyway was also considered something of a miracle for the engineering skill involved in its construction, which enabled it to tower over the roads below like a runway heading off into outer space.

More importantly, however, the story of roads, bridges, and tunnels in New Jersey is the story of people—resourceful, dynamic people with vision and daring, such as the bespectacled engineer who dared to dream that he could build a tunnel under the Hudson River from Jersey City to New York, or the New Jersey family that paid a tragic price for its desire to show the world that suspension bridges could span even the greatest gaps between towns and cities.

This is the story of some of the most memorable New Jersey roads, bridges, and tunnels—and of the people who made them so.

"He builded better than he knew."

This phrase, awkward in its pronunciation but elegant in its sentiment, is on a plaque near the New York City entrance to the Holland Tunnel. The plaque and nearby bust commemorate Clifford M. Holland, the man who designed and oversaw the construction of what was then the first underwater tunnel strictly for automotive traffic. The story of the Holland Tunnel is an old one: a desire to conquer nature's barriers for the convenience of humanity. And, like many similar endeavors, the price of achieving this desire was high.

The idea of a tunnel between New Jersey and Manhattan had long been a dream of far-thinking people. In the nineteenth century Hoboken's John Stevens, frustrated by the delays and unpredictability of ferry service between the two sides of the Hudson, suggested building a stone tube under the river to expedite wagon traffic between New Jersey and New York. The idea went nowhere, simply because it was considered impossible.

The problem persisted, and with the dawning of the automobile age, accelerated into a crisis. Ferries remained the only way for vehicles to move across the Hudson, but most had been built to hold horse-drawn carriages and wagons, not the larger and heavier autos. Consequently, only a few vehicles could make the crossing each time. Cars backed up for miles at Hudson River ferry depots, and it was not uncommon for motorists to have to wait several hours to make the thirty-minute trip across the water. Other vehicles were also at the mercy of the ferries and the weather, a point that was brought home quite clearly when a seven-day freeze of the Hudson caused a food shortage in Manhattan.

Obviously, a quicker mode of travel between New Jersey and New York was needed. After studying various alternatives, in 1919, a bistate commission recommended building a tunnel under the Hudson River that would connect Jersey City and New York City.

Many reacted scornfully to this proposal. After all, they pointed out, in order to reach bedrock wouldn't the tunnel have to be dug nearly one hundred feet below the surface of the Hudson? And wouldn't the tunnel have to be almost two miles long—a distance never before attempted? Finally, and most significantly, how would air circulate in a tunnel that long and that deep? Wouldn't it just fill with lethal carbon monoxide fumes and become a deathtrap for motorists?

All of these were valid objections. But the skeptics hadn't reckoned with the ingenuity and determination of the man hired by the New York State Bridge and Tunnel Commission and the New Jersey Interstate Bridge and Tunnel Commission to do the job: a thirty-six-year-old civil engineer and Harvard graduate named Clifford M. Holland.

Born on March 13, 1883, in Somerset, Massachusetts, Holland was no stranger to building tunnels: he had previously worked on both the Battery and the East River tunnel projects and was recognized as a leader in the field. However, he had two strikes against him when he was interviewed by the tunnel commissioners for the project: not only would the proposed Hudson River Vehicular Tunnel be more difficult than anything he had ever attempted (in fact, it was more difficult than any tunnel anyone ever attempted before), but the panel had already tentatively selected General George W. Goethals, builder of the Panama Canal, as the man for the job.

However, the slim, slightly built Holland made the panel forget the famous canal builder with his visionary and well thought out plans for the tunnel. A main feature of Holland's design was to use smaller tubes lined with both cast iron and concrete for extra strength, rather than the larger tubes lined only with concrete that Goethals had proposed. On July 1, 1919, Holland became the chief engineer in charge of building the tunnel, at a salary of twelve thousand dollars a year.

Because of the uniqueness of the project, Holland was forced to do things no one else had done before. To test the emissions of motor vehicles—a revolutionary concept then—he sealed off an abandoned coal mine near Pittsburgh and measured the exhaust emitted by many different varieties and sizes of motorized vehicles traveling at various speeds. To measure the effects of carbon monoxide on living organisms, blood from student volunteers from Yale University who had inhaled a mixture of air and carbon monoxide was tested. A miniature tunnel was built to the exact scale of the proposed one to gather additional information about emissions and air circulation.

From the data gathered, Holland developed a brand-new method of ventilation called a "vertical transverse flow." This system utilized two ventilating stations on each side of the Hudson, housing a total of eighty-four huge fans that would pump 3,600,000 cubic feet of fresh air per minute into the tunnel. Forty-two fans would suck fresh air in, then force it through special chambers below the roadway; from there it would enter the tunnel through vents in the curbing, mix with the exhaust fumes, and rise to the ceiling, where it would be removed by forty-two suction fans. This would provide a complete change of air every ninety seconds.

Although severely criticized, Holland's plan was adopted. On October 12, 1920, a ground-breaking ceremony for the new tunnel was held in New York. Within a few days, work began on the New Jersey side as well. Crews began tunneling toward each other from opposite sides of the river, sometimes progressing as much as fifteen feet a day and sometimes advancing just a few inches.

To design the tunnel, Holland had been working around the clock. Once the actual digging began, his workdays became even longer. Each laborious foot that the workers dug seemed to bring new problems, and Holland was constantly on call to solve them. Even the few hours of sleep he got each night were frequently interrupted by problems that required his immediate attention. A myriad of decisions both large and small consumed every moment of his life. His wife, Anna, and their four daughters hardly ever saw him. For four years he ate, slept, and breathed the tunnel.

Finally he broke down. On October 8, 1924, it was announced that Holland was taking a one-month vacation from his job necessitated by his "continuous devotion, night and day, during the past five years." With his health rapidly failing, Holland left for Battle Creek, Michigan, to rest so that he could return for the historic joining of both sides of the tunnel, now just weeks away.

He never made it back to New York. On October 27, 1924, Holland suffered a heart attack and died in Battle Creek. His untimely death canceled a special celebration commemorating the "holing through," in which President Calvin Coolidge was supposed to push a button in Washington to set off the final explosion.

Two days later, workers from each side broke through the final barrier of rock between them and shook hands, a moment that Clifford Holland had virtually killed himself to accomplish.

The tunnel was not yet done exacting its terrible price. Holland's replacement, Milton Freeman, died five months later, a death that was also widely attributed to overwork. A third engineer, Ole Singstad, finished the tunnel, but not without regrets. In later life, he lamented the number of cars he had allowed to come into New York City.

On November 12, 1927, Governor A. Harry Moore of New Jersey and Mayor Frank Hague of Jersey City, along with officials from New York, officially dedicated the tunnel. For the next several hours, thousands of people—twenty thousand within the first hour—celebrated this engineering marvel by walking through the long tube from one side of the river to the other. (The tunnel connects Canal Street in Manhattan with Twelfth and Fourteenth Streets in Jersey City.) For the pedestrians, it was a party atmosphere; they laughed, shouted, sang, knelt down to feel the fresh air flowing through the roadbed vents, and talked about establishing restaurants along the tunnel's sides.

Promptly at midnight, the tunnel was closed to pedestrians forever; a few moments later the first cars came rumbling through. On the New Jersey side, more than one thousand cars had been lined up, seven abreast for four blocks, waiting to make the historic trip. The first driver through from Jersey City (not counting dignitaries) was J. Frank Finn, an attorney. He was the first "unofficial" New Jerseyan to enjoy the fact that the trip across the Hudson River had been reduced from thirty minutes to eight.

In honor of the man who gave his life so that it could become a reality, the Hudson River Vehicular Tunnel was renamed the Holland Tunnel. In 1994, because of the tunnel's historic importance, the U.S. Department of the Interior designated it a National Historic Landmark, making it the first vehicle tunnel to gain that status. Thanks to the genius of Clifford Holland, a structure that was built to accommodate eight million vehicles a year today handles double that amount.

He had indeed "builded better than he knew."

DID YOU KNOW?

Just in case you're ever on a game show where winning the grand prize depends on knowing some obscure information about the Holland Tunnel:

Width of the roadway:	20 feet
External diameter of the tunnel:	29 feet, 6 inches
Maximum depth from mean high water to roadway:	93 feet, 5 inches
Length of tunnel, portal to portal:	8,558 feet (north tube)
	8,371 feet (south tube)
Initial construction cost:	$48 million

Even as the Holland Tunnel was being dug, it was becoming obvious that it alone would not solve all the commuting problems between New Jersey and New York City. The tunnel was downtown; something else was needed closer to midtown Manhattan, the daily destination for thousands of New Jerseyans. That something, it was decided, would be a suspension bridge from 178th Street in Manhattan to the rocky basalt cliffs of the Palisades in Fort Lee, New Jersey.

The announcement brought out all the naysayers who had been in hiding after their dire predictions about the Holland Tunnel had gone up in smoke. This time, the skeptics zeroed in on the great distance that the proposed bridge would have to cover: 3,500 feet. No suspension bridge had ever reached that far; the only one even close was under construction at Detroit, and that was a "mere" 1,850 feet.

But again, the doubters had failed to consider the iron will of the man hired to build the bridge, a dour but brilliant Swiss engineer named Othmar Hermann Ammann. As single-minded as Clifford Holland in his pursuit of excellence, Ammann plowed ahead with engineering and topographical studies that showed the only way for the bridge to be feasible was to build massive towers from which to hang the suspension cables. In October 1927, ground was broken for the new bridge.

The bridge transformed the tiny town of Fort Lee, once home to the nation's movie industry (see chapter 11). The fields where Douglas Fairbanks, Fatty Arbuckle, and Mary Pickford had once cavorted for the cameras were paved over in order to build the roadway approaches to the new bridge. Even the great cliffs of the Palisades, where starlets had once hung in death-defying terror in order to make another of the popular cliff-hanger films, were transformed through the building of the bridge's giant supporting towers and cable anchoring supports.

Ammann and his crew labored daily to build what many had said would be impossible. To answer those doubts, the Swiss engineer built two 595-foot-high steel towers (the height of a sixty-story skyscraper) to hold his suspension cables. Each tower was composed of twenty thousand tons of steel erected in single-story sections for twelve successive stories.

The four cables themselves were spun, strand by individual strand, by the Roebling Company of Trenton. Each fifth-of-an-inch thick wire had a strength of 98 tons per square inch. Each cable was 36 inches in diameter, and was composed of 61 strands, or 26,474 wires apiece. In all, the bridge used 105,000 miles of this spaghetti-thin wire, or enough to circle the earth four times.

The major controversy during construction was whether to encase the great steel towers in concrete, as had been done on the Brooklyn Bridge and many other suspension bridges. Ammann opted not to, and to this day, people debate the aesthetics of the naked steel towers of the George Washington Bridge.

Ammann, however, was more interested in results than arguments about beauty, and he was spectacularly successful, On October 25, 1931, the great bridge was opened, one year ahead of schedule. It was, at the time, the largest suspension bridge in the world and immediately provided the traffic relief that New Jersey commuters were seeking. Four and a half million cars traveled over it during the first year.

Exuberance in Fort Lee knew no bounds on the day of the bridge opening. The town pulled out all the stops for the gala event, including a concert by the 310th Infantry Band of Englewood, speeches by various dignitaries to a celebratory crowd of four thousand, and even a nighttime block dance on the bridge plaza.

George Washington. First in war, first in peace, and a great guy to name a precedent-setting bridge after.

DID YOU KNOW?

Names considered for the new bridge were: Gate of Paradise, Bridge of Prosperity, Noble Experiment, Pride of the Nation, Peoples' Bridge, and Bi-State Bridge. Finally, because George Washington had commanded forts on both sites—Fort Lee in New Jersey and Fort Washington in New York—it was decided to name the bridge after the Father of Our Country.

And, because you never know what quiz shows are going to ask:

Length of the bridge:	4,760 feet
Width of the bridge:	119 feet
Width of the roadway:	90 feet
Height of towers, above water:	604 feet
Water clearance of bridge at mid-span:	212 feet
Cost of initial construction:	$59 million

At first, it may seem that the only thing the George Washington Bridge and Green Sergeant's Bridge, New Jersey's last remaining covered bridge, have in common is the word "bridge." After all, the Hudson River bridge, with its fourteen lanes and wide roadbed, dwarfs the one-lane, twelve-foot-wide bridge in Sergeantsville (Hunterdon County). But when you look a little closer, you'll find that both bridges exist today primarily because of the determination of people who wouldn't take no for an answer.

It was on January 14, 1960, that the *Hunterdon County Democrat* first carried the story that was soon to captivate not only all of Hunterdon County but the entire state of New Jersey as well: "Fate of Covered Bridge in Precarious Balance" read the headline. Either decay or the vibrations from a large vehicle had caused the nearly hundred-year-old Green Sergeant's Bridge to slip off one of its massive supporting oak timbers. As a result, the bridge was sagging dangerously over the Wickecheoke Creek below, looking as if it would topple into the water at almost any moment. Initially the county tried to fix the bridge by jacking it up and slipping the supports back into place, but the work was halted when rotting wood was discovered at the base of the bridge. Other components of the bridge, such as iron plates and rods, were also found to be unsafe because of their age.

Repair costs were estimated at between twelve thousand and fifteen thousand dollars, and some thought it not worth the money. The county engineer urged that a new bridge be built for safety's sake. "I've got as much sentiment as anyone," he said. "But if someone gets killed there, people will blame me for permitting such an antique, narrow bridge to remain in use. It's a wonder to me that there never has been a serious accident there."

Entrance to Green Sergeant's Covered Bridge, the last covered bridge in New Jersey.

Others agreed, pointing out that half a dozen school buses used the bridge each day, as well as a large number of other vehicles. Since the bridge could only accommodate traffic heading in one direction at a time, it put drivers in the precarious position of hoping that no one else would come barreling into the span when they were crossing it. Although the Hunterdon County freeholders made no decision at the time, the prevailing mood seemed plain: Green Sergeant's Bridge was a relic of the past that had outlived its usefulness. No one would be sorry to see it go.

The error in that thinking was quickly revealed in the next issue of the *Democrat*. The newspaper was filled with letters urging that the quaint old structure be saved. "It sometimes happens that an undertaking of this sort is pushed thru by a few people of limited vision before the general public is aroused," one Stockton resident wrote. "If it goes we will all lose something of charm and beauty and be much the poorer in spirit." Another letter writer said, "I deplore the destruction of such landmarks. In so many cases there is an utter disregard of the intrinsic value of them. Some parts of these [landmarks] should be preserved, not only for sentimental value, but [so] that the younger generations can see for themselves the methods and arts of former years." From Essex County came a letter from students and teachers at Livingston High School summing up the prevailing mood: "Your idea of tearing down the covered bridge may be good materialistically, but as far as sentiment goes it should not be considered."

Almost overnight, the old bridge became a cause célèbre. Swarms of people visited the ailing structure, some to take photos, others just to view a part of history whose days seemed numbered. Pressure steadily mounted on the freeholders to save the bridge. Even members of Governor Robert Meyner's cabinet got into the act; Salvatore A. Bontempo, commissioner of the New Jersey Department of Conservation and Economic Development, opined that "New Jersey's last covered bridge has a particular appeal not only for camera enthusiasts, travelers and historians, but for all those who appreciate the scenic beauties of New Jersey and strive to preserve them."

At the next freeholders' meeting, a citizen's group that favored saving Green Sergeant's Bridge offered to pay for its own survey of the structure to see if preservation was feasible. One of the leaders of the effort, calling the bridge "a link between today and yesterday," said that replacing the bridge would be like tearing down the Leaning Tower of Pisa and replacing it with a straight tower.

But the pressure on the freeholders was not all one-sided. Others pushed for the bridge to be replaced by a newer and wider modern span better able to handle the modern traffic load. Eighty-one signatures opposing the restoration of the bridge were gathered and presented to the freeholders.

All the while, the fate of Green Sergeant's Bridge hung in the balance. The bridge was built in 1872, after a meeting at Jacob Wilson's hotel in Sergeantsville had produced a resolution to place a wooden bridge over the stream, with "timbers of white oak and rock oak," and to have it "inclosed [sic] with pine boards," Its curious name came from a man named Green Sergeant, a well-known resident of the area who had also given his name to nearby Sergeantsville.

Back then, the only traffic the one-lane bridge had to worry about was horse-drawn, and it was fairly easy for a wagon or carriage coming one way to pull over to the side to let another pass. With the dawning of the Automobile Age, however, the bridge became more and more inadequate. It had already been repaired once, in 1932, by John W. Scott of Flemington for five hundred dollars. Could it be saved again?

For months the preservationists, who had organized into the Covered Bridge Association, and the freeholders struggled to see if Green Sergeant's

Green Sergeant's Covered Bridge, side view.

Bridge could be saved. Finally, with help from the state, a solution was found: a new bridge would be built next to the wooden bridge, to carry eastbound vehicles, while Green Sergeant's would be repaired and made one-way in the opposite direction.

Work began in May 1961. As Green Sergeant's Bridge was taken apart, each piece was marked—A, B, C, and so on—and stored in the county garage in Flemington. Then, like a giant jigsaw puzzle, the span was put back together, using as much of the original materials as possible.

On September 15, 1961, a dedication ceremony was held at the rebuilt bridge, now with a reinforced concrete deck slab in place of the old wooden timbers. "Here it is, mended a little, some new timbers on its east side, but just as lovely as ever, just as beloved as ever," said Mrs. Edward M. Stone, president of the Green Sergeant's Covered Bridge Association.

Today Green Sergeant's Bridge is listed on the state and national historic registers. The bridge is a natural tourist attraction (artists and photographers are drawn to it as well), particularly in the autumn, when the changing leaves of the surrounding woods surround it. At any time of the year, however, Green Sergeant's Bridge is a beautiful symbol of days past—and of the wisdom of preserving that past for future generations to enjoy.

Green Sergeant's Covered Bridge, from the river.

New Jersey once had more than two dozen covered bridges. Today, with the exception of Green Sergeant's Bridge, these quaint reminders of yesterday have vanished into history.

All of the state's counties except Bergen, Monmouth, Atlantic, and Morris had at least one covered bridge spanning a public highway. Some of the more memorable were:

Crosswicks. This bridge in Crosswicks (Burlington County) over the Crosswicks Creek was near the scene of heavy fighting between British and colonial troops during June 1778, when the English were moving through New Jersey on their way to Sandy Hook. The bridge, built in 1833, was adorned with eagles and the United States flag.

Dividing Creek. Built in 1841 to cross Dividing Creek in Cumberland County, the bridge carried a warning that anyone traveling over it at a gait faster than a walk would be fined ten dollars. Cattle would often spend the night inside the bridge, which must have been quite a surprise to anyone using it after dark.

Stockton. This bridge spanning the Delaware River and linking Stockton, New Jersey, and Centre Bridge, Pennsylvania, was first opened in 1814. It had to be rebuilt several times and was destroyed by fire in 1923. When the Delaware was flooded in 1841, George B. Fell of Lambertville was on the bridge while it broke into two pieces. Fell climbed on top of the bridge and was swept down the raging river. He passed underneath two other bridges that collapsed seconds after he went by (New Hope and Yardleyville—now Yardley) before struggling ashore at Trenton—just as the debris of the other bridges came barreling past him.

Raritan Landing. Located about one mile north of New Brunswick (Middlesex County), this was the first covered bridge in New Jersey. Built in 1772, it was partially destroyed by the retreating Continental Army in 1776 to slow the British pursuit of Washington's troops.

South Branch. This bridge across the Raritan River was featured in a Ripley's "Believe It or Not" segment in 1941 that claimed it was more than two hundred years old. In reality, the bridge wasn't erected until 1820.

No chapter on transportation innovations in New Jersey would be complete without the Roeblings of Trenton.

It would be wrong to call John A. Roebling the father of the suspension bridge, since such structures had been built in China, Japan, India, Tibet, and other countries since ancient times. What Roebling did, however, was move the suspension bridge light years ahead, and show a disbelieving nation—and world—that suspension bridges could be used to span great distances.

Before Roebling, the roster of failed suspension bridges was lengthy: a 408-foot bridge over the Schuylkill River in Philadelphia collapsed under the weight of snow and ice; the Lewiston-Queenston bridge over the Niagara River went down in a gale in 1855; the Wheeling Bridge over the Ohio River flipped completely over before plunging into the water; and, worst of all, the Menai Strait Bridge in Wales was destroyed by wind three times (in 1826, 1836, and 1839).

Roebling, however, had a better way. Born on June 12, 1806, in Muhlhausen, Germany, he had emigrated to the United States in 1831. After trying his hand at farming, Roebling, who had studied engineering at the Royal University of Berlin, got a job as assistant state engineer in Pennsylvania. Before long he was building dams, aqueducts, and bridges. Soon he had graduated to constructing suspension bridges at Pittsburgh, Cincinnati, and over the Niagara River, spanning gaps that most people thought impossible.

Roebling knew that part of the problem with suspension bridges had been that their roadbeds were too flexible and that the force of all their weight being swung back and forth by the wind was too much to bear. "That bridge," he wrote about Wheeling, "was destroyed by the momentum acquired by its own dead weight." To rectify this, he devised a truss system to stiffen his own bridges and keep the road in place. Even more important, he perfected a method of twisting strands of wire together into extraordinarily strong, yet flexible, cable. In 1848, on the advice of his friend Peter Cooper, Roebling opened his own wire mill in Trenton, where he produced the cable and perfected techniques to make it even stronger and safer. By 1867, when Brooklyn came calling, he was the undisputed master of the suspension bridge.

Brooklyn, however, might never have sought Roebling's services if the winter of 1866–67 hadn't been so severe. Huge ice floes dotted the East River, making ferry travel (the only way to get from Brooklyn to Manhattan at the time) all but impossible. Finally, when Brooklynites realized that people coming from Albany were arriving in Manhattan faster than they were, they gave Roebling the go-ahead for his suspension bridge.

Roebling was delighted. Here was the ultimate challenge: a bridge from Brooklyn to Manhattan had long been considered a fool's errand. Feverishly, he got to work, planning it so that the length of the span (sixteen hundred feet) and its weight (five thousand tons) would assure the bridge's stability. To this Roebling intended to add massive stone towers, carved as corniced walls and pierced with gigantic Gothic arches. The total effect would be a spectacle to behold. "The contemplated work," Roebling wrote,

". . . . will not only be the greatest Bridge in existence, but it will be the greatest engineering work of this continent, and of the age. The great towers will be entitled to be ranked as national monuments."

Charged with enthusiasm, Roebling began the preliminary engineering work. But fate had other plans for the master bridge builder. On June 28, 1869, as he was standing on a cluster of piles on a ferry taking some measurements, the boat crashed into a slip. The wood moved, crushing Roebling's right foot. Long before, Roebling had decided that conventional medicine and doctors were not necessary and that a person could use the power of his mind to vanquish disease and injury. Now he held firm to this belief, even going so far as to order a surgeon to amputate his damaged toes without an anesthetic.

But John A. Roebling, conqueror of every obstacle nature had ever thrown at him, had finally met his match. Tetanus set in and moved quickly through his body. Racked with pain, Roebling spent his last day inventing an apparatus to help him move around in bed. On July 22, 1869, the famous bridge builder died.

Work on the bridge barely slowed; Roebling's son and assistant, Washington A. Roebling, was appointed to replace him. Cast in the same determined mold as his father, the thirty-one-year-old Roebling was not about to let the bridge that his father had given his life for come to naught. Like his father, Roebling was everywhere, personally supervising every aspect of the construction, which began in 1870.

Two years later, in the summer of 1872, Washington Roebling was carried out of an underwater chamber barely alive. He had suffered an attack of what was then called caisson disease, but is now known as the bends. The illness left him permanently, painfully paralyzed at age thirty-five.

Still, work on the bridge did not stop. Although now an invalid, Roebling oversaw construction every day from his apartment window through powerful field glasses. With his wife, Emily, he devised a hand-tapping code so that he could communicate his orders to her. She, in turn, passed them on to the workers. In this manner was the Brooklyn Bridge ultimately built.

On May 24, 1883, the Brooklyn Bridge was officially opened. Dignitaries, including President Chester A. Arthur, gave speeches, bands played, and people looked up in awe at the massive brown towers. Looking down at all of it was Washington Roebling.

It had cost three million dollars, killed John A. Roebling and crippled his son, and taken fourteen years of backbreaking labor, but the bridge that most people thought would never be built was now a reality—a reality achieved through the incredible determination of the Roeblings of Trenton.

It is, arguably, not only the most famous road in New Jersey, but in the entire United States.

Mention the New Jersey Turnpike anywhere else in the country, and you're almost certain to get a nod or smile of recognition; if people haven't actually been on it they've heard about it. Now try that with the New York Thruway, and see how many blank stares you receive. Love it or hate it, the Turnpike is, as the *New York Times* once said, the "most American of highways."

The Turnpike has come to define New Jersey. No one thinks of the Garden State Parkway, the Atlantic City Expressway, or any of the countless other roads that crisscross the state in the same way that they do the Turnpike. Some people hate the road; for them it calls to mind all the evils of urbanization, like big oil refineries belching stomach-churning flumes into the air and miles of concrete cloverleaves on which you can seemingly travel for days without ever straightening your wheel. Others, however, think of the kinder, gentler Turnpike that runs through the central and southern portion of the state, where the scenery becomes greener, and the road becomes a multilane highway to points south.

Speed was the initial reason behind the Turnpike's existence. As the automobile became the dominant mode of transportation, it became obvious that roadway construction in New Jersey was not keeping up. There are still people who quake at the memory of trying to get from Point A to Point B on such highways as Route 9, which gave red-light district a whole new meaning.. By the end of World War II, stop-and-go travel in New Jersey had become a painfully familiar way of life. As more and more people flocked to the suburbs, and the American Dream was redefined to include how many large cars a person had, New Jersey's roads began to groan under the strain: Route 46, built to carry 32,000 cars per day, was carrying 56,000; Route 1, designed to accommodate 30,000 vehicles, was clogged with more than twice that number; and Route 22 was a virtual parking lot, with over 69,000 cars per day. The state's highways had the highest traffic density in the world. Plainly, drastic measures were needed.

To the rescue stepped Governor Alfred E. Driscoll. A strong and opinionated Republican governor who enjoyed the benefit of a Republican legislature, Driscoll knew the state was drowning in traffic. In his January 1947 inaugural address, Driscoll outlined his plans for the Turnpike.

The inertia-creating cynicism about government that exists today hadn't yet become widespread; the United States had, after all, just swept to victory in World War II. The future was bright and full of promise, and there didn't seem to be anything that a country or state couldn't do. When Driscoll said that the state needed a superhighway running virtually its entire length, people nodded, rolled up their sleeves, and got to work.

In October 1948, the state legislature passed the New Jersey Turnpike Authority Act and the road was off and running. To emphasize the sense of urgency to build the road, Paul Troast, the chairman of the Turnpike Commission, put a sign on his office door: "The Turnpike Must Be Done By November Fifty-One!"

This, of course, was only three years—three years to build a 117-mile road from scratch. Today, it would take two years for people to stop laughing at this kind of deadline, but times were different then; there was a will and a determination to get the job done, and to do it right.

To meet the deadline, the Turnpike Authority divided the construction into seven sections, each of which was to be built simultaneously. Another incentive to get the job done quickly was the $48,000 per day interest charge that was accumulating on the $235 million of thirty-five-year bonds that had been issued to finance the project. The faster the road was built, the sooner the revenues would begin and the bonds could be retired.

Construction began in September 1949 and proceeded at a blistering pace. Along the way, numerous problems that threatened to delay the project were discussed, analyzed, and resolved in record time. The muddy marshes of north Jersey were conquered by using sand to draw off the excess water; the towering Pulaski Skyway, which stood directly in the Turnpike's path, was dealt with by squeezing the road under the Skyway, rather than over it; crossing the wide Passaic and Hackensack Rivers was accomplished by building what were, at the time, the two longest bridges of their type (6,955 feet and 5,623 feet, respectively). To make up for the loss of manpower caused by the Korean War, everyone just worked harder and faster.

Incredibly, the Turnpike was finished on schedule. On November 5, 1951, the first fifty-three-mile section from Deepwater (Salem County) to Bordentown (Burlington County) was opened. Three weeks later, after formal dedication ceremonies, an additional forty miles was opened from Bordentown to Woodbridge. Twenty-three more miles were opened over the next few months. At a total cost of $277 million, the New Jersey Turnpike had indeed "been done by November fifty-one!"

Ironically, considering the abuse that the Turnpike takes today, the initial reaction to the road was euphoric. It was widely hailed as the "Highway of Tomorrow": prestigious national magazines such as *Time, Fortune, Business Week,* and the *Saturday Evening Post* carried articles about the wonderful new road. Drivers accustomed to highways filled with traffic signals and stop signs were stunned by how quickly the Turnpike whisked them to their destinations (it was estimated that a passenger car would save seventy minutes, and a truck ninety minutes, via the Turnpike).

This euphoria did not last. As the years went on, the Turnpike was hammered for everything from its lack of roadside viewing opportunities to just being "ugly." All a comedian looking for a quick laugh had to do was mention the New Jersey Turnpike, and the guffaws came rolling down the aisles.

These criticisms, however, miss the point: The Turnpike was never meant to be pretty, or fun to drive, or an architectural wonder. As Angus Gillespie and Michael Rockland point out in *Looking for America on the New Jersey Turnpike,* the Turnpike was simply meant to be a road that got you where you wanted to go as quickly and efficiently as possible. There are no sweeping curves to maneuver, and no rolling hills to admire, because the whole point of the Turnpike is that a straight line is faster.

So, while we may never come to terms with it, we might still want to take a moment and reflect on the New Jersey Turnpike: It may be all that its critics say it is, but you won't find a better example of the spirit of hope and optimism that once infused the United States than this "most American of highways."

DID YOU KNOW?

Turnpike Trivia

Names of the service areas:	Clara Barton, James Fenimore Cooper, Grover Cleveland, Thomas Edison, John Fenwick, Alexander Hamilton, William F. Halsey, Joyce Kilmer, Vince Lombardi, Molly Pitcher, Richard Stockton, Walt Whitman, and Woodrow Wilson.
Length:	148 miles
Most common vehicular problems:	Mechanical trouble (49,000), flat tires (5,800), out of gas (4,300), battery failure (2,200)
Busiest toll interchange:	#16E/18E, Lincoln Tunnel and George Washington Bridge
1951 traffic volume:	17.9 million vehicles yearly
2013 traffic volume:	205 million vehicles yearly

The Garden State Parkway was designed to be the complete opposite of the Turnpike. Whereas the Turnpike is a no-nonsense, let's-get-where-we're-going-right-now type of road, the Parkway is more of a leisurely Sunday drive. Even the name "Garden State Parkway" conjures up images of men with handlebar mustaches and linen dusters, and ladies with parasols and hoop skirts enjoying an outing. The Parkway, with its tree-lined vistas and wide, grassy medians with bushes and flowers, was made to be visually enjoyed as well as traveled. In fact, the road's forest-like appearance was once considered so inviting to deer that special reflectorized pieces of metal were installed in wooded areas to scare away the animals before they leaped out onto the roadway. It didn't work.

In the beginning, the Parkway was hailed as a liberator, come to rescue the Jersey Shore from its isolation and bring unparalleled prosperity to the entire region. In August 1954, the *Asbury Park Press,* with all the feverish optimism of post–World War II America, raved about the new road that had just opened: "One trip over the parkway will convince any motorist that it measures up to the bright promises with which it was built." The paper went on to laud the road's "smooth, broad roadways . . . carefully planned approaches . . . [and] beautiful vistas."

Prophetically, the newspaper also noted that one result of the Parkway would be "a vast increase in the number of people who move into this area . . . with this growth in population will come serious social and economic problems, upon the successful solution of which the preservation of the Shore as an attractive residential and recreational center will depend."

The Parkway delivered on all that and more. The road ushered in a tidal wave of people and problems that the Jersey Shore is still dealing with: Open space was gobbled up by ravenous development that seemed intent on placing a strip mall on every corner; pollution fouled waterways that had been clean for centuries, not only harming the vital tourist trade but putting fishing boats and related businesses in jeopardy; local property taxes skyrocketed as communities struggled to build schools and other facilities for the sudden flood of new residents.

Worst of all was the traffic. Suddenly driving on formerly quaint one-lane highways with ancient drawbridges became a nightmare, as gridlock strangled the Shore and threatened to turn it into the urbanized community that many had come there to escape. Even the mighty Parkway itself wasn't immune to the automotive influx: travelers who'd been stuck in Sunday-night traffic jams on the Parkway would talk about them around the water cooler the next day like veterans swapping war stories.

Today the Parkway is as much a lightning rod for criticism as the Turnpike. Just as happened to its cousin the Turnpike, the Garden State Parkway is discovering that the days of hailing a roadway are long gone.

DID YOU KNOW?

Parkway Trivia

Average miles between tolls:	15
Mowable acres of land:	3,000
Number of homes and buildings acquired for original right-of-way:	2,000
Amount spent to acquire land for original right-of-way:	$49 million
Length of the Parkway:	174 miles
Cost of original construction:	$330 million

Traveling the Pulaski Skyway is not for the faint of heart.

Towering, at its highest point, a sky-scraping 135 feet above the Passaic and Hackensack Rivers, the Pulaski Skyway is like riding on a road suspended on hooks from the sky. When it was built, the road was the most spectacular highway in the United States, a 3.7-mile viaduct whose black steel latticework made it instantly identifiable from miles away.

Before the Skyway was built, the trip between Jersey City and points north, such as Newark and Elizabeth, was a grueling journey marked by innumerable traffic lights and two drawbridges that were raised more than they were closed. The Skyway, built at a then-record cost of seven million dollars per mile, reduced the travel time between Jersey City and Newark to five minutes. Building the roadway took 88,461 tons of structural steel, more than was used in the construction of the George Washington Bridge.

The road is named for General Casimir Pulaski, a Polish nobleman who fought on the side of the United States in the Revolutionary War. Pulaski was considered one of the finest and bravest men on either side during that war, seeing action in engagements at Haddonfield, Egg Harbor, and Camden, among others. Pulaski died on October 11, 1779, after being shot while (typically) leading a charge in the Battle of Savannah. Both sides mourned his passing.

DID YOU KNOW?

New Jersey was one of the most active states in the Underground Railroad, a network of people and homes that helped slaves gain their freedom in the years before the Civil War. Fleeing slaves would be moved primarily at night from "station" to "station" on the railroad, going city by city and state by state, until they reached their final destination in the north.

In New Jersey, one spur of the railroad crossed from Philadelphia to Camden, wound its way north through Burlington, Bordentown, Princeton, New Brunswick, Perth Amboy, Rahway, and Jersey City, and then to points farther north. A second spur began around Salem, then traveled through Woodbury, Evesham, and on to Bordentown, where it joined the line going north. A third route crossed the Delaware River at Greenwich, then went to Swedesboro, Evesham Mount, and Mount Holly, and then linked with the northern route at either Burlington or Bordentown.

The Call of the Pines

The very first thing that must be understood about the New Jersey Pinelands is that their very existence is one of nature's great jokes on humanity.

Think of it: 337,000 acres of virginal woods and unpolluted water in the middle of the most densely populated state in the union. Mile after mile of nothing but pine forests, sand roads, and a few tiny towns in the center of a state routinely dismissed as nothing more than an urban overflow of concrete and asphalt between the urban complexes of New York and Philadelphia. Over one million acres of woods, rivers, bogs, and open space—an area larger than Rhode Island—that occupies approximately 30 percent of the fifth-smallest state in the country.

The more you talk about it, the more the miles and acreages add up, the more incredible it sounds. Having the Pinelands in the middle of New Jersey is like turning a corner in Manhattan and finding yourself in the midst of Sherwood Forest. It just shouldn't be.

But it is. In a state full of surprises for the depth of its natural beauty, the Pinelands is New Jersey's ultimate prank. And, if you look deeper into the mysteries of this strange and fascinating land, you'll find that the New Jersey Pinelands is more than just a pretty face.

By now, the Pinelands shouldn't be a surprise to anyone. During the last few decades the region has received more warm and fuzzy publicity than a litter of kittens playing with a ball of string.

It all started in the mid-1960s, when John McPhee's insightful *New Yorker* essays on the Pinelands culminated in his 1967 book *The Pine Barrens,* which introduced the region to the country for the first time. Since this coincided with the early back-to-the-land movement, the Pinelands suddenly became a media darling. Magazines tripped over themselves publishing breathless accounts of the joys of wandering through this "primordial" wilderness that, to them, had seemingly appeared out of nowhere in the middle of urbanized, mechanized New Jersey. "Piney Power" hats and T-shirts began popping up faster than crocuses on a spring lawn.

All of this praise was not only a welcome change for the Pinelands but an astonishing reversal of public opinion. For decades before that, the region had the reputation of a worrisome place.

The impetus for this extremely unflattering view of the Pinelands came from a report published in 1912 by Elizabeth Kite, a psychological researcher at the Vineland Training School. Although Kite bore no ill will toward the people of the area, her depiction of them and their woodland lifestyle was notoriously harsh. Besides painting vivid portraits of imbecilic men, women, and children, Kite depicted Pinelands residents as having no more regard for life than most people do when they step on an insect. "They was all insured. I'm still young and can easy start another family," said one woman in Kite's report after finding out that her husband and children had all been killed in a fire.

This report incited a storm of public outrage. The American work ethic—shoulder-to-the-wheel, nose-to-the-grindstone—was never stronger than it was during the early years of the twentieth century, for workers of every class. New Jerseyans were outraged that lurking in their midst was a group of shiftless, lazy people who ignored society's rules.

Politicians then were no less adept at jumping onto the bandwagon of public opinion than they are today. New Jersey's then-governor, James T. Fielder, toured the Pinelands to assess the situation firsthand. He returned a shaken man.

"I have been shocked at the conditions I have found," Fielder announced. "Evidently these people are a serious menace to the State of New Jersey because they produce so many persons that inevitably become public charges. They have inbred, and led lawless and scandalous lives, till they have become a race of imbeciles, criminals, and defectives." To keep New Jersey free from the odious Pineys, the governor suggested that the region somehow be cut off from the rest of the state.

With friends like that the Pinelands didn't need enemies. Soon Pinelands' residents had even more reason to retreat into the deep woods and let the rest of the world spin on its merry way without them. Kite's supervisor at Vineland, H. H. Goddard, took her findings and used them as the basis for a report on a family he dubbed with the fictional name of Kallikak. Boiled down to its essence, Goddard's proposition was that virtually everyone in the Pinelands was descended from one man, Martin Kallikak. Martin and a dim-witted barmaid supposedly conceived an illegitimate son, Martin Kallikak Jr.—called the "Old Horror" by Goddard—who then proceeded to spawn all manner of drunks, prostitutes, imbeciles, and general cretins: "From him [Kallikak Jr.] have come four hundred and eighty descendants," wrote Goddard. "One hundred and forty-three of these, we have conclusive proof, were or are feeble-minded." He then went on to break down the more infamous Kallikak kin into thirty-three "sexually immoral persons," twenty-four alcoholics, three epileptics, three criminals, and eighty-two who died in infancy.

The overall message of all this negative publicity was crystal clear: the Pinelands were a place to be avoided at all costs, and avoid them most New Jerseyans did. (Ironically, Kite was subsequently forced to withdraw her report because of the firestorm that surrounded it. Although she admitted that her conclusions about the Pinelands being populated by sex-crazed misfits were probably not representative of the region as a whole, the damage had been done.)

Even the residents themselves seemed ashamed of their heritage. In the 1930s and 1940s, when pioneering folklorist Herbert Halpert tramped through the woods collecting songs and stories of the Pinelands, he kept asking people he met where the Pineys were. Those in the north said they were farther south, while those in the south told him to look in the north; no one wanted to be known as a Piney. Like an urban dark alley, the Pinelands became a sinister, dangerous place; walk down it, people would say knowingly, and you may not come back.

Today, the breeze of public opinion has sent the pine cone spinning 180 degrees. People flock year-round to the Pinelands for hiking, camping, canoeing, and other outdoor pursuits. The region is celebrated in story and song, and the residents are admired—even envied—for having the sense to live in the peace and serenity of the woods, away from the concrete and constant cacophony of the cities and suburbs. In fact, the same society that was once condemned was afforded a singular honor in 1983, when the Library of Congress's American Folklife Center came to New Jersey to study and document the Pinelands way of life.

Everywhere the folklorists looked, they found something special about the Pinelands. They found it in the way grandparents would tell children stories around a fireplace at night, and in the method used to catch snapping turtles. They found it in the way some folks gathered sphagnum moss, prepared food, or decorated their yards. They found it in the way loggers cut trees, trappers caught game, and craftsworkers made decoys and embroidered dollies for their tables. In short, what they found was an incredible body of life-affirming wisdom and knowledge, passed down through generations, that gave the Pinelands a unique cultural identity. In an increasingly hectic world, the Pinelands still run according to the ancient and much more important laws of the human spirit.

"We often protect knowledge by making it tangible, binding it in books with acid-free pages which are then housed in monumental buildings of marble and granite," said the Folklife Center's final report on the Pinelands, entitled *One Space, Many Places*. "Yet local knowledge has its own life, a life lived independently and dynamically, and which must be monitored at its source if we are to keep up with it at all."

One of the stories that has undoubtedly been passed down from generation to generation in the Pinelands is that of the Jersey Devil. Another, however, concerns the indisputably real-life exploits of a man named Joe Mulliner.

Mulliner's place in Pinelands lore is open to dispute. Some depict him as a Robin Hood–like character, stealing mainly from the wealthy, tipping his hat to women, and generally behaving in a charming and civilized way. Others, however, claim he was a cold-blooded killer, a man who terrorized the countryside, robbing, pillaging, and burning anything and everything in his path. As usual when there are two widely divergent portraits, the truth lies somewhere in-between.

Joe Mulliner was the head of a large gang of robbers that operated in the Pinelands at the time of the Revolutionary War. The gang members were dubbed "refugees" because of their supposed loyalty to England during the war, but since they preyed on Tories and Continentals alike, it's likely that their only allegiance was to enriching their own wallets.

Mulliner himself was a tall, handsome Englishman who almost always had a brace of pistols tucked into his leather belt. A bit of a dandy, the outlaw chief loved to dress up in fancy uniforms and attend lavish parties, where he would dance with the bejeweled, petticoated women until the wee hours of the morning.

Since most of the men in the area were involved in the war, Mulliner's gang usually faced no more than token opposition. The group rampaged through the Pinelands for years, virtually without fear of the law.

According to legend, however, even Mulliner's conscience got the best of him once. The gang—minus Mulliner, who was probably off dancing somewhere—robbed the home of a widow named Bates. When she tried to stop them, they tied her to a tree and burned her house down. Mulliner supposedly felt so badly about this that, several weeks later, Mrs. Bates received an anonymous gift of several hundred dollars. It was whispered with certainty that the donor was Joe Mulliner.

For a long time Mulliner and his gang ran the Pinelands as their own little fiefdom, but once the war was over and the men came home, the countdown to justice began for the robber chief. Mulliner, however, ignored the changing circumstances, and this led to his undoing. One night in the summer of 1781, as he was dancing at a tavern in present-day Nesco, a group of men who had been searching for him surrounded the building and took him prisoner.

Mulliner was taken to Burlington to stand trial. There was little doubt of the verdict, as the *New Jersey Gazette* of August 8, 1781, reported:

> At a special court lately held in Burlington, a certain Joseph Mulliner, of Egg-Harbour, was convicted of high treason. . . . This fellow had become the terror of that part of the country. He had made a practice of burning houses, robbing and plundering all who fell in his way, so that when he came to trial it appeared that the whole country, both whigs and tories, were his enemies.

The sentence was death by hanging. According to the Reverend G. A. Raybold, an eyewitness to Mulliner's incarceration, the always-arrogant outlaw became alarmed at how he would fare in the hereafter and tearfully admitted his "baseness" in the presence of three members of the clergy.

Since so many tales sprang up about Mulliner's life, it was perhaps inevitable that another began on the day of his death. According to local lore, Mulliner was taken back to the Pinelands, where he was hung from a tree on the banks of the Mullica River. Some even embellished the story further by claiming that his ghost can occasionally he seen riding along the road near the hanging tree.

However, Raybold's on-the-spot account of Mulliner's death proves that the bandit met his end very near to where he was tried. "Thousands of peo-

ple, it was computed, were there from all parts of the country," the clergy-
man wrote:

> The music sounded doleful as a wagon approached containing Mul-
> liner [and] his coffin. The procession passed out of Burlington to a
> place called Gallows Hill. Mulliner rose and gazed upon the crowd.
> His countenance seemed unchanged. He spoke at some length. He ac-
> knowledged his gilt [sic] and begged the people to pray for him. Then
> closing his eyes he sat down and appeared to be in an agony of prayer.

A few moments later, the criminal career of Joe Mulliner was over for
good. Some said that he was brought hack to the Pinelands, where he was
buried along Pleasant Mills–Nesco Road. For years a simple tombstone
marked the site. The state even put an historical marker there. The grave-
stone disappeared in the 1960s, however, and has not been replaced. If it is
indeed Joe Mulliner buried there in the soft Pinelands soil, he sleeps the
lonely sleep of the anonymous dead.

It would be wrong to assume that the Pinelands does not contain ghosts.
If a ghost is a phantom of things past, a memory of what was but is not
anymore, then the Pinelands could be the most haunted place in the United
States. There are indeed ghosts in the Pinelands—ghost towns, that is.

These are not garden variety ghost towns like those found in old westerns; you won't find any windblown tumbleweeds or swinging saloon doors
in the Pinelands. Like everything else about the Pinelands, these towns are
unique, primarily because almost all traces of them have vanished. There
are no buildings, roads, or signs to indicate where they once were. In most
cases, the only way to find any evidence of a town is to stumble across an
outline of bricks half-buried in the ground, marking the place where a
building once stood. These are the last indications of the era when the Pinelands was one of New Jersey's, and the nation's, most important industrial
regions.

Many people are shocked to discover that the bucolic Pinelands once
housed industry of any type. Yet for decades the sound of the breeze whispering through the trees was joined by the thunder and lightning of the
hammer and the blast furnace from factories that produced glass, iron ore,
lumber, and paper. Towns with quirky names like Martha Furnace and Atsion Forge sprang up to house those who worked in these factories. Each
industry had its heyday, then, as a result of economic factors beyond their
control, vanished. When the last factories closed down and the work disap-

peared for good, so did the people. The towns were abandoned, and a deep quiet settled over the Pinelands once again.

It is the iron ore industry, which existed in the Pinelands for nearly a century, from 1760 to 1850, that best illustrates the rise and fall of the region's industrial might. There were approximately two dozen "iron plantations" in the region during the industry's peak.

The Pinelands iron industry played a critical role in the early history of the United States. Thousands of cannonballs produced in the New Jersey woods helped Americans win both the Revolutionary War and the War of 1812. (Batsto ironworkers were considered so vital to the Revolutionary War effort that they were exempted from military service.) Before sailing to fight the Barbary pirates, Stephen Decatur's flagship was armed with twenty-four-pound cannons cast at Hanover Furnace. Decatur himself was at the site, checking things over, when he supposedly encountered the Jersey Devil (see chapter 8). The fence that once surrounded Independence Hall was made from Pinelands iron, as was the cylinder for John Fitch's steamboat and firebacks for George Washington's fireplace.

The iron found in the Pinelands was known as bog iron, because it was usually found in swampy ground alongside bodies of water. Bog iron is created by the chemical reaction of iron salts in the area's numerous stream and marsh beds to pine needles and other decaying vegetable matter. As the iron rises to the surface of the water and hits air, it oxidizes, forming brownish blue–colored patches that mix with the mud of stream and marsh beds.

Ironworkers would dig up the ore and transport it by large boats to the furnace. There it was crushed into small pieces (a process called "stamping"), boiled to remove excess water, and cooked to separate the slag, or worthless material. The porous, impure, somewhat soft iron that was left was called pig iron and was used for products like stoves, kettles, and window sash weights. Most of the pig iron wound up at the forge, where it was re-smelted into metal of great strength called bar iron. Bar iron was used for items such as wagon wheels, tools, and horseshoes.

As might be expected, working at the iron forges was a difficult and demanding job. Men labored from sunup to sundown, usually in twelve-hour shifts with few breaks. Workers were usually sweat-streaked, hot, and exhausted at day's end. Holidays were practically unheard of and except for an occasional day off to go fishing or hunting, an ironworker's life was one of almost constant backbreaking labor.

The communities that sprang up around the iron works were company towns in the strictest sense. Workers and their families lived in small, sparsely furnished wood frame houses; luxuries were rare, and necessities often hard to come by. Women purchased practically all of the family's needs at the company store, which usually managed to ensnare most workers in a web of debt before too long.

As it was, many workers and their families never saw real currency. Many were paid either in credit slips or company-issued scrip that was only redeemable at the company store. Since competing businesses were frowned upon, and the towns were so isolated that there was nowhere else to go and spend actual money anyway, the company store was the hub of the town.

By contrast, the ironmasters (those who supervised the ironworks and were responsible for production, much like overseers on southern plantations) lived in large, airy homes fitted out with nice furniture. Stories are told about the incredible luxury that the ironmasters lived in, compared to the abject poverty of most of the workers. While many of these tales are probably the result of the natural resentment between the haves and the have-nots, there's no disputing the fact that the ironmasters had a much greater standard of living than the workers.

In the iron towns, the coming of spring meant the resumption of work. Once the temperature warmed enough to permit water to start flowing freely and turn the water wheels that powered the great bellows, the furnace was fired up. It would not go out until the return of winter froze the water once again. The furnace operated twenty-four hours a day, seven days a week, filling the town with its throaty roar, like an ever-present beast crying constantly for food. To feed the furnace, the woods for miles around an iron town were usually stripped bare of trees. (The perpetual need for wood was another reason why most iron towns were located deep in the forest.)

What destroyed the bog iron industry in the Pinelands was the discovery around 1840 of high-grade anthracite coal and iron ore in the hills of western Pennsylvania. It was easier to extract the iron from this ore than it was from bog ore, which, coincidentally, had begun to be depleted. (It takes twenty years for nature to renew exhausted bog iron beds.) Coal was also superior to wood charcoal as a fuel to fire the blast furnaces. The implications of the Pennsylvania discovery were not lost on those familiar with the Pinelands industry. The *Camden Mail and General Advertiser* of July 1, 1840, observed: "It is suggested that the recent application of anthracite fuel to the smelting of iron ore will be very injurious, if not fatal, to the iron works of New Jersey."

The newspaper was right. Once large-scale iron smelting began in Pennsylvania, New Jersey's bog ore industry was doomed. Death came fairly quickly to what had been a way of life for Pinelands residents for decades. The fires went out at mighty Batsto for the last time in 1848, and the rest of the furnaces followed in short order. Within twenty years not a single ironworks remained in operation in the Pinelands.

When the furnaces shut down, the company store and all the ancillary businesses also closed. The workers discovered that living in isolation deep in the Pinelands made finding another job extraordinarily difficult. People suddenly found themselves with no money and no prospects. It was a time of desperation for many Pinelands families.

DID YOU KNOW?

Who was Charles Read? This forgotten man of the Pinelands can be rightfully called the Father of the region's Iron Age. In 1766, at age fifty-one, Read was consumed with building a business empire in the Pinelands through what he called his "iron works scheme." Within two years Read had built four iron forges: Etna, Taunton, Atsion, and Batsto. Unfortunately, he badly underestimated the amount of capital he would need for such an enterprise and was in financial trouble almost from the start. Beset by business troubles and personal tragedy, and in failing health, by 1773 Read had sold all his interests in his iron forges. Sadly, financial trouble and ill health continued to plague him. On December 27, 1774, he died alone in North Carolina, without ever knowing that his "scheme" would shortly become a thriving industry that would help the United States win the Revolutionary War.

Some iron towns tried to shift their industrial focus when it became clear that bog ore was dying. Paper mills and glass factories were common attempts to fill the void left by the iron industry.

The town of Harrisville is probably the clearest illustration of the evolution of Pinelands industries. Beginning as the Skit Mill, a lumbermill built in 1750, the town also operated a sawmill and then an iron forge before being converted to a paper mill by William McCarty in the early 1830s. By the time brothers Richard and William Harris took control in 1851, the little town—now called McCartyville—had a double paper mill in operation. The Harrises promptly changed the name of the community, enlarged the paper mill until it was more than three hundred feet long, and built a gasoline plant to power both the mill and light the town.

The primary product at Harrisville was a heavy, coarse brown paper made from hay, reeds, rags, and waste paper called "butcher's paper." It is very similar to the type of paper steaks and other cuts of meat are wrapped in today. However, while this paper was great for pork chops, it was not good for writing, which was where the money lay in the paper industry. The Harrises tried to tap this lucrative market by developing a high-quality writing paper, but failed. Even with this handicap, Harrisville prospered for awhile.

At its peak, Harrisville was an ultramodern, sparkling clean city. One of its most distinctive features was a row of ornamental street lamps that lined the town's main road. The Harris brothers were benevolent landlords, who gave their employees rent-free homes, free ice, and other amenities almost unheard of for workers in that day. Richard Harris was a certified neatnik who would chastise adults and children alike if he saw them littering city streets and was constantly after the town's residents to close their gates and keep their properties looking orderly and tidy.

In the end, however, Harrisville failed, like all the other Pinelands industrial towns. Perpetually undercapitalized, the Harrises' finances were stretched to the breaking point by numerous recessionary shocks that shuddered through the national economy. The final nail in the coffin came when the Raritan and Delaware Railroad decided to bypass Harrisville and build a line eight miles to the west of the town. The brothers and their partners were forced to sell their property at a sheriff's sale in 1891. After this, the town bounced from owner to owner. In 1910 a massive fire swept through Harrisville, destroying most of the buildings. Vandals took the rest, including the famous street lamps.

Apparently, the Harrises had a hard time letting go. For years rumors persisted that the brothers had come back to live amid the rubble of their town after its destruction. Although that is unlikely, it is probable that the men returned from time to time to gaze upon the ruins and reflect on what once had been.

The fate of Harrisville was a microcosm of what befell industries and the communities they spawned in the Pinelands. By the second half of the nineteenth century, railroads had become the chief movers of goods in the United States, and the absence of rail service in the deep woods made it difficult to get Pinelands-produced products to the marketplace. Depletion of the wood supply—the iron furnaces used a thousand acres of pine trees each year—also helped to hasten the end of the industrial age, since it removed a chief source of fuel. Typically underfinanced, the owners didn't have enough capital to ride out rough business waters. The industrial focus of the United States was shifting to the cities throughout the nineteenth century, and the isolated Pinelands just didn't fit in. Gradually, all the towns were abandoned, and peace returned to the Pinelands once again.

Until well into the twentieth century, the industrial ghost towns of the Pinelands stood like silent sentinels of another era. Often tucked into the woods, they would suddenly just appear to hikers and campers as they turned a corner, looming stone and brick phantoms from another time and place. Well into the early 1970s, it was still possible to visit many of these abandoned communities.

Today, however, that opportunity is gone. The spotlight of attention thrown onto the Pinelands has led to a massive increase in visitors to the area, and not all of them care about preserving the region's heritage. Many of the abandoned buildings were shamelessly vandalized until they either fell down of their own accord or had to be demolished for safety reasons. Opportunists, seeing the potential for a quick buck, stripped the buildings for material that they could resell, such as tin roofs. Others viewed the ghost towns as open-air building supply stores: stones were taken for fireplaces, cedar shingles for garages and basement family rooms, and bricks for outdoor barbecues.

Once the structures were gone, the relentless forest overgrew what was left. Now a hiker unaware of an iron town's location could walk right through the middle of what was once the company store, or a worker's home, and not even realize it. To view the glory of what once was in the Pinelands, it is necessary to visit such restored villages as Allaire (formerly the Howell Iron Works) and Batsto.

DID YOU KNOW?

Everyone knows that towns in the Pinelands have some colorful names, such as Ong's Hat and Double Trouble. But how many people know the former names of some of these towns? On the left is the current name of some Pinelands towns; on the right is their former name or names. Try to match the past with the present:

1	Vincetown	A	Shamong
2	Retreat	B	Etna Furnace
3	Chatsworth	C	Worthless City

4	Pineworth	D	Shinntown and Nabo
5	McCartyville	E	Edgepollock, Shamong, and Brotherton
6	Pleasant Mills	F	Weepink, Brimstone, and Quakytown
7	Indian Mills	G	Harrisville
8	Medford Lakes	H	Two Bridges
9	Medford	I	Sweetwater

Answers: 1. F, 2. H, 3. A, 4. C, 5. G, 6. I, 7. E, 8. B, 9. D.

When the industries failed, the Pinelands reverted to what they once had been: quiet forests bisected by meandering streams and dotted with brackish bogs. The industrial collapse created a vacuum that others tried to fill with their own ideas of how best to utilize the Pinelands. One of these visionaries was Joseph Wharton.

Wharton was already a wealthy and successful Philadelphia business-man, poet, and artist when he began buying huge tracts of Pinelands prop-erty. In 1876 he bought Batsto, although some probably wondered why. "The buildings were so dilapidated that there was much doubt as to whether they should be repaired or torn down," said Civil War general Elias Wright, who assisted Wharton with his Pinelands purchases.

Wharton spent a lot of money to rehabilitate Batsto, including an esti-mated forty thousand dollars on the former ironmaster's mansion alone. Although he used some of his holdings to work on agricultural projects, such as raising sugar beets, it was really the region's unspoiled, crystal-clear water that Wharton was after. His native Philadelphia needed good drink-ing water, and Wharton thought that the pure, clean water of the Pinelands would fit the bill quite nicely.

Wharton planned to build almost three dozen reservoirs in the Pine-lands that would flow, through a series of canals, to one gigantic reservoir in Camden. From here an aqueduct under the Delaware River would bring the water into Philadelphia. Fortunately, his scheme went for naught. The New Jersey legislature got wind of the plan, and passed a law in 1884 prohibiting the export of drinking water from the state.

To his credit, Wharton took the defeat philosophically. Instead of storm-ing out of the Pinelands and letting his holdings deteriorate, he redoubled his agricultural efforts and was instrumental in developing the region's cranberry industry. His Pinelands property ultimately became the hundred-thousand-acre Wharton State Forest, with Batsto as its heart.

Besides water, the other main asset of the Pinelands following the industrial collapse was land. Unfortunately, where there was land, there were also likely to be dishonest land speculators.

Land speculation was a booming business in the Pinelands in the late nineteenth century. Millions of dollars were lost by people suckered by high-pressure salesmen into buying useless lots in the Pinelands. The typical victims were city residents who had no knowledge of the area, and even less about how to get there. Many people bought, sight-unseen, worthless lots drawn out only on paper, and never actually visited their "holdings." Even if they did manage to find their way to the Pinelands, the lack of roadways and directional signs sent most of them home without ever having laid eyes on their so-called investment.

The most infamous land speculation scheme was called Magic City, which was supposed to be located on fourteen hundred acres between Chatsworth and Tabernacle. Ads promoting the sale of the "finest" farming land began appearing in New York City newspapers in 1888. Investors were promised that for their money (home sites cost from $50 to $100 each, while a five-acre "farm" was priced at $175) they would be living in a community that contained such amenities as a college, a hotel, and a music academy. People responded to the ads enthusiastically. More than ten thousand housing lots and two hundred farm plots were sold by 1895.

The Magic City that was finally built, however, was a far cry from the one advertised. It contained just twelve homes and a small factory. The speculation scheme collapsed, and those who had believed in the magic of Magic City joined the long list of others who had wanted so desperately to believe that the Pinelands was Paradise Regained.

Joseph Wharton is long gone from the Pinelands, as are, fortunately, the land speculators. Not all of those who came, however, wanted only to take something out of the Pinelands. Others wanted to give something hack.

Elizabeth White, for example, spent years at Whitesbog developing the modern cultivated blueberry, finally succeeding in 1916. Just before she died, in 1952, this woman with hands stained dark blue from years of handling blueberries, asked landscape architects for the new highway then being built called the Garden State Parkway to please consider planting blueberry bushes alongside the road. The architects looked at this tall, elderly woman with the long, old-fashioned dress and the years of knowledge in her eyes and didn't know how they could refuse. When the time came, blueberry bushes were planted along the section of the Parkway that cuts through the Pinelands.

Then there were those for whom the Pinelands was merely a source of recreation, the pursuit of which reached a pinnacle in Chatsworth during the late nineteenth century. The membership roster of the Chatsworth Club contained names that one does not normally associate with the Pinelands: Astor, Morgan, Gould, and Vanderbilt. Yet they, along with many other politicians, socialites, and captains of industry came to Chatsworth during the Gilded Age to relax from the pressures of being rich and powerful. When they weren't attending festivities at the Chatsworth Club, which was presided over by Levi P. Morton, vice-president of the United States under Benjamin Harrison, the crème de la crème of society could be found at the White Horse Inn (also known as the Shamong Hotel). Eventually, the rich found other playgrounds in which to amuse themselves, and Chatsworth's brief moment in the spotlight was over.

Wharton, White, and Astor are names forever linked with the Pinelands. Another is that of Emilio Carranza, "Mexico's Lone Eagle." In June 1928, Carranza was making a nonstop goodwill flight from Mexico City to Washington, just as Charles Lindbergh had done in reverse the previous December. The young aviator was already a hero in Mexico, for his role in putting down a rebellion and for his incredible presence of mind in the air, including when he deliberately flew into a thunderstorm so that the rain could put out a fire on the plane's wing.

However, fog over North Carolina forced Carranza to land, thwarting his initial nonstop attempt. Young, proud, and determined, Carranza, after reaching New York City, announced that he intended to fly nonstop back to Mexico.

The day he chose—July 13—was a typical East Coast summer day, hazy and humid, with the risk of thunderstorms increasing as the day wore on. Taking off from New York's Roosevelt Field in late afternoon, Carranza turned his plane south. Somewhere near Chatsworth, he met with a thunderstorm. But this was not a benevolent storm like the one that had put out the fire on his plane, and the storm tossed the small plane around like a child's toy. People in Chatsworth said they heard a plane in trouble that day, the noise audible but faint over the crash of thunder. Carranza's plane went down in a stretch of woods in Tabernacle Township.

Nearly twenty-four hours went by before the young man's body was found, thrown from the wreckage of his small plane, and disfigured so badly that it could only be identified through documents addressed to Carranza found in the pilot's pocket. The plane, according to the July 14, 1928, edition of the

New York Times, "was half buried in the soft bog, and a few feet away was the Wright Whirlwind motor of the craft. The fuselage and the motor had crashed down into a small clearing in the midst of the pines and stunted oaks."

"I pleaded with him not to go," revealed Lieutenant Henry B. Clark, manager of Roosevelt Field. "I told him the weather was too bad and that it would be a miracle if he even got off the ground."

In Mexico City, three hundred thousand people accompanied Carranza's casket to its interment, and the entire nation mourned the loss of one of its best and brightest. Every year the Mount Holly American Legion post holds a memorial service at the crash site, which is now graced by a large, pylon-shaped stone monument. The inscription reads: "Messenger of Peace. The People of Mexico hope that your high ideal will be realized. Homage of the children of Mexico to the aviator Captain Emilio Carranza, who died tragically on July 13, 1928, in his goodwill flight." Although there is a green

The Carranza Memorial, located deep in the Pine Barrens.

highway sign on Route 206 in Burlington County that points the way to the Carranza Memorial, few visit the site today.

There are hundreds of stories like these in the Pinelands—tales of how people came to this vast expanse of sand and pine and met success and sorrow, disappointment and deliverance, triumph and tragedy. These stories began when the first human encountered the Pinelands, and they will continue for as long as the region exists. Like a magnet, the Pinelands will continue to attract those who see in it an opportunity.

This is the Pinelands that has existed since humanity first began exploring the region ten thousand years ago. It is the same place that once attracted men who dreamed of building an empire of iron, and the same place that cast cannonballs to defeat the British in the War of 1812. It is the same place that the Atlantic called "aboriginal in savagery" in 1859, and that Governor Fielder found so frightening a half-century later. It is even the same place that McPhee wrote about in the mid-1960s, and considering how many other dramatic and profound changes have rumbled through the world since then, this is probably the most surprising of all.

Indeed, in many respects the Pinelands today are in better shape than they were when McPhee's book first alerted people to the existence of this culturally and environmentally unique region. Several proposals that were floating around in the mid-1960s that would have ripped the soul out of the Pinelands, including one to build a jetport in its heart and another to construct a new city for several hundred thousand people there (shades of Magic City), have been mercifully shot down.

Grandiose schemes like this led to 1978 federal legislation that declared the Pinelands the country's first national reserve, which is a partnership between the federal, state, and local governments to try and retain the region's singular character while not strangling development or economic opportunity. Under this plan, a core region of 337,000 acres is closed to traditional residential, commercial, and industrial development, thus preserving the Pinelands' pristine natural beauty for generations to come. The Pinelands Commission oversees activity within the entire 1.1 million acres of the reserve, trying to walk the fine line between not impeding development and not allowing it to run amuck.

Today, the Pinelands would seem to have the best of both worlds: preservation and carefully controlled development. However, if there's anything certain about life, it's that uncertainty is the only known constant in an ever-changing world. As New Jersey one day becomes "maxed out" in terms of development, and there is no more land on which to build houses, roads, and shopping centers, will people not point to the Pinelands, with its clean water and miles of unbroken forests, and say: There. There is the next frontier of economic opportunity for New Jersey. We must seize it. And considering how many "budget crises" the state has gone through, and how many more the future promises to bring, who knows what could happen?

In 1967, John McPhee wrote that the Pinelands were "headed slowly toward extinction" because of development pressures. While that journey has been forestalled, even apparently derailed, it has not been canceled. Like a soldier tiptoeing through enemy territory, the Pinelands must always keep looking back to make sure that something unpleasant isn't gaining on it.

DID YOU KNOW?

Pinelands Facts
- The Pinelands is home to 39 species of mammals, 299 types of birds, 59 species of reptiles and amphibians, and 91 various types of fish.
- Thanks to the Pinelands, New Jersey ranks second in U.S. blueberry production.
- The Cohansey aquifer contains over 17 trillion gallons of water enough to cover all of New Jersey with ten feet of water.
- Seven species—the Pine Barrens tree frog, the carpenter frog, the ground skunk, the northern pine snake, the northern scarlet snake, the northern red-bellied snake, and the corn snake—are found in New Jersey only in the Pinelands.
- Population density in the Pinelands ranges from ten persons to four thousand persons per square mile.
- The Pine Plains contains the famous pigmy pine forest, the most extensive area of its type in the country.

Birthplaces and Burial Sites

Although a pessimist will tell you that we're born just to die, an optimist will retort that life is what you make it. All that is a rather roundabout way of introducing this chapter, which is an alpabetical listing of the birthplaces and burial sites of many famous people that can be found in New Jersey.

Born in New Jersey

Abbott, William (Bud), comedian, born October 2, 1900, Asbury Park

Addams, Charles, cartoonist, born January 7, 1912, Westfield

Amos, John, actor, born December 27, 1941, Newark

Barnes, Priscilla, actress, born December 7, 1955, Fort Dix

Barry, Rick, basketball player, born March 28, 1944, Elizabeth

Basie, William (Count), band leader, born August 21, 1904, Red Bank

Bennett, Joan, actress, born February 27, 1910, Palisades

Blaine, Vivian, actress/singer, born November 21, 1924, Newark

Blake, Robert, actor, born September 18, 1933, Nutley

Bon Jovi, Jon, musician, born March 2, 1962, Sayreville

Burr, Aaron, politician, born February 6, 1756, Newark

Cauldfield, Joan, actress, born June 1, 1922, East Orange

Cleveland, Grover, U.S. president, born March 18, 1837, Caldwell

---

DID YOU KNOW?

Stephen Grover Cleveland, the only U.S. president born in New Jersey, is also the only man elected to two nonconsecutive terms as the nation's chief executive. He won his first term in 1884, lost to Republican Benjamin Harrison in 1888, then defeated Harrison in 1892 to become both the twenty-second and twenty-fourth president of the United States.

During his second term Cleveland underwent not one but two operations for cancer of the mouth that were kept completely secret from the national media. Twice during July 1893, while the nation was in the midst of a financial panic, Cleveland had operations to remove cancerous bone and tissue from his mouth in a makeshift operating room on board a yacht. Worried that news about his health would throw the nation into an even worse panic, Cleveland kept both operations secret from the newspapers, passing off the rumors of his ill-health as merely "gout" and "dental trouble." The secret was kept so well that to this day some history books still don't mention these surgeries. (A complete medical analysis of Cleveland's illness is at his birthplace in Caldwell.)

Two weeks after he left the presidency for the second and last time in March 1897, Cleveland and his wife retired to Princeton. Here he spent the last eleven years of his life in a variety of pursuits. Although he enjoyed many honors, including being elected a trustee of Princeton University, nothing delighted him more than putting aside work to spend the day with his children. In March 1908, suffering from heart and kidney ailments, the aging former president celebrated a bittersweet seventy-first birthday in the Lakewood Hotel, one of his favorite spots, which stayed open an additional six weeks after the end of its winter season to accommodate its honored guest. Three months later, on June 24, 1908, after murmuring "I have tried so hard to do right," Grover Cleveland died in his Princeton home. He was buried in Princeton Cemetery two days later.

Cooper, James Fenimore, writer, born September 15, 1789, Burlington
Copperfield, David, magician, born September 16, 1956, Metuchen
Costello, Lou, comedian, born March 6, 1908, Paterson
Cousins, Norman, publisher, born June 24, 1912, Union Hill
Crane, Stephen, writer, born November 1, 1871, Newark
Dancer, Stanley, harness racer, born July 25, 1927, New Egypt
Dee, Sandra, actress, born April 23, 1942, Bayonne
de Palma, Brian, film director, born September 11, 1940, Newark
DeVito, Danny, actor, born November 17, 1944, Neptune
Douglas, Helen Gahagan, congresswoman, born November 25, 1900, Boonton
Douglas, Michael, actor, born September 25, 1944, New Brunswick
Evigan, Greg, actor, born October 14, 1953, South Amboy
Ferrer, Mel, actor, born August 25, 1917, Elberon
Forsythe, John, actor, born January 29, 1918, Penn's Grove
Foster, Preston, actor, born August 24, 1900, Ocean City
Francis, Connie, singer, born December 12, 1938, Newark
Francis, Genie, actress, born May 26, 1962, Englewood

Gandolfini, James, born September 18, 1961, Westwood

Garfunkel, Arthur, singer, born November 5, 1941, Newark

Ginsberg, Alan, poet, born June 3, 1926, Newark

Gore, Lesley, singer, born May 2, 1946, Tenafly

Gray, Barry, radio personality, born July 2, 1916, Atlantic City

Halsey, William (Bull), naval officer, born October 30, 1882, Elizabeth

Harris, Franco, football player, born March 7, 1950, Fort Dix

Hayden, Sterling, actor, born March 26, 1916, Montclair

Hobart, Garrett A., U.S. vice-president, born June 3, 1844, Long Branch

Houston, Whitney, singer, born August 9, 1963, Newark

Keith, Brian, actor, born November 14, 1921, Bayonne

Kilmer, Alfred Joyce, poet, born December 6, 1886, New Brunswick

Kirk, Phyllis, actress, born September 18, 1930, Plainfield

Kirsten, Dorothy, soprano, born July 6, 1919, Montclair

Kovacs, Ernie, comedian, born January 23, 1919, Trenton

Langella, Frank, actor, born January 1, 1940, Bayonne

Lewis, Carl, track and field athlete, born July 1, 1961, Willingboro

Lewis, Jerry, comedian, born March 16, 1926, Newark

Light, Judith, actress, born February 9, 1949, Trenton

Lindbergh, Anne Morrow, writer, born June 22, 1906, Englewood

Liquori, Marty, runner, born September 11, 1949, Montclair

MacRae, Gordon, singer, born March 12, 1921, East Orange

Mailer, Norman, writer, born January 31, 1923, Long Branch

McBride, Patricia, ballerina, born August 23, 1942, Teaneck

Mitchell, Thomas, actor, born July 11, 1892, Elizabeth

Moore, Victor, actor, born February 24, 1876, Hammonton

Murray, Kathryn, dance teacher, born September 15, 1906, Jersey City

Nehemiah, Renaldo, track athlete, born March 24, 1959, Newark

Nelson, Ozzie, actor, born March 20, 1906, Jersey City

Nelson, Ricky, singer/actor, born May 8, 1940, Teaneck

Nicholson, Jack, actor, born April 22, 1937, Neptune

Panghorn, Franklin, actor, born January 23, 1893, Newark

Parker, Dorothy, writer, born August 22, 1893, West End

Pollard, Michael J., actor, born May 30, 1939, Passaic

Previn, Dory, singer, born October 22, 1929, Rahway

Riddle, Nelson, composer, born June 1, 1921, Oradell

Robeson, Paul, singer/actor, born April 9, 1898, Princeton

Rovere, Richard, journalist, born May 5, 1915, Jersey City

Saint, Eva Marie, actress, born July 4, 1924, Newark
St. Denis, Ruth, dancer, born January 20, 1879, Newark
Schary, Dore, film producer, born August 31, 1905, Newark
Shero, Fred, hockey coach, born October 23, 1925, Camden
Simon, Paul, singer/songwriter, born November 5, 1942, Newark
Sinatra, Frank, singer, born December 12, 1915, Hoboken
Springsteen, Bruce, singer/songwriter, born September 23, 1949, Freehold
Stagg, Amos Alonzo, football coach, born August 16, 1862, West Orange
Stieglitz, Alfred, photographer, born January 1, 1864, Hoboken
Streep, Meryl, actress, born June 22, 1949, Summit
Swit, Loretta, actress, born November 4, 1937, Passaic
Symmes, Anna, wife of U.S. president W. H. Harrison, born 1775, Morristown
Theismann, Joe, football player, born September 9, 1946, New Brunswick
Terhune, Albert Payson, writer, born December 21, 1872, Newark
Travolta, John, actor, born February 18, 1954, Englewood
Valli, Frankie, singer, born May 3, 1937, Newark
Vaughan, Sarah, singer, born March 27, 1924, Newark
Von Stade, Frederica, mezzo-soprano, born June 1, 1945, Somerville
Warwick, Dionne, singer, born December 12, 1941, East Orange
Wheeler, Bert, comedian, born April 7, 1895, Paterson
Williams, William Carlos, poet, born September 17, 1883, Rutherford
Wilson, Edmund, writer, born May 8, 1895, Red Bank
Wilson, Flip, comedian, born December 8, 1933, Jersey City
Woollcort, Alexander, writer, born January 19, 1887, North American Phalanx
Wyatt, Jane, actress, born August 12, 1912, Campgaw

Buried in New Jersey

Beach, Sylvia, first publisher of James Joyce's *Ulysses,* died 1962, Princeton Cemetery, Princeton
Berger, Meyer, journalist, died 1959, Riverside Cemetery, Saddle River
Bloor, Ella Reeve, labor organizer, died 1951, Harleigh Cemetery, Camden
Boehn, Edward, creator of realistic porcelain figures, died 1969, St. Mary's Cemetery, Trenton
Burr, Aaron, U.S. vice-president, died 1836, Princeton Cemetery, Princeton

Another permanent resident of Princeton Cemetery is Aaron Burr Jr., who served as vice-president of the United States in Thomas Jefferson's first term. However, it is as the man who killed Alexander Hamilton in a duel at Weehawken, New Jersey, on July 11, 1804, that Burr is best known. Most accounts of the affair claim that Hamilton didn't aim at Burr—supposedly he pointed his pistol up in the air or shot at a tree well over Burr's head—while the vice-president gets portrayed as the blackheart who deliberately murdered one of the country's Founding Fathers. That's history's portrait of Aaron Burr—but it might well be wrong.

As part of the nation's bicentennial celebration, the Smithsonian Institution decided to restore the pistols (which had been supplied by Hamilton) used in the infamous duel. When they did, they found that the guns had been altered in several ways, including being able to use larger-size balls. However, the most significant "adjustment" was that the guns had a special hair trigger; by secretly setting the trigger to fire after only a half-pound of pressure had been applied, rather than the normal ten to twelve pounds of pressure, a duelist could fire much quicker than his opponent. This could have been Hamilton's plan, and most accounts of the duel note that he fired first. Something caused him to miss, however, and Burr's shot found its target.

Aaron Burr Jr. was no saint, as his sordid later career proves. Among the low-lights are his involvement in a plot to have the western states secede from the United States, a trial for treason, and marriage to a former prostitute, whose considerable fortune he squandered in several months. It does seem, though that he has been judged wrongly for his role in the most famous duel of all time.

Butler, Nicholas Murray, helped establish Carnegie Endowment for International Peace, died 1947, Cedar Lawn Cemetery, Paterson

Childs, Samuel, founder of the Childs Restaurant chain, died 1925, Cemetery of the Basking Ridge Presbyterian Church, Basking Ridge

Buried next to Grover Cleveland in Princeton Cemetery is his daughter, Ruth Cleveland. Born in 1891, the little girl was so popular during her father's second administration that the Baby Ruth candy bar was named after her. Sadly, the happy child with the smile of gold was not fated to enjoy a long life; Ruth Cleveland died of diphtheria at age thirteen.

Crane, Stephen, writer, died 1900, Evergreen Cemetery, Hillside

Edison, Thomas Alva, inventor, died 1931, Glenmont, West Orange

Edwards, Jonathan, Calvinist theologian, died 1758, Princeton Cemetery, Princeton

Gilder, Jeannette Leonard, early literary agent, died 1916, Bordentown Cemetery, Bordentown

Gilder, Richard Watson, founder of the Author's Club, died 1909, Bordentown Cemetery, Bordentown

Houston, Whitney, singer/actress, died 2012, Fairview Cemetery, Westfield

DID YOU KNOW?

Two of the most enduring symbols of Americana—Leo, the M-G-M Lion, and Elsie, the Borden's cow—also claim New Jersey as their final resting place. Elsie is buried in Plainsboro (Mercer County) with a tombstone marked with her real name, Lobelia, while Leo rests in Long Hill Township (Morris County).

Lewis, Joe E., comedian, died 1971, Cedar Park Cemetery, Paramus

Lombardi, Vince, football coach, died 1970, Mount Olivet Cemetery, Middletown

McClellan, George, Union Civil War general, died 1885, Riverview Cemetery, Trenton

McGuire, Peter J., father of Labor Day, died 1906, Arlington Cemetery, Pennsauken

Pennsauken grave site of Peter McGuire, considered one of the founders of Labor Day.

Grave site of General George McClellan in Trenton.

Mann, John, watercolorist, died 1953, Fairview Cemetery, Fairview
O'Hara, John, writer, died 1970, Princeton Cemetery, Princeton
Peterson, Thomas Mundy, first black man to vote, died 1904, St. Peter's
  Episcopal Church, Perth Amboy

DID YOU KNOW?

Thomas Mundy Peterson is known as the first black man to vote in the United States because he voted on March 31, 1870, in a Perth Amboy election to revise the city charter, one day after the Fifteenth Amendment to the Constitution, barring race as a qualification for voting, went into effect. In later years Peterson served on the charter commission and was a delegate to the Republican National Convention.

Roebling, John A., bridge builder, died 1869, Riverview Cemetery, Trenton

Shahn, Ben, painter of contemporary American society, died 1969, Roosevelt Cemetery, Roosevelt

Whiteman, Paul, band leader, died 1967, Cemetery of the First Presbyterian Church of Ewing, Trenton

Whitman, Walt, poet, died 1892, Harleigh Cemetery, Camden

Williams, William Carlos, writer, died 1963, Hillside Cemetery, Lyndhurst

DID YOU KNOW?

Walt Whitman's castlelike tomb in Harleigh Cemetery in Camden is quite impressive—but even more so after visiting the small, ramshackle house on Mickle Street in which the poet spent the last years of his life. The story behind the tomb illustrates the type of fierce determination that Whitman possessed even when old and sick.

The Good Gray Poet's move to Mickle Street was not well received by his friends and admirers, who felt the tiny house beneath a writer of Whitman's stature. Accordingly, they raised money for Whitman to buy another home, possibly a retreat down by the seashore that he so loved. Whitman, however, had his own ideas as to what to do with the money; instead of a vacation home, he used it to build his tomb.

On Christmas Day, 1890, Whitman went to Harleigh Cemetery, which had offered to donate the land, to choose a site for his tomb. Aware that he was dying, Whitman had thought a great deal about his final resting place; inspired by a drawing by William Blake, Whitman designed a simple yet imposing structure that was meant to hold him and other members of his family. Originally he had wanted a statue of himself on top of the tomb, but the cost had been prohibitive. As it was, the total cost was four thousand dollars (later reduced to fifteen hundred dollars through his friends' influence).

Needless to say, his friends were aghast when they heard that Whitman was spending his money on what they considered an ostentatious monument. The poet, however, blithely ignored the criticism. On several occasions Whitman journeyed to Harleigh to check on the tomb's progress, sometimes reading the workmen scraps of his poetry. As Whitman grew sicker, the project became a race against time.

It was a race that Whitman won. The brooding stone structure was completed just in time to receive the remains of the great poet after his death on March 26, 1892. Having gotten his own way in life, Whitman also had things his way in death; six other members of the Whitman family are interred with him.

Bibliography

General

Beck, Henry Charlton. *Fare to Midlands.* New York: E. P. Dutton, 1939.

Bishop, Gordon. *Gems of New Jersey.* Englewood Cliffs, NJ: Prentice-Hail, 1985.

Brydon, Norman F. *Of Time, Fire and the River.* Self-published, 1970.

———. *The Passaic River.* New Brunswick, NJ: Rutgers University Press, 1974.

Carruth, Gorton. *The Encyclopedia of American Facts & Dates.* New York: Harper & Row, 1987.

Cohen, David Steven. *The Folklore and Folklife of New Jersey.* New Brunswick, NJ: Rutgers University Press, 1983.

Cunningham, John T. *New Jersey: America's Main Road.* Garden City, NY: Doubleday, 1966.

———. *The New Jersey Sampler.* Upper Montclair, NJ: New Jersey Almanac, 1964.

Johnson, Allen, and Dumas Malone, eds. *Dictionary of American Biography.* New York: Charles Scribner's Sons, 1927.

Kross, Peter. *New Jersey History.* Wilmington, DE: Middle Atlantic Press, 1987.

Lurie, Maxine N., and Marc Mappen, eds. *Encyclopedia of New Jersey.* New Brunswick, NJ: Rutgers University Press, 2004.

Lyght, Ernest. *Path of Freedom.* Cherry Hill, NJ: E & E Publishing, 1978.

McMahon, William. *Pine Barrens Legends, Lore and Lies.* Wilmington, DE: Middle Atlantic Press, 1980.

Mappen, Marc. *Jerseyana.* New Brunswick, NJ: Rutgers University Press, 1992.

Roberts, Russell, *Historic Photos of New Jersey.* Nashville, TN: Turner Publishing, 2010.

Roberts, Russell, and Rich Youmans. *Down the Jersey Shore.* New Brunswick, NJ: Rutgers University Press, 1993.

Stockton, Frank R. *Stories of New Jersey.* New Brunswick, NJ: Rutgers University Press, 1961.

Chapter 1   New Jersey Firsts

Chris, Teresa. *The Story of Santa Claus.* Secaucus, NJ: Chartwell Books, 1992.

"The Evolution of the Colt" and other miscellaneous materials supplied by Colt's Manufacturing Company, Hartford, CT.

"The Father of American Cartoonists," in *TelNews*. New Jersey Bell, November 1991.

Haven, Charles T., and Frank A. Belden. *A History of the Colt Revolver.* New York: Bonanza Books, 1940.

Jones, E. Willis. *The Santa Claus Book.* New York: Walker and Company, 1976.

Kalata, Barbara N., *A Hundred Years, A Hundred Miles*. Morristown, NJ: Morris County Historical Society, 1983.

Lawnside Website. http://www.lawnside.net/index.html

Lee, James. *The Morris Canal: A Photographic History.* quoted in "The Morris Canal," on the Morris Canal Greenway Website. www.morriscanal.org/history.htm

Levins, Hoag, "Who Was Peter Mott?" Oct 2001. Historic Camden County Website. historiccamdencounty.com/ccnews24.shtml

Levins, Sandy, "The Vanished Era of Lawnside's Dreamland," Dec 2007. Historic Camden County Website. historiccamdencounty.com/ccnews126.shtml

Michalsky, Barbara V. *Whitesbog—An Historical Sketch.* Browns Mills, NJ: Conservation and Environmental Studies Center, 1978.

"Negroes End Flight." *New York Times,* July 29, 1933.

New Jersey Gold: Facts and Fables from 50 Years of TelNews. New Jersey Bell Telephone Company, 1984.

One Hundred Years of Brewing. New York: Arno Press, 1974.

"Peter Mott House," Lawnside Historical Society Website. www.petermotthouse.org/museum.html.

Potter, Harry M. "The World's First Drive-In Theatre." *South Jersey Magazine,* October–December 1974.

Reilly, H. V. Pat. *From the Balloon to the Moon.* Oradell, NJ: HV Publishers, 1992.

Rizzo, Dennis, *Parallel Communities.* Charleston, SC: The History Press, 2008.

Segrave, Kerry. *Drive-In Theatres.* Jefferson, N.C.: McFarland, 1992.

Tales of New Jersey: Being a Collection of the Best Tales, Fact and Folklore That Have Appeared in the Pages of Tel-News, the Informal Publication Sent to All New Jersey Bell Customers since 1935. New Jersey Bell Telephone Company, 1963.

Weiss, Harry B., and Grace M. Weiss. *The Early Breweries of New Jersey.* Trenton: New Jersey Agricultural Society, 1963.

Winders, Gertrude Hecker. *Sam Colt and His Gun.* New York: John Day, 1959.

Chapter 2 The Rocks, the Land, and Other Things

Burke, Gary, ed. *Yesterday Today in New Jersey.* Jersey City, NJ: C&S Publications, December/January 1994.

Sattler, Helen Rodney. *The Illustrated Dinosaur Dictionary.* New York: Lothrop, Lee & Shepard, 1983.

Wacker, Peter O. *Land and People*. New Brunswick, NJ: Rutgers University Press, 1975.

Wallace, Joseph. *The Rise and Fall of the Dinosaur*. New York: Gallery Books, 1987.

Widmer, Kemble. *The Geology and Geography of New Jersey*. Princeton, NJ: D. Van Nostrand, 1964.

Wilford, John Noble. *The Riddle of the Dinosaur*. New York: Alfred A. Knopf, 1985.

Wolfe, Peter F. *The Geology and Landscapes of New Jersey*. New York: Crane, Russak, 1977.

Chapter 3   Interesting People

Biographical Sketch of Joseph Napoleon Bonaparte, Count De Survilliers. London: J. Ridgway & Sons, 1833. [No author; probably written by Louis Mailliard].

Bordentown Historical Society. *Bordentown 1682–1976*. Bordentown, NJ: Historical Society, 1976.

Carlisle, Robert D. B. *Clara Maass Medical Center: Building Bridges for 125 Years*. Belleville, NJ: Clara Maass Health System, 1993.

Clara Louis Maass: The Tradition of Caring. Belleville, NJ: Clara Maass Foundation.

Connelly, Owen. *The Gentle Bonaparte*. New York: Macmillan, 1968.

Convery, Frank W. H. "The Life and Times of James Still." *Mount Holly Herald,* January 4, 1962.

———. "More on the Life of Dr. James Still." *Mount Holly Herald,* April 19, 1962.

Cunningham, John T. *Clara Maass—A Nurse, A Hospital, A Spirit*. Belleville, NJ: Rae Publishing, 1968

Daily Herald. Newbury Port, MA. March 30, 1847.

Frankenstein, Alfred. *After the Hunt*. Berkeley and Los Angeles: University of California Press, 1969.

Greenhill, Ralph, and Thomas D. Mahoney. *Niagara*. Toronto: University of Toronto Press, 1969.

Hamilton, Rae. "Doctor James Still, Famous Negro Physician, Was Born Near Medford." *Mount Holly Herald,* July–August, 1938.

Irby, James B. *Black Heritage in Central Burlington County*. Self-published, 1975.

Isaacson, Walter. *Einstein*. New York: Simon & Schuster, 2007.

Johnson, Allen, and Dumas Malone, eds. *Dictionary of American Biography*. New York: Charles Scribner's Sons, 1934.

Kralik, Marilyn, and Pauline S. Miller. *A Century of Art: 1850–1950; Ocean County Artists and Their Works Before 1950*. Ocean County Cultural and Heritage Commission, 1992.

Macartney, Clarence Edward, and Gordon Dorrance. *The Bonapartes In America*. Philadelphia: Dorrance, 1939.

Neffe, Jurgen, *Einstein*. New York: Farrar, Straus and Giroux, 2005.

"New Mystery In Hidden Vault In Bonaparte's New Jersey Estate." *World Magazine,* March 22, 1914.

New York Times, August 25–27, 1901.

Ross, Michael. *The Reluctant King.* New York: Mason/Charter, 1977.

Saturday Evening Post: October 6, 1827, July 26, 1828, August 2, 1828, August 9, 1828, October 17, 1829, November 7, 1829, November 14, 1829, November 21, 1829, and December 5, 1829.

Stacton, David. *The Bonapartes.* New York: Simon & Schuster, 1966.

Still, James. *Early Recollections and Life of Dr. James Still.* New Brunswick, NJ: Rutgers University Press, 1973.

Walsh, William S. "The American St. Helena." *Frank Leslie's Popular Monthly,* February 1894.

Wilmerding, John. *Important Information Inside.* New York: Harper & Row, 1983.

Woodward, E. M., *Bonaparte's Park and the Murats.* Self-published, 1879.

———. *Bordentown and Its Environs.* Self-published, circa 1890.

Chapter 4 The Sporting Life

Briggs, Asa, ed. *A Dictionary of 20th Century World Biography.* Oxford: Oxford University Press, 1992.

Dempsey, Jack, *Dempsey.* New York: Harper & Row Publishers, 1977.

"Dempsey Knocks Out Carpentier in Fourth Round of the Bout." *Newark Evening News,* July 2, 1921.

DiClerico, James M., and Barry J. Pavelec. *The Jersey Game.* New Brunswick, NJ: Rutgers University Press, 1991.

Durant, John, and Les Etter. *Highlights of College Football.* New York: Hastings House, 1970.

"The Football Match." *The Targum,* November 1869.

Herbert, John W. [Article, title unknown]. *Sunday World Magazine,* September 21, 1930.

"Many Prominent Persons Will Witness Big Fight." *Newark Evening News,* June 30, 1921.

Mason, Nicholas. *Football!* New York: Drake, 1975.

Mayer, Ronald A. *1937 Newark Bears.* Union City, NJ: William H. Wise, 1980.

Nash, Bruce, and Allan Zullo. *The Baseball Hall of Shame 2.* New York: Pocket Books, 1986.

"New Jersey." *New York Times,* November 9, 1869.

Overmyer, James. *Eff Manley and the Newark Eagles.* Metuchen, NJ: Scarecrow Press, 1993.

Peterson, Harold. *The Man Who Invented Baseball.* New York: Charles Scribner's Sons, 1969.

Roberts, Randy. *Jack Dempsey.* Baton Rouge: Louisiana State University Press, 1979.

Rogosin, Donn. *Invisible Men.* New York: Atheneum, 1983.

"Small Chance for Crooks at Fight." *Newark Evening News,* July 1, 1921.

Sobol, Ken. *Babe Ruth and the American Dream.* New York: Random House, 1974.

"The Start of It All." *Rutgers Alumni Magazine,* September 1969.

Swinburne, Lawrence, and Irene Swinburne. *America's First Football Game.* New York: Contemporary Perspectives, 1978.

Weiss, Harry B., and Grace M. Weiss. *Early Sports and Pastimes in New Jersey.* Trenton, NJ: Past Times Press, 1960.

Whittingham, Richard. *Saturday Afternoon.* New York: Workman, 1985.

The World, November 23, 1924.

Chapter 5   Canning, Building, Riding, and Other Fascinating Things About New Jersey

Collins, Douglas, *America's Favorite Food.* New York: Harry N. Abrams, 1994.

Levins, Hoag. "Camden's Golden Era of Shipbuilding," March 2001. Historic Camden County Website. historiccamdencounty.com/ccnews05.shtml

"New York Shipbuilding," Destroyer History Foundation Website. http://destroyer history.org/destroyers/newyorkship/

Sim, Mary B., *Commercial Canning in New Jersey History and Early Development.* Trenton: New Jersey Agricultural Society, 1951.

Tourbook: New Jersey and Pennsylvania. Heathrow, FL: American Automobile Association, 1994.

Westergaard, Barbara. *New Jersey: A Guide to the State.* New Brunswick, NJ: Rutgers University Press, 1987.

Zatz, Arline. *New Jersey's Special Places.* Woodstock, VT: Countryman Press, 1990.

Chapter 6   Celebrated Sons and Distinguished Daughters

Acocella, Joan. "After the Laughs." *The New Yorker,* August 6, 1993.

Bacon-Foster, Corra. *Clara Barton, Humanitarian.* Washington, DC: Columbia Historical Society, 1918.

"Clara Barton's Role in Bordentown's History." *The Bordentown Register.* September 6, 1956.

Clark, Barbara Louise, *E. B.* Philadelphia: Dorrance, 1975.

Ehrlich, Scott. *Paul Robeson.* New York: Chelsea House, 1988.

Fishwick, Marshall W. *Illustrious Americans: Clara Barton.* Morristown, NJ: Silver Burdett, 1966.

Frewin, Leslie. *The Late Mrs. Dorothy Parker.* New York: Macmillan, 1986.

Gibson, Emma Ghering. *Pioneer Women of Historic Haddonfield.* West Collingswood, NJ: Varacomp, 1973.

Harwood, Michael. *In the Shadow of Presidents.* Philadelphia: J. B. Lippincott, 1966.

Lunardini, Christine, *Alice Paul.* Boulder, CO: Westview Press, 2013.

Meade, Marion. *What Fresh Hell Is This?.* New York: Villard Books, 1988.

New York Times, January 24, 1976.

O'Malley, Michael. *Keeping Watch.* New York: Viking Penguin, 1990.

Paul Robeson: The Great Forerunner, by the editors of *Freedomways.* New York: Dodd, Mead & Company, 1965.

Pretzer, William S., ed. *Working at Inventing: Thomas A. Edison and the Menlo Park Experience.* Dearborn, MI: Henry Ford Museum and Greenfield Village, 1989.

Robeson, Susan. *The Whole World in His Hands.* Secaucus, NJ: Citadel Press, 1981.

Ross, Ishbel. *Angel of the Battlefield.* New York: Harper & Brothers Publishers, 1956.

Stross, Randall, *The Wizard of Menlo Park.* New York: Crown Publishers, 2007.

Tally, Steve. *Bland Ambition.* New York: Harcourt, Brace, Jovanovich, 1992.

This Is Haddonfield. Haddonfield, NJ: Historical Society of Haddonfield, 1963.

Whisenhunt, Donald T. *Elias Boudinot.* New Jersey Historical Commission, 1975.

"Who Was Alice Paul," Alice Paul Institute Website. www.alicepaul.org.

Chapter 7 Great Storms

Asbury Park Press, December 11–20, 1992.

Asbury Park Evening Press, September 15–16, 1944.

Caplovich, Judd. *Blizzard! The Great Storm of '88.* Vero Beach, FL: Vero House, 1987.

Ludlum, David M. *The New Jersey Weather Book.* New Brunswick, NJ: Rutgers University Press, 1983.

New Jersey Courier, March 14–21, 1888.

New York Times, March 12–15, 1888.

Newark Evening News, March 14–15, 1888.

Savadove, Larry, and Margaret Thomas Buchholz. *Great Storms of the Jersey Shore.* Harvey Cedars, NJ: Down the Shore, 1993.

Star-Ledger. *When Sandy Hit: The Storm That Forever Changed New Jersey.* Battle Ground, WA: Pediment Publishing, 2013.

Chapter 8 Ghosts, Tall Tales, and Legends

Beck, Henry Charlton. "Ghosts of 1800s Haunted Church in Jersey City." *Sunday Star-Ledger,* March 29, 1964.

Cohen, Daniel. *Phantom Animals.* New York: Pocket Books, 1991.

Cohen, David Steven, *The Ramapo Mountain People.* New Brunswick, NJ: Rutgers University Press, 1974.

Halpert, Herbert. *Folktales and Legends from the New Jersey Pines.* Bloomington: Indiana University Press, 1947.

Jarvis, Sharon. *Beyond Reality: True Tales of the Unknown.* New York: Bantam Books, 1991.

McCloy, James F., and Ray Miller. *The Jersey Devil.* Wallingford, PA: Middle Atlantic Press, 1976.

Quarrie, George. *Within a Jersey Circle: Tales of the Past, Grave and Gay, as Picked Up from Old Jerseyites.* Somerville, NJ: Unionist-Gazette Association. 1910

Weird New Jersey 4, Summer 1993. Compiled by Mark Sceurman, Bloomfield, NJ.

Chapter 9 Historical Happenings

Asbury Park Evening Press, October 31, 1938.

Booth, Sally Smith. *The Women of '76.* New York: Hastings House, 1973.

Brady, Frank. *Citizen Welles.* New York: Charles Scribner's Sons, 1989.

Bridgeton Chronicle, November 13, 20, and 27, 1874.

Cantril, Hadley. *The Invasion from Mars.* New York: Harper & Row, 1966.

Gilman, Col. C. Malcom B. *Monmouth Road to Glory.* Red Bank, NJ: Arlington Laboratory for Clinical and Historical Research, 1964.

Hicks, Brian, *When the Dancing Stopped: The Real Story of the Morro Castle Disaster and Its Deadly Wake.* New York: Free Press, 2006.

Koch, Howard. *The Panic Broadcast.* Boston: Little, Brown, 1970.

Learning, Barbara. *Orson Welles.* New York: Viking, 1985.

Lender, Mark. "The Battle of Monmouth." Unpublished manuscript.

Mulford, William C. *Historical Tales of Cumberland County.* Bridgeton, NJ: Evening News Company, 1941.

Newark Evening News, October 31–November 1, 1938.

Sickler, Joseph S. *Tea Burning Town.* New York: Abelard Press, 1950.

Smith, Samuel Stelle. *The Battle of Monmouth.* Monmouth Beach, NJ: Philip Freneau Press, 1964.

———. "The Search for Molly Pitcher." *Daughters of the American Revolution,* April 1975.

Stryker, William S. *The Battle of Monmouth.* Port Washington, NY: Kennikat Press, 1927.

Witcover, Jules. *Sabotage at Black Tom.* Chapel Hill, NC: Algonquin Books, 1989.

http://www.njhm.com/morrocastle.htm

Chapter 10 A Town Treasury

Asbury Park Press, June 29–30, 1994.

Baker-Carr, C. D. T. *Sand and Glass.* Garden City, NY: Doubleday, 1960.

Baver, W. John. *William Carlos Williams, Stephen Crane, and Philip Freneau.* Trenton,: New Jersey Historical Commission, 1989.

Daniels, Morris S. *The Story of Ocean Grove.* New York: Methodist Book Concern, 1919.

Grover, Kathryn. *Hard at Play.* Amherst, MA, and Rochester, NY: The University of Massachusetts Press and the Strong Museum, 1992.

Harris, Howard. "The Transformation of Ideology in the Early Industrial Revolution: Paterson, New Jersey, 1820–1840." Ph.D. diss., City University of New York, 1985.

Herbst, John A., and Catherine Keene. *Life and Times in Silk City.* Haledon, NJ: American Labor Museum, 1984.

Hewitt, Louise. *Historic Trenton.* Trenton, NJ: Smith Press, 1916.

History of Ocean Grove. Ocean Grove, NJ: Ocean Grove Times, 1944.

Johnson, Virgil S. *Millville: 1802 to 1952.* Self-published.

———. *Millville Glass: The Early Days.* Millville, NJ: Delaware Bay Trading, 1971.

McMahon, William. *Historic South Jersey Towns.* Atlantic City: Press Publishing Company, 1964.

———. *South Jersey Towns.* New Brunswick, NJ: Rutgers University Press, 1973.

Miller, John C. *Alexander Hamilton: Portrait in Paradox.* New York: Harper & Row, 1959.

Millville, NJ. Centennial Souvenir, 1860–1906. Millville Centennial Corporation.

The North American, October 11, 1908.

Norwood, Christopher. *About Paterson.* New York: E. P. Dutton, 1974.

Osborn, W. B. *In the Beginning, God.* New York: Methodist Book Concern, n.d.

Podmore, Harry J. *Trenton Old and New.* Trenton, NJ: MacCrellish & Quigley, 1964.

Quigley, Mary Alice, and David E. Collier. *A Capital Place: The Story of Trenton.* Woodland Hills, CA: Windsor, 1984.

Raum, John O. *History of the City of Trenton.* Trenton, NJ: W. T. Nicholson 1871.

Stokes, Reverend E. H. *Ocean Grove: Its Origin and Progress.* Philadelphia: Press of Haddock & Son, 1874.

Trenton Times, June 30, 1994

Tripp, Anne Huber. *The I.W.W. and the Paterson Silk Strike of 1913.* Urbana: University of Illinois Press, 1987.

Whittemore, Reed. *William Carlos Williams: Poet from Jersey.* Boston: Houghton, Mifflin, 1975.

Chapter 11 When New Jersey Was Hollywood

Altomara, Rita Ecke. *Hollywood on the Palisades.* New York: Garland, 1983.

"American Bicentennial News," 1776–1976.

Balshofer, Fred J., and Arthur C. Miller. *One Reel a Week.* Berkeley and Los Angeles: University of California Press, 1967.

Hendricks, Gordon. *Origins of the American Film.* New York: Arno Press and the *New York Times,* 1972.

New Jersey Motion Picture and Television Commission, "1993 Annual Report," 3–25.

Jersey Journal, May 24, 1971.

New York Herald Tribune, October 26, 1947.

New York World Telegram, October 29, 1947.

Nye, David E. *The Invented Self.* Odense, Denmark: Odense University Press, 1983.

The Record, January 29, 1964.

Spehr, Paul C. *The Movies Begin.* Newark, NJ: Newark Museum, 1977.

Sunday Record, March 6, 1983.

Sunday Record Call, July 6, 1969.

Chapter 12   It's the Natural Thing to Do

Axel-Lute, Paul, *Lakewood-In-The-Pines.* South Orange, NJ: Paul Axel-Lute, 1986.

Cavanaugh, Cam. *Saving the Great Swamp.* Frenchtown, NJ: Columbia Publishing, 1978.

Chernow, Ron, *Titan: The Life of John D. Rockefeller, Sr.* New York: Random House, 1998.

Leek, Charles. *The Birds of New Jersey.* New Brunswick, NJ: Rutgers University Press, 1975.

Niles, Lawrence, Kathleen Clark, and Sharon Paul. *Comprehensive Management Plan for Shorebirds on Delaware Bay.* Joint publication of the Endangered & Nongame Species Program & the Nature Conservancy.

Roberts, Russell. "Next Stop Delaware Bay." *New Jersey Living,* April 1987, 24.

Miscellaneous pamphlets, handouts, and data sheets from the Edwin B. Forsythe National Wildlife Refuge and the Great Swamp National Wildlife Refuge.

Endangered and Nongame Species Program, New Jersey Department of Environmental Protection and Energy, Division of Fish, Game and Wildlife. *1992 Annual Report.*

Riley, Laura, and William Riley. *Guide to the National Wildlife Refuges.* Garden City, NY: Anchor Press, 1979.

Wheeler, David, *Wild New Jersey.* New Brunswick, NJ: Rivergate Books, 2011.

Chapter 13   Roads, Bridges, and Tunnels

Asbury Park Press, August 7–10, 1994.

Beaver, Patrick. *A History of Tunnels.* Secaucus, NJ: Citadel Press, 1973.

Cranmer, H. Jerome. *New Jersey in the Automobile Age.* Princeton, NJ: D. Van Nostrand, 1964.

"Fort Lee to Block Access to George Washington Bridge." *Trenton Times,* October 14, 1994, A-10.

Gillespie, Angus Kress, and Michael Aaron Rockland. *Looking for America on the New Jersey Turnpike.* New Brunswick, NJ: Rutgers University Press, 1989.

Hankins, Grace Croyle. *True Stories of New Jersey.* Philadelphia: John C. Winston, 1939.

Miscellaneous materials provided by the Port Authority of New York and New Jersey.

New York Times, October 28, 1924, November 13, 1927, and October 25, 1931.

Olney, Ross R. *They Said It Couldn't Be Done.* New York: E. P. Dutton, 1979.

Plowden, David. *Bridges.* New York: Viking, 1974.

Shirley-Smith, H. *The World's Great Bridges.* New York: Harper & Row, 1953.

Silverberg, Robert. *Bridges.* Philadelphia: Macrae Smith, 1966.

Steinman, D. B. *The Builders of the Bridge.* New York: Harcourt, Brace, 1945.

Trachtenberg, Alan. *Brooklyn Bridge: Fact and Symbol.* New York: Oxford University Press, 1965.

Chapter 14 The Call of the Pines

Carter, James H. *A Trip Through the Pines.* Self-published, 1969.

Goddard, Henry Herbert. *The Kallikak Family.* New York: Macmillan, 1912.

Hufford, Mary. *One Space, Many Places.* Washington, D.C.: Library of Congress, 1986.

McPhee, John. *The Pine Barrens.* New York: Farrar, Straus & Giroux, 1967.

Moonsammy, Rita Zorn, David Steven Cohen, and Lorraine E. Williams. *Pinelands Folklife.* New Brunswick, NJ: Rutgers University Press, 1987.

New York Times, July 14, 1928.

Pierce, Arthur D. *Iron in the Pines.* New Brunswick, NJ: Rutgers University Press, 1957.

Pinelands Guide. New Jersey Pinelands Commission.

Pinelands Collection. Pinelands Room. Burlington County College.

Chapter 15 Birthplaces and Burial Sites

Arbeiter, Jean, and Linda D. Cirino. *Permanent Address.* New York: M. Evans, 1983.

Canby, Henry Seidel. *Walt Whitman: An American.* Boston: Houghton Mifflin, 1943.

Cantor, George. *Historic Landmarks of Black America.* Detroit: Gale Research, 1991

Chupack, Henry. *Walt Whitman in Camden.* Ph.D. diss., New York University, 1952.

Hoyt, Edwin P. *Grover Cleveland.* Chicago: Reilly & Lee, 1962.

Johnson, Otto, ed. *The 1992 Information Please Almanac.* Boston: Houghton Mifflin, 1992.

Nigro, Dana. "Saving a Famous Mascot's Grave." *Independent Press,* August 3, 1994.

Sarapin, Janice Kohl. *Old Burial Grounds of New Jersey.* New Brunswick, NJ: Rutgers University Press, 1994.

Stetler, Susan L. *Almanac of Famous People.* Detroit: Gale Research, 1989.

Index